The Poisoner

The Poisoner

The Life and Crimes of Victorian England's Most Notorious Doctor

Stephen Bates

OVERLOOK DUCKWORTH
NEW YORK • LONDON

This edition first published in hardcover in the United States and the United Kingdom in 2014 by
Overlook Duckworth, Peter Mayer Publishers, Inc.

NEW YORK
141 Wooster Street
New York, NY 10012
www.overlookpress.com
For bulk and special sales, please contact sales@overlookny.com,
or write us at the above address.

LONDON
30 Calvin Street
London E1 6NW
info@duckworth-publishers.co.uk
www.ducknet.co.uk
For bulk and special sales, please contact sales@overlookny.com,
or write us at the above address.

Cataloging-in-Publication Data is available from the Library of Congress

Book design and typeformatting by Bernard Schleifer

Manufactured in the United States of America
ISBN US: 978-1-4683-0911-9
ISBN UK: 978-0-7156-4750-9
1 3 5 7 9 1 8 6 4 2

For James Meikle, who enjoys a good murder . . .

Contents

List of Illustrations

The Poisoner

Ever yours
Wm Palmer

William Palmer, at the racecourse, assessing the odds, betting book in his hands and mourning band around his hat.

1

Stafford, 14 June 1856

THE NIGHT HAD BEEN UNSEASONABLY COLD AND WET FOR JUNE, BUT HOUR after hour the tramp of boots and clogs and the grind and clatter of iron-rimmed wheels could be heard down the country lanes and village streets of the Midlands. Children lying awake in their beds would never forget the sound. It seemed as if the whole world was quietly on the move through the darkness. Thousands of people, heedless of the intermittent gusts of rain, were converging on the county town of Stafford. There was to be a public hanging on the morning of one of the most notorious murderers Victorian England had ever known or read about, and they did not want to miss it. Dr William Palmer, the infamous Rugeley Poisoner, a respectable professional man from a wealthy family yet a serial killer, was going to swing for his crimes and it would be quite something to watch – it would be a tale they could tell their grandchildren. Perhaps there would be an affecting scene, a breakdown, tears or, best of all, a confession and repentance: a true spectacle. That would be worth the sleepless night, the damp and the hours of walking in the pitch dark – 10 miles, 20 miles some had done, then the same journey home to follow later. Why, it would be almost as good as a public holiday.

At Stafford's new railway station, the excursion trains were pulling in every half-hour through the night: from Manchester and Liverpool, up from Birmingham and the industrial towns of the Black Country, Walsall and Wolverhampton, Tipton and Dudley, and across from Shrewsbury and Stoke. The passengers crowding the trains were joining the throng in the streets. They too were avid to see a man die before breakfast.

Stafford was bursting with revellers that night: the gathering crowd would swell it to at least twice its normal size. Later, it would be estimated that 30,000 spectators had been present, but no one could have done a head-count. The streets were packed and the pubs were open and doing a roaring trade as the visitors drank through the evening and into the early hours, sheltering from the rain, keeping their courage up and singing songs to while away the time. It was, said the *Staffordshire Advertiser* sanctimoniously in its next edition,

> a miscellaneous company and occasional snatches of a Bacchanalian or a rustic song were heard as small parties moved unsteadily onwards – the song being suddenly checked as the chaunters remembered where and for what they were going.
> Hundreds, tired, footsore and travel stained had evidently tramped many miles to reach Stafford and for five hours carriages of every kind, laden to the very extreme capacity . . . poured into the town in an unremitting stream . . . there was a complete procession of over-laden spring carts, omnibuses, many with four horses and all descriptions of vehicles. We heard one aged man boast he had walked from a place 14 miles off to see the sight and that he meant to walk back again. No doubt many others walked as far, or further, urged and supported by that indefinable, morbid taste which causes such large and miscellaneous gatherings of spectators at the execution of any criminal of peculiar notoriety.

Not everyone was drinking. Moving among the crowd were preachers and peddlers of improving tracts and ballads, men carrying placards warning of the wages of sin and others carrying Palmer's last words before he had had a chance to make them and his confession before he had made that too.

Many journalists were also stalking the town that night. More than forty had been sent from the London papers, and the regional press from Liverpool, Manchester, Birmingham, Nottingham and many other towns and cities. The execution was a big story: the biggest of the year, bigger in column inches than the ending of the Crimean War. Even Queen Victoria had been following it: "That horrible Palmer," she had written in her private journal the day after his trial, "A doctor and a blackleg . . . everyone was convinced he had done it . . . the scoundrel." And the case of William Palmer was not only filling the newspapers of Britain: the *New York Times* had reported it – "the Borgia of the betting ring", it had called him, "a story that outdistanced the best-selling romances of Bulwer Lytton". Even the *Ballarat Star* in far-off Australia had written up the story.

So great had been the expected crowd – public executions always brought a rowdy mob, craning for a view and disappointed if they didn't get a spectacle – that about twenty stands had been erected in the private gardens and on the roofs opposite the front of the prison where the hanging was to occur. The mayor had sent out the borough surveyor to inspect the structures' sturdiness and to issue licences. Spectators would pay for such a view, even more if they could secure a place in the warm, at a window overlooking the road in front of the jail where the execution was to take place at 8 a.m. The last thing Stafford would want was a stand collapsing and crushing its occupants. They had had that once before: executions had formerly been carried out on the prison gatehouse roof, which had allowed everyone to get a good view, but the scaffold on that occasion had collapsed in mid-execution, so now there was a portable gallows and the sentence of the law was carried out only a little way above the ground. By three o'clock in the morning the gallows, set on a large, black-hung box six feet high, had been wheeled into place on its four iron wheels outside the front gate. It had two stout beams, one at each end, and a cross-beam from which the rope dangled above a trap-door. Chains attached to the prison wall secured it in place.

Now crowd barriers were also erected, and Captain Hatton, the cadaverous chief constable of the county, had deployed 200 police officers and special constables to keep order outside the prison and all along the route to the railway station. The town officials had issued instructions that women and children should keep away. The public notice issued the previous week stated:

> the police have received instructions to prevent all young persons under the age of 14 from mixing in the crowds and they also suggest the propriety of all females abstaining from any attempt to approach the county prison as the risk of personal injury from the presence of so great a crowd as may assemble on the occasion will be extremely great.

It made no difference, of course. The *Manchester Guardian*'s anonymous correspondent, shivering in the rain and cold, reported:

> The bulk of the spectators were of the lower classes . . . working men from town and country with a plentiful sprinkling of "roughs" and of the "dangerous classes". Well-clad middle class men and tradesmen were there too, but most of that description could afford to pay for the sight of the rope, the convict, the hangman, the white cap and the quivering body . . . it was a matter of bargain – and of taste.
>
> It must be recorded that women were there, as anxious for the sight as the lowest and most degraded among the crowd. We saw one, not eighteen years old, who stood for hours . . . she seemed to shiver occasionally, but that was due to the cold and wet, not to any appreciation of her false position or to a feeling of the horror of the scene. We saw several smartly-dressed women especially upon a stand whence, with the aid of glasses – and they were used, we believe – a "good view" could be obtained. Public reprobation of the conduct of such disgraces to their sex would have but little effect. We state the fact and we leave the subject with disgust.

Inside the prison's condemned cell, William Palmer must have been able to hear the distant noise of the crowd and the rumble and rattle of the scaffold being wheeled into place. He was having a disturbed night, constantly woken and harried by the prison chaplain, the Rev. Robert Goodacre, and another clergyman, Henry Sneyd, who were trying to secure, finally, his confession. They woke him from a deep sleep at half past two and he rose "with outward propriety and seeming earnestness" to pray with them until five o'clock. An hour and a half later and they were back for another go: "the chaplain was most earnest in his exhortations to the convict to confess his offence before quitting the world; and the convict listened but said nothing."

Palmer was thirty-one but looked older: pink-cheeked and running to fat like many a sporting gentleman and follower of the turf. When he had appeared in court at the Old Bailey for his trial a month before, the reporters

**This is thought to be a photograph
of William Palmer.**

were astonished at just how ordinary he looked – not like a murderer at all, the monster that the pre-trial publicity had led them to expect. "His coun-tenance is clear and open," the *Times*'s man recorded:

> The forehead high, the complexion ruddy and the general impression which one would form from his appearance would be rather favourable than otherwise, although his features are of a common and somewhat mean cast. There is certainly noth-ing to indicate to the ordinary observer the presence of either ferocity or cunning and one would expect to find in him more of the boon companion than the subtle adversary.

This very ordinariness of course made him all the more sinister. Here was the respectable classes' worst nightmare: wickedness incarnate and insidi-ous, disguised as normality. The worst of it was that you could have passed him in the street without ever noticing his villainy. Charles Dickens, with his fascination for the macabre and the criminal, took a keen interest in the case, attended the trial and wrote to his friend John Forster afterwards:

> Everywhere I see the late Mr Palmer . . . Mr Palmer sits next to
> me at the theatre; Mr Palmer goes before me down the street . . .
> I look at the back of his bad head repeated in long, long lines
> on the race course and in the betting stand . . . and I vow to God
> I can see nothing but cruelty, covetousness, calculation . . . and
> low wickedness.

The one thing the chaplains couldn't do, however hard they tried, was make William Palmer confess. Disturbingly, he stubbornly refused, even now in the last few minutes of his life. The only two words he had spoken publicly in his own defence had occurred at the start of his trial: "Not guilty." He was polite, he was obsequious, he expressed his gratitude to the prison staff and the governor Major Fulford. All he would say now, finally, when asked again if he accepted the justice of his sentence, was that he admitted nothing. The *Observer* reported the next day that, "using a great deal of gesticulation", he had exclaimed with vehemence: "I am not guilty. I am not guilty. I am a murdered man." In a last gesture of defiance he declined to wear his own clothes to his execution, as was his right. He knew that the hangman could claim what he was wearing and that it would almost certainly end up bought for Madame Tussaud's waxworks, so he chose to wear the rough, grey woollen prison uniform and blue striped flannel shirt instead. His auburn hair had been shaved and he would march now to the scaffold looking like a convict rather than a professional man.

Now, the hangman was ready. George "Topper" Smith was a stern, hatchet-faced Black Country nail-maker who had seen the inside of prison himself several times, for debt, for failing to support his family and, once, after being caught running naked through Wednesbury while drunk. He had been conducting hangings locally in his spare time for nearly twenty years and performed them wearing a labourer's white smock and a top hat to add dignity to the occasion. Smith had apparently underbid the national hangman William Calcraft, the Newgate executioner in London, by offering to do the job for £5 instead of the normal £10, and so had been chosen by the authorities. He had invested a pound of his fee in buying a new smock to make the day a bit more special. Smith's other nickname around the pubs and taverns of the Black Country was "Throttler", for that is what he and his kind did. There was no science to a hanging, no quick drop to break a man's neck in an instant; rather, it was a slow strangulation which frequently took several minutes once the trap-door opened beneath a condemned man's feet. To hasten death, Smith would race below and pull on the legs, especially if the prisoner had paid him to do so to quicken his end. Calcraft, more of a crowd-pleaser, would sometimes leap on the victim's shoulders to tug him downwards. It was always a gruesome and excruciating ceremony.

As the prison bell tolled and eight o'clock approached, Palmer and the execution procession arrived at the scaffold. From there, he would have looked out at a sea of upturned faces as far as the eye could see, all craning to watch him die. They were falling silent now, expectant for what they were about to witness. There were cries of "hats off" and "umbrellas down", not as marks of respect but to clear the view. The *Manchester Guardian*'s man remarked that the spectators were "not worse than crowds generally . . . at executions, possibly better than is usual . . . thick steam arose from the drenched and sweltering mass".

Palmer managed a smile. He inclined his neck as Smith adjusted the noose and shook his hand. "God bless you," he said. Smith stood back, ready to spring the trap. Palmer was still staring at the crowd and then the executioner remembered something. He returned to place the white hood over the condemned doctor's head. In a moment it would all be over.

But even as the bolt was pulled, there were many who questioned Palmer's guilt and, even if he was guilty, whether it had been proved beyond reasonable doubt in one of the longest and most sensational murder trials of the nineteenth century. How could a man be hanged for poisoning when not a grain of strychnine had been found in his victim's body?

2

"Oh doctor, I shall die!"

FOR JOHN PARSONS COOK, A YOUNG SPORTING GENTLEMAN, TUESDAY 13 November 1855 was the most satisfactory day of his life. His jaunt to Shrewsbury races with his friends had culminated in his horse Polestar winning the main race at odds of seven to two, gaining him the enormous sum of £3,000, the equivalent of perhaps £180,000 today. The money would clear his pressing debts and the partying would go on for two nights. One of his friends declared of Cook:

> I knew he was very anxious as the winning of the race was of great consequence to him. After the race was run he was so excited that for two or three minutes he could not speak to me. He was elated and happy for the rest of the day, but he was not at all intoxicated.

The whole of the Shropshire county town was in party mood for the races. It was one of the events of the local season. Farmers were riding over from the Welsh Marches and down from the Cheshire Plain, while trains were bringing spectators, revellers and bookmakers, trainers and touts from across the country into Shrewsbury for the big week of the year, the last races of the season. They were coming down from Manchester and up from Birmingham and the Black Country, and from even further afield. Some of Cook's cronies had travelled all the way from London. The Raven Hotel in Castle Street, where Cook and his friends were celebrating with brandy and "beakers of provincial champagne", was heaving with race-goers. They would undoubtedly have been jostling in the corridors, singing in the bars and reeling from private room to private room, crashing parties and waving tankards and wine glasses. Outside the streets were thronged with country bumpkins and fancy men in their coloured waistcoats, artisans in sturdy worsted clothes and hobnail boots, farmers in tweeds and gaiters, lords and ladies, butlers and servants, shop assistants, horse fanciers and whores.

The autumn nights were drawing in after damp and chilly days and, at the Raven, surely the best celebration was John Parsons Cook's. A sallow, pale-faced, perspiring young man, just twenty-eight years old and not in the best of health, he cut a singular figure among the guffawing, red-faced members of the racing fancy. He was, said one who as a young boy had carried Cook's cricket bag to a match that summer, someone who had gone the pace pretty extensively. The lad, George Fletcher, wrote seventy years later that Cook "dressed rather showily, with a good many rings and a conspicuous watch-chain . . . a cheerful fellow enough, fond of a good drink and always hopeful that he would regain the fortune he had lost upon the Turf". Polestar's victory went a long way towards doing that. Cook was an owner and gambler, working his way through his inheritance. He had come into £12,000, left to him by his father who had died when he was a child, and Cook had given up training in a solicitor's office in Worthing on the Sussex coast, in favour of a more congenial, self-indulgent life with racing cronies in the Midlands. His closest friends gossiped that he had been treated for syphilis earlier in the year. Cook had been worried about that too. He had had mouth ulcers all summer and been dosing himself with mercury, against his doctor's advice. Only the previous week at Liverpool races his friend John Sargeant observed that he was surprised he could eat or drink anything as his blackened mouth was "in a complete state of ulcer".

The celebration resumed in the evening following the next day's races. After drinking at the Unicorn, the revellers reconvened later at the Raven. The party in the first-floor rooms Cook had booked consisted of a group of male mates: independent gentlemen such as himself, professional types including his friend William Palmer, tradesmen such as Ishmael Fisher, a wine merchant from Holborn in London, and George Myatt, a saddler who had come across to the races from Staffordshire with Palmer, and various other friends, acquaintances and hangers-on. As Cook lived in Lutterworth,

Shrewsbury Races

south of Leicester and 80 miles from Shrewsbury, he would probably break his journey halfway home with them in Rugeley, the quiet little town north of Wolverhampton where Palmer and Myatt lived.

William Palmer was Cook's closest racing crony. They had known each other for at least two years. Palmer was three years older than his friend. He had medical training enough to have been admitted to the Royal College of Surgeons, but he was no longer practising, though people still called him doctor. Palmer was a familiar figure around the racecourses of the Midlands – nattily, even prosperously dressed, stove-pipe hat perched on his head, betting book in hand, no side in his manner and a good word for everyone, including the servants. He had the sort of roguish charm that made him popular around the men of the turf and a habit of losing that made bookmakers smile in anticipation. He was a good loser, too. One of his horses, Nettle, had been running second in the Oaks the year before, until it had veered off the track and thrown its jockey. Palmer had simply shrugged it off with the remark: "It's a bore though, isn't it?"

It was a convivial party that night in Shrewsbury – everyone agreed about that later – with brandy to warm them up after a damp day at the races. The cheery middle-aged Midlanders and Londoners would have had to endure their young, generous friend repeating the story of Polestar easily winning the Shrewsbury Handicap and flourishing his winnings. The money would enable Cook to pay off the moneylenders circling around, and now he would be able to continue following the pursuits of the turf. He boasted that there would be £1,000 waiting for him in winnings to be collected from Tattersall's, the racehorse auctioneers and centre of the betting industry, at their office near Hyde Park Corner in London the following Monday when the money from bets was released. Ishmael Fisher later recalled: "He was in high spirits and appeared to be in as good a state of health as ever I had known him to be." Others were less sure: they thought Cook was pallid and delicate. And he seemed to be well on the way to getting tipsy. George Myatt, the saddler, said: "He was not very drunk, but I could see he was the worse for it."

Fisher, whose own room was next door – separated from the party in Cook's sitting room only by a wooden partition – joined the gathering between 11 p.m. and midnight to find them all drinking grog, in time to hear Cook calling on Palmer to have some more brandy with him. Palmer said: "I shall not have any more until you have drunk yours", whereupon Cook took several gulps. Suddenly the young man exclaimed: "There is something in it. It burns my throat dreadfully." Palmer took the glass from him, swallowed the rest and said, "Nonsense. There is nothing in it", before handing the tumbler over to Fisher and George Read, another wine merchant, to see if they could taste anything. "Cook says it's drugged," Palmer explained helpfully. "What's the use of handing me the glass when it's empty?" Read replied. Fisher said that the only smell he could detect was brandy.

The party broke up a little while later, with a now groggy Cook, going into his bedroom and then coming out again, wanting to talk to Fisher. In Fisher's room he said he thought "that damned Palmer" had dosed him and gave him a wad of £800 in banknotes from his winnings to take care of for him. He had already been sick, and when Fisher took him back to his room, he vomited repeatedly, badly enough for his friend to call for a doctor. The man who arrived, William Scaife Gibson, was actually a surgeon's assistant, not a doctor, but that was all the same. Cook told him he thought he had been poisoned and Gibson suggested he should drink some warm water to make himself sick. Then he stuck a toothbrush down his throat, but what he threw up was perfectly clean, as was his tongue. He prescribed Cook an emetic: two rhubarb pills, three grains of calomel and a so-called "black draught" of *mistura sennacum* – a tincture of liquefied senna pods – to clear his bowels, which he thought were distended. "I treated Cook as if he had taken poison. I took him at his word, not from his symptoms. He seemed a little excited by drink but quite sensible what he was doing and saying . . . his brain had been stimulated with brandy and water," he said. But Gibson did not bother to bring his poisoned patient to the attention of the authorities and did not linger to see whether the medicine was working. It was, after all, an era of nostrums and self-medication, when what a later generation would ascribe to biliousness or gastroenteritis could easily stem from quack remedies and medicines copiously laced with easily obtainable substances such as arsenic.

Palmer, supposedly the professional medical man, had gone to bed through all this, leaving Fisher and another friend, a stationer named Robert Jones, to sit up with Cook and administer the draught. When Fisher saw Palmer the next morning, the latter was still grumbling that the young man was accusing him of putting something in his drink: "I never play such tricks with people," Palmer told him. "I can tell you what he was; he was damned drunk." Fisher did not think so, certainly not. That morning he had given Cook his money back, after removing about £200 to settle one of his debts. What he did know was that Cook and Palmer were very thick with each other: "They were a good deal connected with racing transactions. They appeared to be very intimate and were a great deal together." The two men loaned each other money, generally stayed in the same hotels and often bet on each other's behalf.

It was only later that someone recalled that Palmer had left the party at one stage before the brandy arrived in its decanter. She was a Mrs Anne Brooks, from Chancery Lane, Ardwick, in central Manchester: by her own description, "a married woman . . . in the habit of attending race meetings, but my husband does not sanction my going when he knows about it." Mr Brooks may have been a maths teacher, according to the census, and she would have been in her late twenties. Whether her husband approved or not, it did not stop her going to the races when she chose. "Brooks is the name of my husband. He never goes with me to races. I live with him. I don't attend many races in the course of a year." A court-room artist caught an image of a respectably dressed, sly-looking woman in a bonnet and shawl. Brooks was an old friend of Palmer's and, having bumped into him in the street earlier that evening, knew him well enough to come up to his room at the hotel to get his tips for the following day's races. In the corridor, she said she saw him standing outside his room, holding a glass tumbler with a clear liquid in it. By the flickering light of a gas lamp she watched Palmer holding it up and shaking it, murmuring to her as he did so that it was fine weather for the time of year. Then, saying "I'll be with you presently", he had taken the glass into a nearby sitting room, before returning with it to his room. Shortly afterwards he came out once more and offered her the same tumbler, or an identical one, now containing brandy and water, which she drank. "It produced no unpleasant consequences in me," she said. "We had some conversation regarding the next day's racing and he said he should back his own horse, The Chicken."

What Mrs Brooks did remember, however, was that a great many racegoers had been taken ill on the Wednesday of that week. "There was a wonder as to what had caused their illness and something was said about the water being poisoned. People were affected by sickness and purging. I knew some persons who were so affected." She did not think any more about it at the time and neither, it seems, did anybody else.

By the following day, Thursday 15 November, Cook was feeling well enough to get out of bed and attend the meeting again, to see The Chicken racing in Palmer's all-yellow colours. It was not a bad horse. It had been placed in a number of important races and ridden by the celebrated young jockey George Fordham. The Chicken would later sell for 800 guineas and was probably Palmer's best in a stable of seventeen racehorses that he owned but could not afford. But it lost on this day. The result was more of a disaster for Palmer than he let on to his friends. Had his horse won, it might have netted its owner about £5,000, enough to pay off his most pressing creditors, though not enough to land him clear of debt. He really needed about £25,000 – a modern equivalent would be approximately £1.5 million – and he needed it desperately. Only the day before he had received a letter from Thomas Pratt, a London solicitor with a profitable sideline in moneylending, demanding urgent payment. Worse, Pratt was also threatening proceedings not only against Palmer but also against his mother who, all unknowing, was also a debtor because her son had borrowed money in her name as well. So was another moneylender called Henry Padwick, who had offices in Berkeley Square and was also a racehorse owner. A third, Edwin Wright of Birmingham, was also making threatening noises. Palmer had been intercepting their letters, so his mother remained in blissful ignorance, but that would not last if Pratt, Padwick and Wright went to court. It would spell ruin for the family.

There was another expedient that Palmer had adopted to raise money that was causing him trouble too. He had taken out an insurance policy on his older brother Walter's life, which in itself might have paid off most of his debts, except that Walter, a hopeless alcoholic at the age of thirty-two, had died just three months earlier, shortly after William had paid the first premium, and the Prince of Wales Insurance Office was now suspicious. It was refusing to cough up. It had been aware of Walter's precarious health when it issued the policy, but Palmer's medical friends in Rugeley, who had attested to his robustness, had not bothered to tell the company that he might not survive beyond payment of the first premium.

Nor was Walter's death the first time someone close to Palmer had died suddenly and the insurance company was taking increasing notice of his misfortunes. His wife Annie, also insured through the Prince of Wales Insurance Office for £13,000, had died only the previous September, after just one payment had been made. That time the company had paid up, but now it had sent two inspectors up to Staffordshire, one of them a large, bluff, canny former policeman called Charles Field, the most famous detective in the country, to check out the unfortunate doctor and particularly the latest life Palmer was hoping to insure: that of his part-time groom George Bates.

The choice of Field to investigate the case was significant and showed how seriously the insurance company was taking the matter. As a detective he was a celebrity. A friend of Dickens – who modelled the character of Inspector Bucket in the recently published *Bleak House* on him – Field had retired from the Metropolitan Police and was by this time running his own agency, though he tended to retain his old rank of inspector to impress clients and miscreants. Field was, said Dickens, "a middle-aged man of portly presence, with a large, moist, knowing eye, a husky voice and a habit of emphasising his conversation by the air of a corpulent forefinger, which is constantly in juxtaposition with his eyes or nose". He cannot have found the latest case very hard to resolve. Bates had been represented on the policy proposal by Palmer and his friend, the Rugeley solicitor Jeremiah Smith, as a gentleman "living independent, with good property and possessing a capital cellar of wine". Smith was acting as a local agent for a number of insurance companies and Bates's life was being touted round for several policies. Other local friends of Palmer, including John Parsons Cook and Rugeley's postmaster Sam Cheshire, had vouched for the accuracy of the representations being made. According to them, Bates was worth £400 a year (instead of less than £100, as was actually the case), in good health and industrious. They wanted to insure his life for £25,000, which would have meant a first year's premium of £500 (for which Smith would have received £25 in commission). Bates had willingly signed up after they gave him dinner at Palmer's house and talked him into it.

Yet when Field and his colleague Simpson subsequently turned up, they tracked down Bates and found him in his work clothes hoeing turnips and spreading manure on a field: hardly a fit job for a gentleman in possession of good property and a fine cellar. The simple soul told them that he had been a farmer but was now out of business. He actually rented a cottage for six shillings and sixpence a week and intermittently received £2 from Palmer for looking after his horses. He didn't know much about insurance policies and told the detectives that he thought he was insured for £4,000 and had been told by Palmer and the other proposers that he himself would receive a quarter of that when it was paid out on his life. Bates may not have been the sharpest knife in the box, but in mitigation the concept of insurance was less well developed and understood in those days, perhaps particularly by those without the means to take it out. A later line drawing of Bates for the newspapers shows a portly middle-aged man with an open, trusting countryman's face and side-whiskers, his hair smeared down neatly across the top of his head with an elegant kiss-curl for the big occasion in court. The picture has him wearing a respectable, rustic cutaway coat over a waistcoat and a spotted tie, which was perhaps more Sunday than daily wear for him.

Probably it was just as well for the sake of Bates's health that the application was not proceeded with as a result of Inspector Field's report. In fact he had gone further and told Palmer that Walter's death was suspicious

Inspector Field, the ace detective, Dickens's friend

and there ought to be an inquiry. The word "murder" was mentioned. The detectives apparently suggested to Palmer that he had better not apply to insure Bates's life any more or there would be a criminal investigation, and – satisfied that they had saved the Prince of Wales Insurance Office from being defrauded – they left without taking the matter further. Field and Simpson did not bother to tell the police that they had uncovered a potential fraud, still less a murder. So much for the ace detective: Palmer was not caught by astute policing or cunning detection. Neither the celebrity inspector, nor his colleague, was called at his trial.

The failure to get the insurance to pay out on Walter's death, or to insure George Bates, meant that Palmer was still pressed for money to pay off Pratt, Padwick and Wright. Each of the horses in William Palmer's stables was costing him hundreds of pounds a year to keep, and since he had taken up racing seriously about four years earlier, he had lost more than he had won. Now the £25 he had borrowed, probably from Cook, to fund the

Shrewsbury trip and bet on The Chicken had gone too. The expedients to keep ahead of his creditors were growing increasingly desperate.

If Cook really thought he had been poisoned, it did not stop him leaving Shrewsbury with Palmer. After the race, the two of them, together with George Myatt, the saddler, returned to Rugeley: by train to Stafford and then in a hired horse-drawn "fly" carriage for the remaining nine miles home. The trip had been something of a treat for Myatt, because Palmer had paid for the bedroom at the Raven Hotel that they had shared and for his train tickets. Clattering along the country lanes in the dark, Palmer himself was sick and vomited out of the window. The party decided it was probably due to the water at Shrewsbury, or because he had eaten food cooked in a brass utensil there. If the real explanation was Palmer's desperate anxiety about his mounting debts, he did not let on. When they arrived in Rugeley in late evening, Palmer went to his home, a pleasant, double-fronted two-storey house, set slightly back from the road behind iron railings in Market Street, while Cook booked into Room 10 on the first floor of the Talbot Arms Hotel, the town's coaching inn, directly opposite. He had stayed there several times before, but in the remaining five days of his life he would scarcely leave his room again.

The small town of Rugeley lies just north of the industrial Black Country, but shielded from it by the ancient woods and heathland of Cannock Chase. Around the town were large aristocratic country estates and, now as well as then, prosperous farming land and pastures grazed by plump cattle. It is a peaceful rural area dotted with picturesque ancient villages. Rugeley was the sort of place where everyone knew everyone else and their business, a close-knit, small community where a man could wander down the street and greet everybody he met – as Palmer did. He was well liked locally, having been born and raised in the town, friendly with other professional types, but also amiable with the locals he met in the inns. He always had time for a chat and, more importantly, tipped well. Next to the front door of his house, which he rented for £25 a year from the local landowner Lord Lichfield of nearby Shugborough Hall, he had attached a brass plate stating in bold print that he was "Wm Palmer, Surgeon and Member of the Royal College of Surgeons", though these days he hired as an assistant an older man, 44-year-old Benjamin Thirlby, to do the job instead.

A rustic view of Rugeley, from the South

Rugeley was – and is – a typical small provincial town. Its population in the 1850s was about 4,500 (today it is 22,000). Journalists who later descended on the place described it as picturesque and dull. Nowadays they might describe it as dull with a question mark against the picturesque. In Market Street, where Palmer lived at Number 7, the 1851 census shows the Sleighs at Number 2 industriously working away at various trades: father Benjamin, aged eighty-seven, and his 58-year-old son James were hatters (Benjamin added that he was also a gardener) and 43-year-old daughter Ann was a milliner, while another daughter, 49-year-old Lucy, was a confectioner. With them lived two teenagers, 15-year-old Jane Cheshire (maybe related to Sam, the local postmaster) who was apprenticed to Ann, and 14-year-old Elizabeth Myatt (presumably related to George, the saddler). The Myatt clan lived next door at Number 3: George and his wife Mary, who was a dressmaker, 14-year-old son George who was apprenticed to his father, and six-year-old Mary Jane, still listed as a scholar, as was four-year-old

Frances. Further down were the Wrights – father Thomas, a blacksmith; next to them, Charles Wootton, a stone-cutter, and his family; then Henry Bennett, a plumber and glazier, and his family, living next to the Palmers. Beyond them, at Number 8, was Moses Levi, a commercial traveller, and further on still a watchmaker's apprentice, a shoemaker, a journeyman tailor, and another ageing hatter, 75-year-old Edward Rice. Palmer and Thirlby were the nearest to professionals living in the street, a fact emphasised by the census entry which, unusually, gave both Palmer's occupation (surgeon and apothecary) and his place of qualification (St Bartholomew's, London). Virtually everyone listed their place of birth as Rugeley, though by the time of the next census in 1861 only the Myatts and the Wrights were still living in the same street.

The Talbot Arms was a typical Georgian coaching inn, a three-storey building with a flight of steps up to the front door and a large bay window sticking out onto the pavement. Further along the building there was an arch through which coaches could come and go. Room 10, where Cook stayed, was on the first floor, directly over the inn's main entrance, with a large sash-window looking out over the narrow street and straight across to Palmer's house, only a few feet away. It was a large room, big enough for two beds, which were hung about with drab damask curtains. The walls were plastered and painted light blue, and there was a fireplace on one side.

It was probably the best place in the town. Cook went straight to bed on his arrival and woke the next morning feeling better. Taking it gently, he had breakfast in bed – a cup of tea and two glasses of brandy – and did not get up until after lunch, when he dined with Palmer and their mutual friend Jeremiah Smith, the local lawyer, known as Jerry (often spelled "Jere" in contemporary accounts). Between them that Friday evening, 16 November, they polished off some beefsteak, champagne and afterwards three bottles of port. "Cook drank his share," said Smith. Afterwards the two of them wandered down to Smith's house, bickering over £50 the lawyer said Cook owed him, then went next door to the Albion Hotel and had some more brandy before Cook ambled back to his room at the Talbot Arms. It was the last time he left the hotel alive.

The following day – Saturday 17 November – Cook woke up feeling ill once more. Palmer visited him in his room several times, prescribing a number of cups of coffee during the course of the day and calling in another

The Talbot Arms, Rugeley in 1856. Room 10, where Cook died, is directly above the entrance.

local doctor, 82-year-old William Bamford, to come and see him too. Bamford was the doctor who had certified Walter Palmer's robust health for insurance purposes. It is probably fair to say that the elderly country doctor – he described himself as a surgeon and apothecary – was not at the cutting edge of medicine. He had been in practice since the turn of the nineteenth century more than fifty years before, and there is no evidence that he had any formal medical qualifications whatever, though that was not necessarily a bar to setting up before the Medical Act of 1858, passed in the aftermath of the Rugeley case, required the registration of doctors for the first time. Medical doctors were few and far between in the early years of the nineteenth century – many people would have passed their lives without ever seeing one – and even those who were educated, at the universities of Oxford, Cambridge or Edinburgh, had little practical training with patients. Bamford would have had decades of experience, but at best only very limited knowledge of a very narrow range of curable illnesses: the rest would all have been guesswork, though that did not necessarily make him worse than any other country doctor.

By the evening Cook was again vomiting repeatedly. Smith volunteered to stay with him and spent the night in his room, offering him toast and water which only made him retch more. When he awoke, Cook felt more comfortable. "I am rather better this morning," he told Smith. "I slept from about two or three o'clock after the confounded concert was gone."

Later that Sunday, however, Cook took a decided turn for the worse, and Palmer and Bamford were called in again. Bamford had certainly seen a lot of death in the course of his long career, including eight of Palmer's relatives and acquaintances. He had known the Palmers all their lives and may have helped to deliver William when he was born in 1824, so if anyone knew Palmer he did. The younger man told him that Cook had been drinking too much champagne. Bamford said: "I asked Cook if he had taken too much wine and he assured me that he took but two glasses. I found no appearance of bile about Cook, but there was constant vomiting. I prescribed for him a saline effervescing draft and a six ounce mixture [but] I never saw him take any of the pills." The medicine Bamford prescribed was two opiate pills, which he himself made up with two grains of morphia, half a grain of calomel and four grains of rhubarb.

During the day, Palmer sent over some broth, but that made Cook even worse. The soup had been prepared down the road at the Albion for some reason, instead of downstairs in the kitchen at the Talbot Arms. Its delivery to the patient's bedside was further delayed because earlier it had been carried over to Palmer's house by his charlady Anne Rowley and kept warm over the fire in the kitchen there. Later, Palmer poured it into a cup and told Rowley to take it across to Cook. He instructed her to tell him that Jerry Smith had sent it – "he did not say why," she said. Elizabeth Mills, a chambermaid at the Talbot Arms, remembered much later that she had tasted some of the soup that had been left over in the cup and had become violently sick too, although she had not remarked upon it at the time. "About half an hour afterwards it made me very sick and I vomited violently all the afternoon until about five o'clock. I was obliged to go to bed. Up to that time I had been quite well. I had taken nothing that I am aware of that had disagreed with me."

On Monday 19 November, Palmer went down to London for the day

The elderly Dr Bamford, who signed the death certificate

by the newly established train service from Stafford, taking Cook's betting book – containing the record of the bets he had placed and his winnings – with him. That afternoon, at Beaufort Buildings, a boarding house on the Strand where he normally stayed, he called in a racing man called George Herring – another of those who had been at the party at the Raven – and asked him to draw money against Cook's winnings at Tattersall's and send cheques to several debtors, including the money-lending attorney Pratt. Palmer had to do this because he himself was not allowed to darken the doors of Tattersall's on account of his record of bad debts, but Cook's winnings on the Shrewsbury Handicap were only payable at Tattersall's under the club's rules a week after the race. He was effectively asking Herring to pay his debts with Cook's money. Herring said afterwards:

> Before he left he pressed me to send the cheques to Pratt and Padwick immediately before the closing of the bank. He said: "When you have settled this account write down word to either me or Cook." I replied: "I shall certainly write to Mr Cook," because I

thought I was settling Mr Cook's account. He said: "It does not matter which." I asked him if I addressed the letter to "Mr Cook/Palmer, Rugeley", would that be correct, and he said yes.

George Herring was a respectable commission agent, collecting and disbursing winnings for clients for a fee, though he may have had his suspicions when asked to pay well-known moneylenders like Pratt and Padwick. He would eventually die, fifty years later, a millionaire – he became a successful businessman in the City of London – and a friend of King Edward VII. He might have known of Palmer's reputation and been surprised to be approached. Cook usually used Ishmael Fisher for such jobs, but Palmer probably knew that his friend owed Fisher £200 and would not have wanted that to be subtracted from the amount paid over. He possibly did not know that Fisher had already taken it from the roll of money Cook had handed him on the night the previous week he was taken ill at Shrewsbury.

Herring sent a cheque for £450 in the post to Pratt, but he did not pay off all the debts he was asked to because Palmer had additionally tried to convince him to use his own money in advance of Palmer paying off the debt he already owed him. Herring was too smart for that: "He asked me to send a cheque at once. I refused to do so as I had not received the money. He said it would be alright." Palmer himself went round to Pratt's office in Queen Street, Mayfair and gave him £50. There were already many signs of exasperation from the moneylender, who was used to receiving repayment from Palmer – and presumably many other clients – in dribs and drabs. In all, Palmer paid off £1,300 that day: a tenth of what he owed and enough only to cover a month's interest on his borrowings. Earlier in November Pratt had warned that there would be writs against Palmer and his mother, and he was still writing him threatening letters, one of which he had received during the Shrewsbury race meeting the previous week. The letters were getting nastier and more urgent: two days later Pratt would cryptically let him know, "If anything unpleasant occurs, you must thank yourself", which still sounds pretty chilling. Pratt was indeed getting his pound of flesh: the interest rate he was charging was 60 per cent. Now he was also trying to write to Palmer's mother, so things were getting more serious: William had not told her about the loans taken out in her name. She had paid his debts before, but this time, being dunned for a huge sum of money she knew nothing about was likely to be different. He might have depleted his own credit with her too.

After a day of financial wrangling and juggling debts, Palmer returned to the Midlands by train to Stafford and then hired a horse and trap to take him home. On the way back, at about 9 p.m., he may have stopped at the house of Mr Salt, another Rugeley surgeon, to pick up three grains of strychnine – the alkaloid organic poison – from Salt's assistant Charles Newton. The poison, distilled from the seeds of the nux vomica (poison nut) tree of southern Asia, was commonly used to slaughter vermin, but even small amounts could quickly kill humans too, within minutes or hours. The modern equivalent of a grain would be about 64 milligrams. *Simpson's Forensic Medicine* estimates a fatal dose at between 30 and 60 milligrams, so a single grain could easily kill and three would be more than enough. It causes convulsions and asphyxiation as the muscles tighten. "I weighed it accurately and gave it to him in a paper," Newton recalled. "He did not pay me for it as I did not sell it, but gave it to him. I and Mr Salt are surgeons and do not sell drugs to ordinary persons." Palmer was only with him for two or three minutes, Newton added, though his evidence was tainted as he only remembered the incident months later.

Newton is an ambiguous figure in the story. Aged about twenty-two at this time, he may have been the illegitimate son of Palmer's assistant Benjamin Thirlby. His evidence, perhaps more than anyone else's, contributed to the conviction of Palmer, who had thought of him as a friend. Palmer maintained that Newton could not have remembered him visiting the shop that night, because his 5 p.m. train from Euston to Stafford must have got in at 8.50 p.m. and he could not have driven the nine miles to Rugeley by horse and trap in 10 minutes. As damaging to Palmer was Newton's belated recollection in the witness box six months later that they had discussed how much strychnine would be needed to kill a dog – the ostensible reason for his needing the poison in the first place. Newton also testified that he had seen Palmer buying six further grains of strychnine at Rugeley's third chemist, Hawkins, on the following morning. This hugely lethal amount was just sixpence worth and could be purchased over the counter. The six grains, if they existed, were never seen again.

During that Monday Cook had been feeling much better, even managing to keep some coffee down. He had got up, dressed, had a shave and chatted to friends. Then, in the evening, Palmer paid a visit following his return from London and afterwards Cook again took a turn for the worse. He began to vomit and scream and then started suffering terrifying convulsions which jerked him almost out of bed. The candle-lit scene in Room 10 must have been gothic in its horror, with the young man writhing and shouting as he cast shadows against the walls. The servants who ventured upstairs to attend him were terrified. Lavinia Barnes, the hotel's waitress, was tidying up in the kitchen when she was called to his room. "About 12 o'clock I was alarmed by the violent ringing of Cook's bell. I went upstairs and saw Cook who was screaming out with pain. He said he was suffocating. His eyes were very wild and standing a great way out of his head; he was beating the bed with his hands. I left for the purpose of sending the boots for Palmer." She then called for help from Elizabeth Mills, the chambermaid who said she had become ill after drinking the broth two days earlier but was now well again. She was in bed in the room above Cook's, trying to get to sleep. Mills said:

> I heard the noise of violent screaming while I was dressing . . .
> as soon as I entered the room I found him sitting up in bed. The
> pillow was on the floor and there was one candle burning. I
> picked up the pillow and asked him would he lay down his head.
> He was beating the bedclothes with both his arms and hands
> stretched out. He said: "I cannot lie down. I shall suffocate if I
> do. Oh, fetch Mr Palmer."

His body, his hands and neck were moving then – a sort of jumping or jerking. His head was back. Sometimes he would throw back his head upon the pillow and then he would raise himself up again. This jumping and jerking was all over his body. He appeared to have great difficulty breathing. The balls of both the eyes were much projected. He was so short of breath. He called aloud: "Murder" twice. He asked me to rub one hand. I found it stiff, stretched out as if the fingers were paralysed . . . all the way up the arm.

Lavinia Barnes described the same harrowing scene:

> He screamed: "murder!" and "Christ have mercy on my soul."
> I never saw anyone in such a state before. Palmer came and I

Rugeley High Street in 1856: the Talbot Arms's inn sign can be seen on the left, Palmer's house is behind the railings on the right and the town hall where Cook's inquest would be held is in the distance.

again went up to the room. He then appeared to be more quiet and composed. Cook exclaimed: "Oh doctor, I shall die!" and Palmer replied: "Oh you won't. Don't be alarmed, lad." I saw Cook drink a darkish mixture out of a glass but I cannot say who gave it to him, but Palmer was in the room. He snapped at the glass with his teeth when it was presented to his mouth. I both saw and heard the snapping of the glass. The fluid did not remain on his stomach; he vomited it up.

Barnes and Mills fled the room. Remarkably, considering that Cook kept accusing Palmer of trying to poison him, he was still calling for his friend as the crisis took hold. Perhaps he did not really believe Palmer would do such a thing. More likely, fear made him desperate; or possibly his debilitating illness had made him apathetic, or too weak to object. In his state, it might anyway have been hard to think ill of such a kindly and solicitous friend as Palmer, for whom nothing was too much trouble. Gradually Cook subsided into sleep. The following morning, Tuesday 20 November, after the frightening scene in the middle of the night, Cook seemed better once more. Elizabeth Mills talked to him as she tidied his room. "I saw Cook," she said. "He asked me whether I had ever seen anyone suffer such agony as he had last night and I replied I never had. He said he should think I would never like to see anyone like that again. I asked him what he thought was the cause of all that agony and he said: 'The pills Palmer gave me at half-past ten.'"

That afternoon, another friend turned up from Leicestershire. William Henry Jones, who was yet another medical man (he described himself as a surgeon and medical practitioner with fifteen years' experience), arrived in response to a letter Palmer had sent him two days earlier. Jones had shared in the champagne celebration at Shrewsbury the previous week and had himself been ill after going home, which delayed his return to look after his friend. Jones, who was also an acquaintance of Palmer's, was the fourth doctor to attend to Cook during his illness. He was the one who knew his usual health the best, for he had been a friend of the young man for five years and Cook stayed in his house when he was in Lutterworth. "His health was generally good," Jones would later say. "But he was not very robust. I think he hunted and played cricket." When he had left him in Shrewsbury the day after Polestar's triumph, Jones said Cook had seemed in his usual health and not in the least the worse for liquor.

But then the letter he had received from Palmer five days later had asked him to come at once:

My dear Sir,
Mr Cook was taken ill at Shrewsbury and obliged to call in a medical man; since then he has been confined to his bed here with a very severe bilious attack, combined with diarrhoea and I think it advisable for you to come and see him as soon as possible.

Jones found Cook sitting up in bed and talking of getting up the next day. He examined the patient with Palmer standing by and found his pulse to be normal and his tongue clean – "You should have seen it before," said Palmer. When he was given toast, though, Cook vomited again. In the early evening old Dr Bamford came round once more and the three medical men stood by Cook's bed discussing his future medication. Cook said he did not want any more of the pills he had taken the previous evening because they had made him ill, so the other three retreated out of his earshot and Palmer suggested that Bamford should make up the same morphine pills as before, but not tell Cook what was in them. The old doctor then went home to make them and Jones paid return visits to Room 10 several times during the course of the evening. His friend seemed very comfortable now: no more vomiting or diarrhoea and no signs of biliousness. Cook sat up in a chair. "He seemed very jocose," said Jones. "Speaking of what he should do during the winter and of his future plans and prospects."

Later, at about 11 p.m., Palmer turned up with a box of pills he said had come from Bamford, opened it and pulled out the handwritten note accompanying it. This just said: "Night Pills, John Parsons Cook Esq." Palmer pointed out the neatness of the handwriting: "What an excellent hand for an old man upwards of eighty to write." It was very good writing indeed, Jones agreed. If Palmer was trying to make a point about the old man's professional and mental competence, or emphasising that Bamford had made up the pills himself, it passed Jones by. They had to force the pills upon Cook, who spewed immediately he had taken them. The two medical men solemnly inspected the vomit and agreed that it only contained toast and water, so he had at least kept the pills down. It had been arranged that Jones would stay in the same room as Cook, so while his friend seemed comfortable he went downstairs for some supper, returning at midnight, by which time Cook was sleepy but "quite as well as usual – nothing to excite any apprehension".

But within ten minutes of Jones getting into his bed, Cook suddenly called out: "Doctor, get up! I am going to be ill; ring the bell for Mr Palmer!" Jones called for Elizabeth Mills, who had waited downstairs in the kitchen in case she was needed – "anxious to see how he got on," she said – and she rushed up to the room to find the doctor trying to support his friend. "Oh Mary," he had said – Mary being the common name for chambermaids if you could not remember their real name – "Go for Mr Palmer." Mills rushed the few yards across the street and rang Palmer's bell. He answered by opening a small pane in his first-floor bedroom window – she could tell it was him by his voice – and he followed her back. Palmer bustled into the room within a couple of minutes of being sent for, to find Jones rubbing Cook's neck which had gone into spasm. Cheerily remarking "I was never so quickly dressed in my life" – too quick, some said later, almost as if he had been waiting for the call – Palmer now gave Cook two more pills, which he said were ammonia, and they had an immediate effect. Cook screamed loudly, threw himself back on his bed and went into convulsions, worse than before. Jones maintained that it could not have been the pills which caused this, as he had only just taken them:

> He said to me: "Raise me up or I shall be suffocated." All the muscular fibres were convulsed; there was a violent contraction of every muscle of the body and a stiffening of the limbs. When he called out to me to raise him, I endeavoured to do so with the assistance of Mr Palmer but found it was quite impossible owing to the rigidity of the limbs. When he found I could not raise him up, he asked me to turn him over, which I did. He was quite sensible.

If Cook was fully conscious, he must have been terrified by what was happening to him. The convulsions were so powerful that his body arched like a bent bow. Jones could now sense that Cook's heart was failing and asked Palmer to fetch some ammonia spirits to try and revive him. Palmer trotted out of the room to fetch smelling salts from his house and found Elizabeth Mills hovering in the corridor, probably too afraid to go in. He said to her encouragingly that Cook was not so ill, "not by one fiftieth part" as he had been previously. "What a game to be at every night," he added jovially as he went downstairs.

By now Lavinia Barnes was also outside the open bedroom door. "I heard Mr Cook scream as I stood on the landing by the door . . . I said to Mr Palmer, 'Mr Cook is ill again,' Palmer said: 'Oh is he?' and went in." Palmer was back with a bottle of *sal volatile* within a minute or so, but by then Jones could tell it was too late and it was never administered. Cook's convulsions and screams stopped and his life was nearly extinct. "He died very quietly," said Jones. "It was very soon after Palmer returned that he died. From the time he raised himself in bed and called upon me to go for Palmer to the time when he died would be from ten minutes to a quarter of an hour."

The maids saw Jones with his head against his friend's chest, listening for a heartbeat. Cook had died on his side, his heart stopping as a result of the convulsions. Jones said: "The outward appearance of the body after death was very dark. As there was only one candle in the room, I could not make the observation I otherwise should have made. Both his hands, the left hand particularly, were clenched . . . the head was quite bent back . . . the body was twisted like a bow; the backbone was twisted back. If I had placed the body at that time upon the back, on a level surface, it would have rested on the head and the heels . . . the jaw was not in its natural condition." The chambermaids ventured back into the room and Mills asked Palmer: "Is it possible Mr Cook is dead?" "Oh yes," he replied. "He's dead." When Barnes exclaimed "Oh, Mr Cook can't be dead!" she said that Palmer had replied: "Oh yes he is – I knew he would be." Someone remembered afterwards that he had said something like "The poor devil has gone" – a phrase which was inevitably later relayed to his detriment, but which a doctor, used to and expecting a death, perhaps might well say.

That was the end of John Parsons Cook, some time after midnight on Wednesday 21 November 1855, on the eighth day after Polestar's triumph in the Shrewsbury Handicap and the parties and the foaming beakers of "provincial" champagne. The question was: how had he died? And, if his demise was unnatural, why and at whose hands? But nobody considered querying such matters at the time. On that November night in the Talbot Arms there was no suspicion that Cook had been murdered. He had been attended by three medical men in his last hours and, despite the patient's exclamations, none of them thought his death unnatural or suspicious.

Old Dr Bamford, summoned by Palmer while Cook was still writhing, arrived within a few minutes of his death. Palmer asked him to fill in the death certificate, as he had done so many times before. "I filled up the certificate and gave it as my opinion that he died from apoplexy." Then, as if to cover his back, the old man added: "When Palmer asked me to fill up the certificate, I told him that, as Cook was his patient, it was his place to fill it up. He said he had much rather I did it and I did so." Apoplexy was the contemporary term for a stroke.

Jones, forty years younger than the old doctor and probably much better qualified, disagreed with Bamford's diagnosis. He thought Cook had died from tetanus, a not uncommon disease which could cause convulsions. Its hugely toxic bacterium, embedded in the soil and substances such as horse manure, spreads infection through open wounds and cuts; its symptoms, developing over six to ten days, include spasms and muscular contractions, eventually arching of the back and neck, asphyxiation, seizure of the heart, and the rictus smile that gives it its common name. "In my judgement, as a medical man, he died from tetanus," said Jones. "Or in ordinary English parlance lockjaw . . . Locked jaw is one of the symptoms." Jones admitted that he had only ever seen one death from tetanus, from an infected wound, but he knew that whatever had killed Cook, it was not what old Bamford thought. "I am satisfied that Cook's death was not caused by apoplexy," he insisted. "I thought Cook's sore throat was syphilitic and Cook told me that several other medical men had told him so also." By then, though, such speculation was too late and a murder trial was underway.

William Palmer, the youngest of the doctors at the bedside, did not give his opinion on the night of Cook's death. He just seemed worried about money. When Elizabeth Mills came back into the bedroom 10 minutes after Cook had died, she said she found him going through the pockets of the dead man's coat and reaching under the pillow and bolster on the bed as if looking for something. Jones saw him with the coat too, and Palmer handed over to him Cook's watch and his purse, containing five guineas and five shillings. In the week since his horse had won its race, hundreds of pounds of his winnings had gone missing, even though he had been too ill to spend anything. It would never be accounted for. Equally importantly, the small pocketbook in which he kept a note of his bets and his winnings had also vanished. Mills said she knew what it looked like: a dark book, not very large, rather more long than square, with gold bands around the edges, a clasp at one end and a little case along the side for a pencil. She had seen him with it on earlier occasions – her memory for such a trivial item was quite precise – and she had handed it to him when he had asked for it on the Monday evening. If Palmer had taken it to London that day, he had also returned it. The book had been on the dressing table then and she had given it to him, together with some paper, a pen and ink, as he lay in bed. Cook had taken out a postage stamp and she had then replaced the book on the frame of the mirror sitting on the dressing table. Mills said she had never seen the book afterwards, but she had certainly watched Palmer later as he went through the dead man's clothes which were lying on a chair. Neither book, nor banknotes, were ever seen again.

Jones recalled: "Before Palmer left, he said something to me on the subject of affairs as between Cook and himself. He said, as near as I can recollect: 'It is a bad thing for me, as I was responsible for £3,000 or £4,000 and I hope Mr Cook's friends will not let me lose it. If they do not assist me, all my horses will be seized.'"

Palmer did more than that. Later in the day he would sit down to write to his chief creditor, the Mayfair solicitor Thomas Pratt. His mind was full of ways to stave off Pratt, whose threats of writs and ruin were becoming daily more pressing. One way out he saw was to gain ownership of Polestar, Cook's horse that had won at Shrewsbury the week before, from the trainer William Saunders.

> My dear Sir,
> Ever since I saw you I have been fully engaged with Cook and not able to leave home and am sorry to say after all he <u>died</u> this day, so you had better write to Saunders but mind you I must have Pole Star if it can be so arranged & should any one call upon you to know what money or monies Cook ever had from you don't answer the question till I have seen you. I will send you the £75 tomorrow & as soon as I have been to Manchester you shall hear about the other monies.
> I sat up two full nights with Cook & am very much tired out.
> Yours faithfully,
> Wm Palmer
> Rugeley
> Nov 21 '55

What none of Palmer's friends and acquaintances knew, though, that night or probably for ever after, was that his debts to his creditors such as Pratt were not the only worries on his mind. He was also being blackmailed by a mistress, for whom he may have procured an abortion a few months before

– he certainly thought he had done so. Her name was Jane and she had recently demanded £100 to keep quiet about the thirty-four letters he had written to her over the course of the previous year – letters he had expected her to destroy but which she had recently informed him she had kept.

By the time he sent money to buy her off, however, William Palmer had even more urgent problems on his mind. Within forty-eight hours of Cook's death, his nemesis arrived. William Stephens, a wealthy retired London businessman and Cook's stepfather, took the train up to the Midlands as soon as he heard the news, determined to find out what had happened to the young man. He for one would be immune to Palmer's charm. The death of John Parsons Cook was becoming more problematic by the hour.

3

"They won't hang us yet"

B Y HIS OWN ACCOUNT, WILLIAM VERNON STEPHENS WAS TAKEN BY SURPRISE on the evening of Wednesday 21 November to receive a visit at his London home from William Henry Jones, coming down straight from the Talbot Arms to tell him that his stepson had died the previous night. Stephens is a central figure in the story, for without his insistence – and money – there would have been no investigation into John Parsons Cook's death and no trial, or notoriety, for its suspect, William Palmer. Stephens's background is largely obscure. He told the later court hearing in evidence that he was "a merchant in the city, but now out of business". He lived in a stuccoed terrace at 11 Campden Grove, Kensington. Jones, materialising out of the night, must have bounded up the steps to reach the front door and break the news. The houses would have been for the genteel middle classes: not grand exactly but reasonably spacious, four-storied, bow-windowed and in a congenial part of town. The area was well-to-do if not as exclusive as it is today. Stephens lived with his sister Frances and a middle-aged servant, Elizabeth Pugh. The census shows he was born in Devon and described himself as a fundholder, so presumably he had done reasonably well for himself in the City and was now living off the income from savings. In 1855 he would have been fifty-four years of age; a line drawing of him from the court case shows a well-dressed and well-fed figure, avuncular and balding, with small oval spectacles. He would not be at all genial, or forgiving, towards Palmer, however, but both vengeful and implacably determined.

John Parsons Cook was his stepson. Stephens had married his mother eighteen years before, after she had been widowed, but she had soon died herself, in about 1839, and so was long dead by this time, though he had not remarried. Cook had older stepbrothers and a sister, but he had never lived with Stephens much: he would have been about 10 years old when his stepfather married Cook's mother and 12 when she died. The men seem to have been on reasonable terms: he called his stepfather "Papa" and Stephens described him as "my poor boy". They were, Stephens said, "in constant weekly intercourse". In his witness statement, written a few months after his stepson's death, signed in a neat, precise hand, Stephens said his stepson had a delicacy of appearance but was in general good health, with no illness to keep him in bed since childhood: "he was always temperate in his habits and capable of great exertion as he shewed by hunting and cricketing. I have never known him to be hysterical, or subjected to fits."

In saying this, Stephens was either being economical with the truth, or he was not entirely aware of his stepson's less temperate habits. Cook had stayed at Campden Grove for a month the previous January when he had been ill, unable to shake off the sore throat that gave him trouble all that year. Stephens clearly thought he had gone off the rails when he gave up his training as an articled clerk in Worthing after his inheritance had come through a few years earlier and had warned him about his bad habits, his betting and race-going, and probably about his louche circle of friends too. "I did everything in my power to withdraw him from that pursuit," Stephens insisted. "In point of appearance he was not a robust man," he added. Cook was delicate – as was his sister – and their father had died at the age of thirty, some said having committed suicide. Stephens had last seen Cook on 5 November at Euston station. "He looked better than I had seen him for some time," he said. "I said: 'My boy, you look very well; you do not look anything of an invalid now.' He struck himself firmly on the chest and said he was quite well." Cook's doctor, Henry Savage, thought much the same. In a letter written a few months later he stated:

> I saw [him] several times between January and March and then in May. In the meantime he had resorted to a mercurial course for sore throats and superficial ulcers of the tongue, lips, inside of cheeks. I recommended him to discontinue the mercury and the ulcers etc immediately began to improve . . . When I saw him

The remorseless stepfather, William Stephens

in November I thought him in very good health. He appeared to be in good spirits. He often mentioned his turf affairs and alluded to his 'partner' but never mentioned his name.

So it must have been quite a shock only a fortnight later for Stephens to find Jones on his doorstep, saying that his stepson had been ill for a week and then died. "I desired him to give me some particulars of my son's illness and death," the older man said in his witness statement, adding that he had immediately been struck with suspicion. "As soon as he had described his last struggles to me, a vague recollection of some case of poisoning which I had somewhere heard of, or read of, passed across my mind in which the symptoms were so much like those Mr Jones had been describing I at once exclaimed: 'Good God, Sir, there is something wrong, he has been poisoned!'" This part of his statement, showing how instantly Stephens concluded his son had been murdered, was understandably never aired in court.

Already predisposed to believe the worst, Stephens set about things in a businesslike fashion, packing an overnight bag and first thing the following morning heading for Lutterworth to explore Cook's room at Jones's home in Princes Square in search of a will and any other papers he had left. They found the will – which named Stephens as executor – and the next day went on to Rugeley, where they bumped into Palmer in the passage at the Talbot Arms. Stephens had met Palmer once before and immediately disliked him because of his influence over Cook. In the traumatic aftermath of his stepson's death, Palmer certainly did not make a favourable impression on him. "I did not like his manner," Stephens said in his statement:

> He did not look me frankly, or directly, in the face. In short, he looked and carried himself like one who felt he had something to answer for and explain. I felt somewhat there had been foul play of some sort and it was impossible for me to doubt [from] Palmer's look and manner that he had been concerned in it. I at once determined that I must investigate this, but I resolved to keep [it] to myself.
>
> I have struggled against my suspicions and tried to erase them from my mind and heart. I have used a decent civility towards him. I have indeed so far persuaded myself that my suspicions ought not to have any foundation.

This did not stop him in the months to come trying to follow up every possible lead to convict Palmer. In a letter to his solicitor from his home in Campden Grove, he wrote: "There is an entry in Palmer's diary, November 24th, as to the train by which he came to London that day. If you will let me know the time, I will try to find the cab he hired and where it took him." He added (and one can sense the pain): "For seventeen years since the death of my wife, I have lived generally here in quiet and almost in seclusion, owing no man anything and giving no man offence . . . I think I might walk up half the town of Kensington to say that at worst I am a harmless and inoffensive old fellow."

Perhaps Palmer's manner was caused by insouciance, recklessness or desperation – maybe all three. There is even a story that, on hearing of Stephens's arrival, Palmer exclaimed: "But he doesn't have any relatives!" Whatever it was, practically everything he said seems to have rubbed

Stephens up the wrong way. In fact he only inflamed his suspicions.

The three men went upstairs to inspect Cook's body, now lying in an open cheap wooden shell coffin but still in Room 10, two-and-a-half days after his death. It was trussed up to push the contorted limbs back into place, so that it could be fitted into the box. The corpse had been prepared for burial by a local woman, Mary Keeling, who had been called out in the middle of the night immediately after Cook's death. She had been at the bedside within an hour, long before rigor mortis would have set in. "I never saw one so stiff before," she said:

> We had difficulty in straightening the arms. I passed a piece of tape under the back and tied it round the wrists to fasten the arms down. We were obliged to tie the feet together. The eyes were open. We were a considerable time before we could close them, because the eyelids were very stiff. The fingers were very stiff and I had difficulty getting off the rings. I got them off and when I had done so the hand closed again . . . I have laid out a great many of all ages . . . I never knew of the arms being tied before this instance . . . I have never known the eyelids so stiff as in this case. I have put penny pieces on the eyes.

Viewing the body two days later, Stephens said that he "was greatly struck by the appearance of the countenance, the tightness of the muscles across the face". He said he could not see any signs of emaciation or disease.

Stephens, Jones and Palmer then trooped back downstairs again and went into a sitting room. Stephens asked Palmer what he knew of Cook's affairs and Palmer immediately launched into a moan about how much he himself was due. He reckoned that the dead man owed him thousands of pounds but, fortuitously, he already happened to have a lawyer's letter, signed by Cook, acknowledging the debts. Palmer said: "There are £4,000 worth of bills out and I am sorry to say my name is attached to them; but I have got a paper drawn up by a lawyer and signed by Mr Cook to show that I never had any benefit from them." Palmer had apparently earlier attempted to persuade the local postmaster Samuel Cheshire, who knew both men (Palmer and he had been at school together) and had been present at

Shrewsbury races with them, to sign the letter as a witness to the signature. But Cheshire, who was prepared to do quite a lot for his old friend, refused on this occasion on the not unreasonable grounds that he had not seen Cook signing it. He did, however, admit to writing out a cheque for £350 at Palmer's dictation on the day before Cook died. Palmer told him that it was money he was owed by Cook, but as his friend was currently so ill, if Cheshire would just write out the details on Cook's behalf, he'd get his sick friend to sign it. It seems to have been presented subsequently to Charles Wetherby, the secretary of the Jockey Club, to settle Palmer's debts, but as there was insufficient money in Cook's account – his winnings on Polestar's race had not been paid in – the cheque bounced. It looks as though Palmer was trying to double-dip – expropriating his friend's winnings and present-ing a cheque supposedly drawn on them. Palmer himself had only nine pounds in the bank at this stage. Both the letter and the cheque disappeared and were never seen again. There were those who suspected Cook's signa-ture must have been forged, for signing cheques written out by someone else would probably not have been a priority for him on his last day alive. Other sums, which Palmer owed to Pratt and to a local farmer and a draper, were settled with banknotes.

In the sitting room of the Talbot Arms, Stephens listened to Palmer's woes about the money he claimed Cook owed him and then said ruthlessly that he doubted whether there would be 4,000 shillings in the dead man's estate to settle the debts. He certainly was not going to offer to pay them himself. Stephens then twisted the knife by asking Palmer whether he owned property, or horses, he could sell to meet his own debts. Palmer sighed that they were already mortgaged. At any rate, said Stephens, Cook must be buried, whether he had any money or not. Palmer immediately replied: "Oh! I will bury him myself if that is all."

No, Stephens retorted, irked. As executor it was his duty to ensure his stepson's burial and he intended to do it in London, in his mother's grave. He would arrange it within a day or two and meanwhile the body would have to remain at the hotel. Did Palmer happen to know of a suitable local undertaker from whom he could order a coffin? It was at this point that Palmer possibly made his greatest mistake in dealing with the stepfather. "Oh, I have been and chosen that," he said. "I have ordered a shell and a strong oak coffin." Stephens was outraged at the usurpation and told him he had no authority to do so. Having seen the body and at that time of year, he did not see the necessity for a quick burial – "the body did not quite look to me like a dead body" – and he was furious that Palmer had made the decision for him. Perhaps Palmer really had forgotten all about the stepfather, or thought that he would not mind or care what happened to the young man's body. Perhaps he genuinely thought he was saving him trouble, or expense. More likely, he wanted to get the body underground as quickly and cheaply as possible, just in case any inquiries were made. If so, Palmer must have begun to realise that things were starting to go wrong. With restrained politeness, the party then adjourned to have a hurried lunch together, so that Stephens could catch the mid-afternoon train back to London. During the meal, he asked Jones to go upstairs and fetch Cook's betting book and any papers from the bedroom. Palmer and Jones went up to the room together but returned shortly afterwards to say they had been unable to find anything.

Stephens again expressed astonishment, at which Palmer said insouciantly, "It's of no manner of use if you find it", adding that a dead man's bets died with him. Stephens, increasingly exasperated and with civility wearing thin, said he would be the judge of what use the book was and added that he knew his stepson had won a great deal of money at Shrewsbury. The book, he insisted, must be found; it contained notes of all Cook's bets and the monies claimed and owed as a result – a gentleman's record of his gambling. Palmer answered quietly: "Oh, it will be found, no doubt." The question of what had happened to the money Cook had won was left hanging in the air. With that, Stephens left to catch his train, ordering the bedroom containing his stepson's body to be locked until he returned.

Stephens spoke to his London solicitor on the Saturday morning, then made to catch the early afternoon train back to Rugeley. On the platform at Euston he was surprised to see Palmer, who told him he had been summoned up to town by telegram that morning. They bumped into each other again when the train stopped at Wolverton station in Buckinghamshire (now part of Milton Keynes) so that the passengers could get out, stretch their legs and buy refreshments. Stephens said meaningfully that it would be as well to know how his stepson had died and he should like his body to be opened, to which Palmer replied words to the effect that it could be easily done.

Railway travel could be both slow and uncomfortable in the days before connecting corridors, on-board toilets or refreshments. Trains would customarily pause for 10 minutes at stations so that passengers could stretch their legs, relieve themselves and buy refreshments. Not heading straight to Stafford but stopping at local halts, the train stopped again at Rugby, where Stephens resumed his conversation with Palmer in the station refreshment room. He said he intended to employ a solicitor and asked Palmer whether he knew of a suitable one in Rugeley. He probably knew that Palmer could name several, not least his friend Jerry Smith. The two men got back on the train and Stephens found that Palmer had joined him in the same carriage. They did not speak, but presumably sat glowering at each other for the rest of the journey. At Rugeley station, Palmer buttonholed Stephens again to tell him that he could indeed find him a solicitor. Stephens now retorted coldly that he would find one himself. "I then immediately, purposely changed the tone of my voice and manner and said: 'Mr Palmer if I should call in a solicitor to give me advice, I suppose you will have no objections to answer him any questions he might choose to put to you?'" Stephens added that Palmer replied, "with a spasmodic affection of the throat, which was perfectly evident, 'Oh no, certainly not.'" In fact, Stephens already had a solicitor in mind, a man named James Gardner, who had been recommended to him by his London lawyers. Now Stephens told Palmer that he was thinking of taking a solicitor with him to Hednesford, just down the road from Rugeley, across the other side of Cannock Chase, because that was where Cook kept his racehorses. Palmer kept his horses there too.

That weekend, Stephens kept bumping into Palmer. The latter was still worried about getting paid. "It is a very unpleasant affair for me about these bills," he told Stephens at one point, but Stephens shut him up by saying that he had heard different accounts of his stepson's finances and accordingly the whole matter would have to be resolved in the Court of Chancery. "Oh indeed," Palmer gulped. Later, Palmer approached him and suggested he should not go to Hednesford, at which Stephens snapped that he would be the best judge of what he should do. The next time, Stephens asked him who Jerry Smith was and whether he would know anything about the missing betting book. Palmer thought not. Then, bumping into each other once again, Palmer asked who would be carrying out the post-mortem and Stephens said he did not know. Stephens, or his Rugeley lawyer James Gardner, wrote to the county coroner during the weekend requesting an inquest.

Gossip was getting around by now that Cook had been poisoned. How else to account for his death? He had had so much to live for. And who could have done it, except his best friend Palmer? In an era of sudden, inexplicable deaths, untreatable illnesses, quack medicines and ineffective remedies, the focus fell remarkably quickly onto the local doctor. There had been just too many deaths with Palmer in close proximity, and Cook's excruciating death and Stephens's loud complaints and all too evident suspicions now crystallised into local certainties, confirming what must previously have been murmured after earlier deaths. They were rumours that Palmer's panicked actions fuelled rather than dispelled. Had it been the first such death, it might not have been noticed, and the evidence might be circumstantial and, at this stage, insubstantial. But on the streets of Rugeley folk were putting two and two together.

On that Sunday evening, the chemist's assistant Charles Newton testified later, Palmer summoned him to his house. He found him sitting in the kitchen, and Palmer, having already bought the strychnine grains the previous week while Cook was still alive, now asked him how much he thought would be needed to kill a dog and whether it would be found in the animal's stomach after death. "I told him a grain and that there would be no inflammation and I did not think it would be found," Newton said he had told him, adding: "I think he said, 'It is all right,' as if speaking to himself, and snapped his fingers."

The post-mortem took place on the Monday morning, downstairs in the assembly room at the Talbot Arms. This would not have been uncommon in that period. Inns often had the largest public rooms locally at a time when there were no facilities for refrigerating and storing bodies, or indeed for transporting them to more specialised laboratories, under the supervision of professional experts. Undoubtedly, often such events were relatively cosy, perfunctory affairs, conducted haphazardly under the guidance of a local surgeon or solicitor in front of a jury of worthies who all knew each other – and who had probably known the deceased as well: all this with entirely predictable outcomes. Coroners hold the longest-established legal office in England (their courts date back to the eleventh century) and have traditionally had considerable leeway in conducting their investigations into unexplained deaths. The inquest into the death of John Parsons Cook would be no exception, but before they got that far, there would have to be an autopsy to try and determine the cause of his death. Had Stephens not insisted, old Bamford's initial verdict that Cook had died of apoplexy would almost certainly have stood unchallenged and unexamined. Perhaps that is what Palmer had been counting on.

On this occasion, though, what happened was one of the most shambolic post-mortems that can ever have been held. Things began to go awry even before the proceedings started, with the arrival of Dr John Harland, a surgeon from Stafford who, apparently much to his surprise, was to conduct the post-mortem. He thought he was just going to be watching, so he had not brought any surgical instruments with him, or even a notebook. If the later sketches of him in newspapers are any guide, Harland was a tall, sardonic-looking man with large mutton-chop whiskers. Clearly, he was less professional, or perhaps just more casual in relation to his duties, than he appeared.

On arriving at Rugeley, Harland's first port of call was Dr Bamford's house, but even before he got there he found Palmer strolling up the street to meet him. He knew William Palmer well, so well in fact that he had been one of the doctors who had certified his alcoholic brother Walter Palmer as fit to be insured only the previous summer: one of the little courtesies a closed local circle of professional men could perform for each other in the run of things. In return for the favour and for his trouble, Palmer had sent him a dozen bottles of port. Not surprisingly, therefore, Palmer was pleased to see him, all the more so when he learned why he had come to Rugeley. Stephens could have had no idea of their connection when he had written the previous day to ask for the doctor to attend. "I am glad you have come to make a post-mortem examination," Palmer declared, relieved. "Someone might have been sent whom I did not know – I know you." Harland then quizzed him about the case, saying there might be a suspicion of poisoning, but Palmer replied: "Oh no! I think not: he had an epileptic fit on Monday and Tuesday night and you will find an old disease in the heart and in the head." No one had mentioned epilepsy before. By now, he was chattering on about "a queer old man" who seemed to suspect him of something: "He thinks that I have got the betting book, but Cook had no betting book that would be of use to anyone." The issue was evidently playing on Palmer's mind, because it could have been of no relevance to Harland.

With the doctor incapacitated without his scalpels, the task of actually cutting up and examining Cook's body fell to none other than Charles New-

**Dr John Harland, who left his instruments
behind when he attended Cook's post-mortem**

ton, the chemist's assistant who had sold Palmer the strychnine the week
before and had had the conversation about dog poisoning the previous
evening, and to Charles Devonshire, a medical student at London University, who was an assistant to another local doctor called David Monkton,
probably as some sort of vacation job. Neither had ever dissected a corpse,
still less conducted an autopsy, or even watched one, before. Devonshire
had borrowed Monkton's surgical instruments to do the incisions.

Now, Palmer met Newton at the door to the assembly room at the
Talbot Arms. Newton later explained:

> Palmer and I were left alone together in the entrance. He re-
> marked that it would be a stiff job and asked me to go over to
> his house for some brandy. We did so. While we were taking the
> brandy he said: "You will find this fellow suffering from a dis-
> eased throat; he has had syphilis." We then returned. I was ex-
> amined before the coroner, but I said nothing about giving
> Palmer three grains of *strychnia*.

So, tanked up and perhaps realising by now that he had a secret of his own to hide about his recent dealings with Palmer, the chemist's assistant and the medical student began the gruesome job of cutting open the still rigid figure on the hotel dining table. Harland said from his observation that the cadaver was stiffer than bodies generally were after six days, the muscles strongly contracted and thrown out and the hands clenched. But the organs were not diseased and he could see nothing to account for the young man's death. Around the table were not only Harland and Bamford but a number of other interested and curious parties and onlookers: Stephens was there, of course, to see his poor boy being dissected, but also Sam Cheshire, the local postmaster, Jerry Smith and Thomas Masters, the elderly landlord of the Talbot Arms. There was a sort of general milling around the table, with Palmer, grinning nervously, wandering about and peering over the shoulders of the two young men bent over the body of his friend. Stephens had made clear that he wanted his stepson's viscera to be examined by an expert pathologist down in London. He had in mind Professor Alfred Swaine Taylor of Guy's Hospital, regarded, certainly by himself, as the foremost and most famous pathologist and poisons expert of the day. Stephens must have heard local rumours about Palmer and poison, quite apart from his own suspicions, for he had already contacted Taylor by the weekend to ask for his help, which he would have to pay for himself. Accordingly, Newton and Devonshire procured a single glass jar to contain all Cook's vital organs and their contents so that they could be sent to Taylor.

Devonshire and Newton started with the stomach. Devonshire lifted it out of the body, cutting it wide open with a pair of scissors and turning it inside out. As he did so, he felt a nudge from behind. It was Newton, who had been shoved in the back by Palmer. The brown and murky fluid in the stomach dripped onto a chair and into the body cavity; Devonshire steadied himself and then tossed the stomach itself into the jar. Devonshire said: "As I was opening the stomach there was a pressure or a push from behind. I did not pay any attention to it and I do not think any of the contents of the stomach escaped." Then, contradicting himself, he added: "I punctured the anterior surface of the stomach and a spoonful of the contents fell out on the chair. I tied up where it was punctured and it was put into the jar and sealed by Doctor Harland." Harland had noted the brown fluid – there were some two or three ounces of it, he recalled – and also the shove:

Palmer was standing to the right of Mr Newton . . . while Mr Devonshire was opening the stomach I noticed Palmer pushed Mr Newton on to Mr Devonshire and he shook a portion of the contents of the stomach into the body. I thought a joke was passing among them and I said: "Do not do that," to the whole. Palmer was the only one close to them when [they] were pushed together.

It was perhaps Harland's only professional comment all day.

Cook's intestines were now drawn out – in Harland's estimation, like the stomach, they contained nothing in particular – and they too were placed in the same jar, which Harland then sealed with a double layer of pig's bladder tied round with string and placed on the table next to the corpse. They did not trouble to examine much else: heart normal and of "no remarkable appearance", spleen and pancreas healthy, pleura fine, brain altogether healthy, a few wart-like follicles at the base of the tongue and epiglottis, but they were natural too. The blood was still fluid, which was unusual, but not particularly remarked upon. There was nothing, Harland said, in the state of Cook's organs to account for his sudden death. It would be three days later, at the request of Professor Taylor, that Devonshire was sent back to the corpse to have another go and remove the liver, kidneys and spleen so they could be belatedly sent to London too. All this was most satisfactory and Harland heard Palmer chuckle loudly to Bamford: "They won't hang us yet."

Then someone noticed that the jar was missing from the table. Harland called out, "Where is the jar?", and everyone looked around for it. After a minute or two, from the far end of the room, yards away near the door, Palmer piped up: "It's here; I thought it more convenient for you to take it away." When the jar was passed to Harland, he saw that there was an inch-long cut through the bladders sealing the top. "The cut was quite clean as if nothing had passed through. I asked who had done this and Palmer, Mr Devonshire and Mr Newton all seemed to say they had not done it." Harland resealed the jar with the same bladder skins so that the slit was not at the top. He planned to take the jar to another local surgeon for safe keeping, before it was sent down on the train to London, either that evening or the following morning. "I would rather you take it to Stafford yourself," Palmer said. No wonder that Dr George Rees, Taylor's assistant at Guy's, said later: "It was the most shamefully conducted post-mortem I ever heard of and little or nothing could be expected from our analysis." The jar, wrapped in brown paper, was actually passed to James Gardner's law firm, whom Stephens had engaged, and they sent their clerk up to London with it overnight, to give to Taylor the following morning at Guy's Hospital. The day after that, after Devonshire had dug about further in Cook's body to retrieve the other organs that Taylor requested, they too, together with three feet of intestine, were sent to London in a jar. It was entrusted to John Myatt, the postboy at the Talbot Arms – a relative of George Myatt, the local saddler, Palmer's neighbour and horse-racing friend – to put on the southbound train at Stafford. This was convenient as he was also driving William Stephens to the station at the same time. What Stephens thought about sharing the fly with a jar of his stepson's organs is not recorded, though as he had already seen the body being cut up he was probably sanguine about it. Death and corpses were not unusual sights in Victorian times.

As Myatt was getting ready, Palmer approached and asked whether he was driving to Stafford and taking the jar. When Myatt said he believed he was, Palmer said there would be a £10 note in it for him if he would upset the trap on the way. Myatt said he would not do it and Palmer wandered off, muttering that it was all a humbug anyway. Myatt was asked whether Palmer had actually said, "I should not mind giving £10 to break Mr Stephens' neck", but he did not recollect that.

In any event, Palmer had another scheme up his sleeve. He buttonholed Sam Cheshire, his old friend the postmaster, who had been with the party at Shrewsbury races. Palmer sometimes loaned Cheshire his horse and trap so he could take Mrs Cheshire for rides on a Sunday afternoon, and he often called on the postmaster to pick up any correspondence that arrived for him or his mother, in case it contained threatening missives from the moneylenders. After Cheshire had refused to witness Cook's supposed letter acknowledging his debts, Palmer suggested he might help in another way. He now asked to be kept informed of any letters sent from London to the Staffordshire coroner William Webb Ward, who was to hold the inquest within a fortnight or so at Rugeley town hall. Palmer and Ward knew each other well and probably regarded each other as friends. "He asked me to let

John Myatt, the postboy at the Talbot Arms,
who Palmer tried to bribe

him know if I had seen or heard anything fresh. I understood that was a temptation for me to open a letter and I told him I could not do that," said Cheshire. "He said he didn't want me to do anything to injure myself." Opening letters was of course a serious breach of trust for a postmaster, strictly illegal and sternly punished. Nevertheless, when Taylor's letter arrived from London giving the results of his examination of Cook's viscera, Cheshire succumbed to temptation and looked inside. It had been sent to Stephens's lawyer, James Gardner, in Rugeley and reported that the professor had been unable to find any trace of strychnia. As if to justify himself, Cheshire said: "I did not give, nor send that letter to Palmer. I merely told him in few words of its contents. I only read part of the letter and told Palmer the contents as much as I remembered. He said he knew they would not [find poison] for he was perfectly innocent." For this favour, Sam Cheshire, "an extremely respectable looking man", not only lost his job but was sent to prison for two years.

William Webb, the disgruntled Staffordshire coroner who Palmer attempted to bribe, slumps in his chair at the inquest

Despite the reassuring news, Palmer was by now in a full panic. First he sent a hamper of game from London to Coroner Ward at his private address in Stoke-on-Trent: a codfish, a barrel of oysters, a brace of pheasants and a turkey. Then he sent George Bates round with a second parcel of game – "nice pheasants and a good hare" from Frantz, a poulterer, in Stafford – and again, a few days later, with a letter enclosing a £10 note. Meanwhile, Palmer retired to his bed, claiming illness.

The coroner had opened the inquest on Cook at the Talbot Arms a couple of days after the post-mortem, but it had then been adjourned to be held down the road in the chamber of Rugeley town hall on 12 December, awaiting Professor Taylor's report of his findings. The gifts therefore arrived on Ward's doorstep while the hearings were in abeyance. Then the inquest was postponed for a further two days to allow Taylor to attend in person and give evidence. Meanwhile, Palmer's letter was sent on 13 December 1855, the day before the resumption. The letter, which Bates was instructed to give personally to Ward, was extraordinarily improvident, not to say reckless. Later, fearful that he himself might be prosecuted as an accessory, the coroner sent it to the home secretary, so it was not a piece of evidence that mysteriously disappeared, like the betting book or Cook's cheque, as it might otherwise have done. Palmer's letter began by pointing out that Cook's last illness had stretched over at least three days and suggesting that Ishmael Fisher could prove that he had received Cook's money after the races. Fisher, of course, had received some of the money at Shrewsbury on the night Cook was taken ill, but he had given most of it back after taking what he was owed.

> Dec. 13th, 1855
> RUGELEY.
> MY DEAR SIR,
> I am sorry to tell you that I am still confined to bed. I don't think it was mentioned at the inquest yesterday Dec 12th, that Cook was taken ill on Sunday and Monday night, in the same way as he was on the Tuesday, when he died. The Chambermaid at the Crown Hotel (Master's) [sic: Palmer must have meant the Talbot Arms] can prove this. I also believe that a man by the name of Fisher is coming down to prove he received some money at Shrewsbury. Now, here he could only pay Smith £10 out of £41 he owed him. Had you better not call Smith to prove this? And again whatever Professor Taylor may say tomorrow; he wrote from London last Tuesday week . . . to say 'We (Dr Rees and I) have this day finished our analysis and find no traces of either strychnine, prussic acid, or opium.'
>
> What can beat this from a man like Taylor, if he says what he had already said and Dr Harland's evidence? Mind you I know and saw it in black and white, what Taylor said . . . but this is strictly private and confidential, but it is true.
>
> As regards his betting-book, I know nothing of it and it is of no good to anyone. I hope the verdict tomorrow will be that he died from natural causes and thus end it.
> Ever yours,
> W.P.

Bates found Coroner Ward in the smoking-room of the Dolphin Inn in Stafford and – "tipping him a knowing wink", according to a contemporary newspaper report – took him outside to the stable yard to give him the letter, which Ward put in his pocket unopened. The newspaper's reporter also noted that the Dolphin had the only billiard room in Stafford as if further to highlight its iniquity and damn the coroner with loucheness.

Perhaps Palmer believed local folk and officials like the coroner would rally round against the inquisitive outsiders such as "the queer old man" Stephens, or the London expert Taylor. That must account for the insinuating tone, but the letter also exposed his friend Cheshire, who had risked his job to do him a favour. Far from proving Palmer to be a cunning criminal mastermind, as he was later depicted in court and in the press, it surely shows him instead on the verge of desperation, clumsily attempting to manipulate Ward for all he was worth. Taylor's conclusion in his letter – that it was impossible to tell "whether any strychnine had, or had not been given just before death since the contents of the stomach had been drained away" – had not yet been read to the inquest jury, so Palmer's letter served only to show that he had managed to obtain clandestine access to the correspondence. The only other explanation is panic. He must surely have assumed that Ward would destroy it and preserve some local code of silence.

We know what the scene at the inquest looked like because what the newspapers were beginning to call the Rugeley Poisoning Case was starting to attract national attention and a court artist was sent to sketch the scene, much as one would today. The picture inside the court-room on the first floor of the town hall shows Coroner Ward looking disgruntled and apathetic, slumped in a high-backed chair at the head of a table around which some of the key witnesses are sitting, resplendent in their side-whiskers and high-collared shirts, diligently reading and taking notes. At the far end there is the sturdy, middle-aged chemist Benjamin Thirlby and smooth-faced Jerry Smith, sitting next to the chief constable of Staffordshire, Captain John Hatton. Across the table from them sits John Smith, Palmer's solicitor from Birmingham, looking plump, prosperous and astute. In another corner, with all the benign appearance of a Toby jug, there is old Tom Masters, the landlord of the Talbot Arms. The elegant room is heaving with respectable middle-aged Midlands gentlemen – all men – craning to watch, moving about, or even arguing among themselves. It must have been quite a babble. At the middle of the table, dapper in a bow-tie and with fashionable, curly side-burns known then as Dundreary weepers, sits George Rees, Professor Taylor's colleague. But dominating the proceedings, standing at a lectern high above the rest of the crowded court-room, is Taylor himself, depicted in the process of laying down his findings. Assured of his professional pre-eminence, he does not look like a man accustomed to doubt, or one who would expect to be contradicted by the yeomen of Staffordshire.

Taylor is now considered the father of British forensic medicine and he had a formidable reputation. He had just celebrated his forty-ninth birthday, two days before the inquest (perhaps that was the real reason the hearing had had to be postponed, because he did not want to travel on that day), but he had already been lecturer in medical jurisprudence at Guy's for twenty-five years and was a fellow of the Royal Society. He had edited the *London Medical Gazette* and was the author both of the *Manual of Medical Jurisprudence* – in use for many years on both sides of the Atlantic – and, in 1848, of the large, standard textbook, *On Poisons in Relation to Medical Jurisprudence and Medicine*. It is likely that Palmer had attended his lectures when he was a student, if he was diligent enough to do so, and in any event he would certainly have been aware of his illustriousness. Taylor was well used to giving evidence in criminal trials and was admired by lawyers for his cogency and fluency in the witness box. If he fostered an air of infallibility – rather like his twentieth-century successor, the pathologist Bernard Spilsbury – it was because he knew, or thought he knew, more about his subject than anyone else. He was, says his biography in the Royal College of Physicians' 'Lives of the Fellows' website, a commanding figure in court, unbending and relentless. Palmer's case was one of his most famous and he would write a book about it in due course. Such an eminent professor, having come all the way up from London, was not to be kept waiting outside, or confined to the witness stand: he was invited into court to sit next to the coroner and even asked pointed questions on his own account. His evidence took on the nature of a prosecution case. Taylor was convinced that, although he could not find any trace of poisons in the specimens he had been sent from the two autopsies, Cook must have been murdered, and by Palmer, using strychnine. He believed that he had found traces of antimony, which might have produced a similar effect. Strychnine, however, would be more sensational: a new drug of devastating lethalness.

The inquest hearing at Rugeley: from left to right at the table: Coroner Ward, at far side: 4th left: Dr George Rees, 5th: Ben Thirlby, left, 6th left: Jerry Smith (pointing), 7th left: the chief constable Captain John Hatton (reading papers); at nearside 4th left: Palmer's solicitor John Smith. Meanwhile Alfred Swaine Taylor lays down the law from the stand on the right.

The only person missing from the scene was William Palmer. He was in bed at home a hundred yards from the town hall, though there were those who said he could be seen occasionally, furtively slipping across the road and into the Talbot Arms. Palmer was not usually someone who drank heavily – he liked to remain in control too much for that – but some said he was now seen drunk. He was said to be buying drinks for all and sundry, something he only usually did when he wanted something. He was loudly protesting his innocence before anything had ever been proved, or even alleged, against him. "Why George," he was said to have told Bates, "As to this poor fellow Cook, they will find nothing in him. He was the best pal I ever had in my life and why should I have poisoned him? I am as innocent as you, George."

When Taylor said he had found no evidence of the drug, Palmer, kept informed of the proceedings by Jerry Smith, must have rejoiced. When Taylor later added, "I believe the pills administered to Cook on the night of Monday and Tuesday contained strychnine which killed him", the die was cast. The inquest lasted two days but from that point its outcome was never in doubt.

Very late at night on Saturday 15 December, it took the jury only seven minutes to deliver the verdict that Cook had died of poison "wilfully administered to him by William Palmer". They should not have done it and Ward should have stopped them. It was not their job to declare the name of a murderer, especially one who had not been arrested, charged or convicted. The coroner should not have allowed such a decision, and the following year he was duly censured by the Lord Chief Justice at Palmer's trial and at the annual meeting of the Coroners' Society of England and Wales: they said his behaviour had been discreditable. With only circumstantial evidence and nothing forensic to prove a case, the charge against Palmer was far from established.

The chief constable of Staffordshire himself, Captain John Hatton, a tall, cadaverous-looking former military man, proceeded round to Palmer's house that night at midnight with an arrest warrant to take him into custody at Stafford prison. This was the first involvement of police officers in the case. There was only an inspector and two constables stationed in Rugeley, and they played no part in investigating any of Palmer's alleged crimes or misfortunes at any stage. Hatton found the accused man already under arrest by two sheriff's officers on a civil warrant for forgery taken out by another of his creditors, Henry Padwick. Palmer's troubles were mounting. Outside his house, an angry mob could be heard gathering to see him being carted off, but it was decided that he was too ill, or the crowd too menacing, for him to be taken to jail that night so he was left with two policemen sitting in his room. One of them, named Thomas Woollaston, later left a memoir of the occasion in typical constabulary prose:

> During that night I . . . remained in charge of accused, then a prisoner, ill or professing to be so and in bed. Throughout the next day we were engaged in searching prisoner's house for papers that might throw light on his transactions with deceased and also with respect to other crimes with which he was suspected to be implicated.

It was the last night Palmer would ever spend in relative freedom. The *Illustrated Times*'s reporter Augustus Mayhew would shortly imagine his plight in purple prose:

> He doubtless did not pass one of the calmest nights in that well-known room in the old familiar house where he had lived so long . . . Alas! He sees the officers of justice crowded around his bed, watching for the slightest change in his disorder which will warrant them in carrying him off a prisoner to Stafford gaol.

By the following evening, either the crowd had thinned, or Palmer was well enough to be moved and he was bundled into a cab – though not before he had had a chance to embrace his maidservant Eliza Tharme, who had herself just lost her five-month-old illegitimate baby son, and to thrust a £50 Bank of England note – a year's wages – into her hand. Palmer was never to be free again. Nor would the man who was already being called the Rugeley Poisoner ever see his hometown again.

4

"The great days of England"

ENGLAND AT THE TIME OF THE RUGELEY POISONING IN 1855 WAS RECOGNISABLY the land we know today: its main cities, towns and villages, its routes and railway lines, and many of its buildings were already in place. But it was also a society very different in outlook, attitudes and spirit. Nearly half its 30 million people still lived in the countryside and in the small market towns and villages dotted across it – though they were gravitating fast towards the rapidly expanding cities. People still dwelt in the dark: after nightfall their homes were lit by candles and the flickering flames from the fire in the grate. When they wrote notes, letters, formal documents or legal opinions, they wrote with a pen dipped in ink, sometimes in neat copperplate, occasionally in a scrawl as indecipherable as a scribble today. The smells in their nostrils each day were often of unwashed bodies and rumpled clothes, of horse manure and coal smoke; the marks on their clothing were usually flecks of soot and mud.

Towns and villages remained extremely parochial places, with rigid social hierarchies and entrenched attitudes. The squire, or local aristocratic landowner, such as the Earl of Lichfield with his mansion and 900-acre estate just outside Rugeley, could expect deference from all and unquestioning obedience from his employees; the parson and schoolmaster would anticipate respect; and the men of business would get together to fix the terms of trade. Professionals, solicitors and doctors, standing slightly apart in society by reason of their skills and qualifications, would naturally form local cartels. Co-operation might slip into rivalry, but it did no one any good to undercut or undermine a colleague. You might know – or guess – another fellow's weaknesses, but it was bad for business to criticise, certainly if outsiders came along, poking their noses into local affairs. Solidarity was only natural and expected. As a famous phrase in *Punch* magazine had it in February 1854: "Who's 'im, Bill?" "A stranger!" " 'Eave 'arf a brick at 'im!" After all, you might scarcely understand the accent if a visitor came from a different part of the country.

The mid-Victorian social order was hard to penetrate or change. Almost everything they heard or read – sermons on a Sunday, newspapers in the week – conveyed conformity. Despite the growing numbers who could claim to be members of the professional or middle class, they were still only a small proportion of the population. They might be free to rise to prosperity by their own efforts, luck or commercial enterprise – and some did, spectacularly – but not to marry into, or be accepted by, their social betters. A married woman's property still became her husband's, divorce required an act of Parliament, prisoners could not give evidence in their own defence, and it was only a few years since more than 220 crimes had been punishable by death (murder still was). Penalties for many crimes and even misdemeanours were savage, if a person was caught by the newly formed and inefficient local police forces. Men and women convicted of a capital offence would be hanged in public, in their hometowns, in front of often baying mobs.

But it was also a country that had grown rich and prosperous in the forty years of peace since the Battle of Waterloo. It stood at the forefront of the world in prosperity, inventiveness and mechanical progress. The Great Exhibition, held four years earlier, in 1851, had shown 6 million visitors the products of proud British manufacturers bristling with innovation and self-confidence, promising a brighter, easier, more comfortable future. "Whatever human industry has created you find there," wrote Charlotte Brontë after her second visit. "It seems as if only magic could have gathered this mass of wealth from all the ends of the earth." There were domestic gadgets and steam-engines, electricity generators, knick-knacks and furniture, such as would – as the young Queen Victoria confided in her diary – "fill one with admiration for the greatness of man's mind, which can devise and carry out such wonderful inventions, contributing to the welfare and comfort of the whole world".

Few would disagree with Lord Macaulay – the second half of whose *History of England* appeared in 1855 – who wrote in a famous, ringing phrase that: "The history of our country during the last one hundred and sixty years is eminently the history of physical, of moral and of intellectual improvement." The British empire stretched from the Antipodes to the Arctic wastes of Canada, wider and further than any empire had ever reached before, and it was still being added to across the world. British trade was exporting four times as many goods from the country's factories as the United States and more than France, Germany and Italy put together. In the previous decade, 5,000 miles of railway lines had been built across Britain, from Cornwall to the Highlands, enabling ordinary men and women who had never left their own neighbourhoods before to travel cheaply. Scarcely a significant town now lacked a railway station. As *The Times* declared in 1850: "Thirty years ago, not one countryman in one hundred had seen the metropolis. There is now scarcely one in the same number who has not spent the day there." In 1854 there were 92 million passenger journeys. The trip might be long, uncomfortable and bumpy, but you could get from the north of England to London for five shillings.

The English middle classes now had the leisure and the money to take holidays by the seaside and to attend distant sports events, and racing was one of the most popular. Sixty-eight new horse-racing meetings were inaugurated between 1845 and 1854. The public could read about current events inexpensively and almost contemporaneously. The repeal of newspaper stamp duty in June 1855 meant that the price of newspapers plummeted and suddenly there were many more of them; papers cost much less and the companies that produced them could afford to print more pages, more frequently. Newspapers were within reach, for the first time, of even the only moderately affluent and their readers were avid for news and – as editors would soon discover – for sensation. Each copy sold would be read by numbers of people, or even read to them at public meetings as great events unfolded. The price of *The Times* came down from one shilling to four pence, while the newly established *Telegraph* slashed its price to a penny and saw its sales rise from 27,000 to 141,000. Rotary presses – invented in the 1840s, patented in 1847 and displayed at the Great Exhibition – now enabled newspapers to print in huge daily quantities. The railways brought these papers and hundreds like them – local and national, specialist and general, serious and gossipy – to breakfast tables across the land every morning. The English middle classes and tradesmen no longer had to wait days to borrow a paper from an affluent neighbour, or to pick one up in an inn: they could find out what was happening, in Parliament or at the Old Bailey, within a day and read the latest news from the distant Crimean War within three weeks. The columns of densely packed prose, thousands of words long and without illustrations, could spur outrage and sensation or shivers of excitement. And editors found that murder, especially, with all the gory details verbatim and unexpurgated, sold copies like nothing else.

Yet, however proudly the richest country on earth might choose to celebrate its progress, it still had yawning problems. Britain's cities were spawning overcrowded, insanitary slums; its factories and mines were slowly being shamed into curbing child labour; many of the country's rural peasantry still lived in hovels; and its inadequately equipped, incompetently led army had been starved and frozen to death in the Crimean War the previous winter. In 1854, 10,000 Londoners died in a cholera epidemic and soon Parliament itself would have to be prorogued – driven away by the foul smells emanating from the sewage-laden Thames outside its windows.

There was an uneasy malaise beneath the surface. George Hudson, "the railway king", the great entrepreneur whose energy had built the east coast railways from London to York, had just been exposed for embezzling investors' funds and bribing his fellow MPs to pass the legislation that would allow his companies' lines to be built. And in February 1856 the City banker, Irish MP and former Treasury minister John Sadleir committed suicide by drinking prussic acid on Hampstead Heath after being exposed as a fraud and forger. Thousands of middle-class investors had been ruined by the collapse of his Tipperary Bank whose assets he had plundered to support his lifestyle. "No other panic was ever so fatal to the middle class," wrote one contemporary:

> There was scarcely an important town in England [that did not] behold some wretched suicide. It reached every hearth, it saddened every heart in the metropolis . . . Daughters delicately nurtured went out to seek their bread. Sons were recalled from academies. Households were separated, homes were desecrated by the emissaries of the law.

Sadleir's suicide note read: "I cannot live – I have ruined too many . . . I have committed diabolical crimes, unknown to any human being." That did not deter anyone. The system could be got round, in banking, on the stock exchange, in insurance and in gambling. If you could get rich quick, why wouldn't you do it?

In the summer of 1855, an exasperated Charles Dickens called his latest work *Nobody's Fault*. It was to be his third great "condition of England" novel, after *Hard Times* and *Bleak House*, but he decided to change the title as he wrote it to *Little Dorrit*. The story was set in a world of corruption and poverty, greed and posturing; of the Circumlocution Office, the Marshalsea Prison and a seething city where "every miserable red-tapist flourishes". The novel might be set in the 1820s, but it was aimed squarely at the 1850s. The story was "a physical force . . . breaking out all around me . . . I have no present political faith or hope – not a grain," Dickens wrote. He was "blowing off steam which would otherwise blow me up". In this, John Sadleir and his equally crooked brother James were transformed into Mr Merdle, "the greatest forger and the greatest thief ever to cheat the gallows". Rather than taking poison, Merdle ultimately borrows a tortoise-shell penknife from Fanny Sparkler to kill himself when he is found out, though Dickens admitted he had the Sadleirs in mind in creating the character. The serialisation of *Little Dorrit* in the autumn of 1855 was an immediate bestseller: 35,000 copies a month, bringing its writer £600 for every episode – a colossal sum when a labourer earned a pound a week and a professional man £125 a year, but small change compared with the £600,000 Hudson had just leeched from his companies. (Multiply the figures by sixty to get a very rough estimation of twenty-first-century values.)

While Dickens was excoriating the corruption of mid-Victorian society, however, an altogether earthier author was proving equally popular with his depiction of another segment of English life. Robert Surtees's *Mr Sponge's Sporting Tour* appeared in 1853. Here were rascally, conniving, hard-up figures among the huntsmen and race-goers of rural England, with whom a different audience could identify. These were the members of the sporting fancy, gentlemen who were "generally spoken of as having nothing a year, paid quarterly": men running through their inheritances, borrowing from loan-sharks, borrowing money at high interest, gambling recklessly, hopelessly, to keep up. Palmer knew all about that world.

Suddenly in the winter of 1855, as news of Cook's death and Palmer's arrest seeped out, the story became a new, real sensation, all the more shocking for emerging from an upstairs room in an obscure inn in a quiet Midlands town. It was a murder case that would thrill and absorb not only the British newspaper-reading public but half of Europe. Fascinated, Dickens squeezed into court to see "the greatest villain that ever stood in the Old Bailey dock", as he watched from the public gallery alongside the cream of the aristocracy, foreign princes, generals returning from the Crimean War, celebrities and scientists. The trial was the sensation of the year. It had, wrote the diarist and gossip Charles Greville, "excited an interest almost unprecedented", unlike anything seen for thirty years. The *Law Times* called it "the longest, greatest, gravest and most important criminal trial of the nineteenth century". What shocked respectable households everywhere was that Dr William Palmer, the man arraigned for cold-bloodedly poisoning his friend, was himself so seemingly respectable. He was not a villain with a twisted face and a knobbly-bumped head, cowering and gibbering like Fagin in the condemned cell at the conclusion of *Oliver Twist*. They were fascinated by his very ordinariness. You just couldn't tell. As the *Morning Chronicle* reported, William Palmer was

> rather under than over the middle height, of a fair, florid complexion and sanguine temperament and with nothing in his round, ordinary face to indicate criminal inclinations or dark and deep designs. A casual observer would set him down as a respectable, good-humoured farmer and a physiognomist would be more inclined to give him credit for social and convivial habits than those elaborately planned crimes which the indictment lays to his charge. His forehead is high and open and altogether the expression of his countenance is the reverse of disagreeable.

He was a doctor, or at least a surgeon, which counted as almost the same thing: a caring professional, someone you visited in the distant hope of being cured. But it seemed, if the press were to be believed – and why wouldn't you believe what they reported? – that he had diabolically wiped out not only Cook but also a host of other victims wholesale: his wife, his children, his brother, his mother-in-law and goodness knows who else. How many was it? Some put the total at ten, others at twenty; at least a dozen victims seemed likely – the worst mass-murderer for centuries. He had stood by, this respectable Englishman, and coolly watched them writhe in agony as they choked their last: the devil incarnate, a monster. Yet he was silent and enigmatic, refusing redemption by acknowledging his culpability.

Palmer's trial came at a significant moment as contemporary fears about poisoning were amounting almost to panic. It was an insidious crime, subtle, sophisticated and underhand, often hard to detect and so particularly villainous. Newly accessible poisons such as strychnine were a modern *scientific* assault that called for new, professional methods of detection by specialist experts rather than the county constabulary. It was, people said, a crime of civilisation and it was on the increase. Criminal poisoning cases were becoming more common: formerly rare, they were now both more frequent and more sensational. Fifteen cases were tried nationally between 1810 and 1819, fifty-nine between 1830 and 1839, 140 between 1840 and 1852: a small proportion of the total number of murders, but ever more sensational, especially as more newspapers were reporting such cases. Like modern alchemists, professional men were seemingly deploying their education and expertise to perverted, calculated, calibrated ends, using new poisons against their spouses, relatives and those from whose deaths they might benefit. This was a subversion of the expected order and women could be as bad as men: in 60 per cent of the poisoning cases of the 1840s women were the accused parties, many of them doing away with their husbands and lovers. Strength was not needed, just guile and wickedness. A poisoner might smile and smile and yet be a villain. And in 1856 the worst of them was William Palmer.

Ballads were composed about him, broadsheets written, pottery figurines and models run off in the kilns up the road in Stoke-on-Trent. Newspapers would increase their print runs and see their circulations rise to unprecedented heights as they disclosed every detail of the case. Literary men such as Dickens had their say. The *Illustrated Times* doubled its normal sale when it printed a special edition and sold 400,000 copies. The cash-strapped *Manchester Guardian* devoted long columns, thousands of words, sometimes more than half its editorial space to the case every day. *The Times* immediately issued a book about the trial. Verbatim transcripts and sensational accounts were published; medical men earnestly discussed the symptoms of strychnine. Pamphlets debated the rights and wrongs of the case.

A campaign was mounted for his acquittal in the face of an unjust trial. In due course, "Topper" Smith, the hangman, would himself give talks, describing the execution while "an exact model of the culprit dressed in corresponding clothes as he appeared on the morning" would swing from a gallows behind him. The story intrigued society both high and low. Party leaders such as Mr Gladstone and Lord Derby would sit in the public gallery during the hearings. Michael Faraday spent time away from his laboratory to attend the trial, along with the Duke of Cambridge and Lord Lucan, recently returned from the Crimean War. Prince Albert was said to be avidly reading *The Times*'s lengthy reports over breakfast – and, evidently, so was the queen herself. Across Europe, princes and aristocrats were fascinated by reports of the English sensation. It was the society event of the year. As the Lord Chief Justice Lord Campbell noted proudly in his diary, it was "the most memorable proceedings for the last 50 years, engaging the attention of not only this country, but of all Europe". Campbell, although well into his seventies, was determined to preside over such a famous event: as his entry in the *Oxford Dictionary of National Biography* said later, he was somewhat too open in his love of applause. When the *Annual Register*, an almanac of the year's events, was published, it devoted 142 pages to the case, more than for any other crime it recorded in the entire Victorian era.

The Palmers of Rugeley were indeed in many ways an archetypical, aspiring British family. They had done well out of the Industrial Revolution and had grown wealthy in business and commerce. They were members of the respectable, church-going bourgeoisie who had risen from the labouring classes into affluence and the professions. William Palmer's father had run a prosperous timber business and held the leases on two coal-mines which had passed to his wife and eldest son after his death. One of William Palmer's brothers had been a businessman, another became a solicitor, a third was ordained and Palmer himself had qualified as a surgeon. In two generations the family had gone from being manual labourers to joining the professions. There was no ostensible reason why William should then have gone to the bad when his brothers did not.

The young lawyer James Stephen, who also attended the trial and was later to become a judge (and, incidentally, uncle of Virginia Woolf), watched the defendant closely in court. Many years later, after a third of a century at the bar, he wrote:

[Palmer's] career supplied one of the proofs of a fact which many kind-hearted people seem to doubt, namely ... that such a thing as atrocious wickedness is consistent with good education, perfect sanity and everything in a word that deprives men of all excuse for crime. Palmer was respectably brought up; apart from his extravagance and vice he might have lived comfortably enough. He was a model of physical health and strength and was courageous, determined and energetic. No one ever suggested that there was even a disposition to madness in him; yet he was as cruel, as treacherous, as greedy for money and pleasure, as brutally hard-hearted and sensual a wretch as it is possible even to imagine. If he had been the lowest and most ignorant ruffian that ever sprung from a long line of criminal ancestors, he could not have been worse than he was.

James Hannay, the London correspondent of the *New York Tribune*, was intrigued by the emergence of a modern phenomenon arising from the revelations about the case: a crime facilitated by the innovations of progress. He told his readers with heavy irony: "The nineteenth century in spite of its enlightenment can do little in the way of villains; and when such a one arrives it appears to have a glimmering that the devil is still extant, will travel by rail as readily as by old coach and hides his hoofs jauntily in patent leather."

This was indeed a modern story, told for a modern audience by modern means of communication. The newspapers called Palmer the "Prince of Poisoners", building him up into a devious mastermind of cruelty. But, except in the degree of his villainy, he was more like Surtees's comic character Soapey Sponge:

a good-looking, rather vulgar-looking man. At a distance – say ten yards – his height, figure and carriage gave him somewhat of a commanding appearance, but ... plainly showed he was not the natural, or what the lower orders call, the *real* gentleman. That Mr Sponge might have lost a trifle on the great races of the year, we don't mean to deny, but that he lost such a sum as eighteen hundred on the Derby and seven on the Leger, we are in a position to contradict, for the best of all possible reasons, that he hadn't it to lose.

Palmer knew just what that was like: he had lost on the Oaks and many other races. He may well have read Surtees's books with rueful recognition. And he certainly didn't have the money to lose either.

Here was the respectable classes' worst nightmare: wickedness incarnate and insidious, disguised as normality. And the worst of it was that you could have passed him in the street without ever noticing his villainy.

5

"A thoroughly bad boy"

WILLIAM PALMER WAS BORN IN RUGELEY IN AUGUST 1824, IN HIS PARENTS' house opposite the parish church, a few hundred yards from the centre of the town. He was the fifth of seven children of Joseph Palmer, who was in his late forties when William was born, and his wife Sarah Bentley, who was in her early thirties and would be the woman closest to her son and most indulgent towards him all his life. He was christened across the road at the newly built St Augustine's church on 21 October that year.

The family home still stands opposite the church: a rather handsome, square, brick-built late Georgian building with sash-windows and a white mock-Grecian portico around the front door. The front garden has a tarmac drive these days, with Range Rovers standing on it – it is now the offices of an electronic data-storage company – but in the early nineteenth century it had flower-beds and an iron gate and, to the side, running down to the nearby canal, was where Joseph Palmer conducted his business as a timber merchant. There was a crane to lift tree-trunks from barges and stands of wood and planking in the yard, where now there is a small housing estate. After the old man died suddenly in 1837, most of the timber went and was replaced with a lawn running down to the water's edge.

Following William Palmer's arrest, there was no shortage of sightseers coming to stand outside the front of the house, at least one of them a correspondent picking up the local gossip about the family and peering judgementally at the décor as assiduously as any tabloid reporter today. Augustus Mayhew, a sharp young man from the *Illustrated Times*, came up from London to write the paper's special supplement, published on 2 February 1856 while Palmer was still awaiting trial, and he gave his assessment of the property:

> If the front of the house has an imposing aspect, the back part at least lets you into the mystery of the attempt that has been made to obtain the admiration of the passer-by in the road. The back premises are dirty and full of dirt. The garden is uncultivated and the mould trodden under foot until it has grown as hard as the remains of the gravel walks that surround them.

Mayhew took aesthetic exception to a bay window at the side of the house, which he pronounced tawdry and "having no right to be there", and to the rich silk curtains which were apparently "in the public house school of fancy". It was all for show, he decided with the sort of lofty metropolitan disdain that young reporters still exhibit. He was confident that he could tell much about the character of a family by their curtains, an infallible principle acknowledged by reporters ever since. The Palmers were evidently people who liked the respectable look of fresh paint, he decided, but he noticed that the stable round the back was roofed in mouldy black thatch, had rotting wooden walls and was no better than a hovel. It was a place that a London cabman would scorn to occupy, he wrote. It is probably no wonder that in years to come Sarah Palmer would march out of the front door and sail down to the front gate to berate the gawpers who gathered there. "Well! I am Mrs Palmer the mother of Doctor Palmer. The judges hanged my saintly Billy and he was the best of my lot," she shouted at them, according to George Fletcher, who wrote a book about the Palmer case in the 1920s and remembered watching the old lady's performance when he was a small boy, taken to see the house in 1859.

Very soon Gus Mayhew from the *Illustrated Times* had decided that, whatever their façade, the Palmers were no better than they should be. Old Joseph Palmer had prospered in business, though the gossip Mayhew picked up nearly twenty years after his death was that his methods had been distinctly underhand. It was a trait that went back through the family line. Sarah Palmer's father – according to Mayhew – was said to have cheated his former mistress, who kept a brothel in Derby, out of her life savings. She had allegedly been "an ignorant woman of somewhat faded attractions" – though, as this was at least sixty years earlier, the source for this information was unlikely to have been first-hand. Joseph Palmer himself was rumoured to have seduced his wife away from her intended, the steward of the Marquis of Anglesey. He had risen from sawyer to timber merchant by defrauding his customers and "everyone speaks of [him] as a coarse, vulgar fellow", who had no friends and yet made a fortune buying up stands of oak during the clearances of neighbouring land – "those excrescences of nature grown by Providence to pay the debts of gentlemen," Mayhew wrote, deploying ponderous irony and meaning trees. Perhaps he was on a penny a line, in which case, since he filed 40,000 words, he did quite well.

Some of the neighbouring gentry had great debts: the first Earl of Lichfield had to sell off the entire contents of Shugborough Hall in the early 1840s to meet gambling obligations of more than £600,000 and the family only narrowly kept possession of the house itself. The countryside around Rugeley included Cannock Chase, but also many large, aristocratic country estates. There was not only Shugborough Hall, but the Marquis of Anglesey's Beaudesert, the Whig politician Lord Hatherton's lands around Penkridge ("from which half the Navy dockyards are supplied – oaks, sir, as big as cartwheels", according to locals), Lord Bagot's estate at Blithfield Hall, five miles north of Rugeley ("the finest woods in Europe") and Earl Talbot's Ingestre Hall near Stafford. The prime minister Sir Robert Peel and his family were not far away at Drayton, near Tamworth. Weston Hall was also nearby and Hagley only a little further off, near Stourbridge.

This was a rich, fertile area with growing and ready markets close by in Birmingham and the Black Country; and there were many rich, ambitious and improving landowners, clearing their lands for farming and maximising their profits by selling off the timber in their woods, so there was a ready supply and considerable profit to be made by dealing in it. When Joseph Palmer died of apoplexy one night at dinner in 1837 at the age of fifty-nine, falling back with the bread and cheese he had been eating still clutched in his hand – the readers were spared no detail – he left the immense sum of £70,000 and no will. It may even have been more than £100,000, for he held the lease on two local collieries at Brereton on Cannock Chase as well. When a parliamentary commission investigating children's employment in coal-mines called in 1842, its officials found prosperous collieries "conducted in a very orderly manner", with boys of ten years and upwards "all robust and healthy without personal injury or deformity" as they worked their twelve-hour days. The Palmers' agent, Mr Grice, told the commissioners: "I do not ever employ a man or boy without first ascertaining his moral character. My men and boys are at this moment as good, steady, industrious, orderly and regular as any class of men in the country." This, though, was not entirely borne out by the teenagers they interviewed: "The men all behave very well to us, except one man, John Mills . . . he knocks me down [and] thrashes me with anything he can lay hold of," said fourteen-year-old Thomas Holland, giving the game away – "We seldom see Mr Grice. He would not allow it if he was told." At any rate, the commissioners do not seem to have taken much exception to what they saw. Whatever his personal foibles and failings, Joseph Palmer had evidently been a considerable Midlands businessman. He had profited from a rich seam of coal and cashed in on the demand for timber – for the ships of the Royal Navy during the Napoleonic Wars and in the building boom that accompanied the industrial revolution in the Midlands. The Palmer family did not lack money. If they threw their weight around in Rugeley and used their money to cajole, threaten and overawe their local critics, as was alleged by some residents to the newspapermen after William Palmer's arrest, they certainly had the means to do so. Mrs Palmer could also ensure that her son would have adequate legal representation at his trial.

Joseph Palmer left a middle-aged wife and seven surviving children. Mary Ann, the eldest of the children, was a bad lot – "her character was not of the best", according to George Fletcher many years later – and, having survived to adulthood and married, she died in 1853, allegedly of drink. The oldest son, Joseph Junior, born in 1818, moved to Liverpool to follow his father's trade as a timber merchant, then returned to Staffordshire, where he bought the lease of a colliery on Cannock Chase and died, also in 1853, before his younger brother's disgrace. The next son, George, who was sixteen when his father died, became a solicitor. He had a twin sister named Sarah who died in infancy. Then there was Walter, fourteen, who came to a sticky end after being insured by his brother, followed by William, thirteen, still at school when his father died, and Thomas, ten, who would become a clergyman, serving for many years in a parish on the Suffolk coast. Finally, there was another daughter, also called Sarah, who was born in 1832 and grew up to marry a Scottish evangelical clergyman named Alexander Brodie later in the year of her brother's execution – though she did so in London, not locally. Brodie, a handsome if bandy-legged man when photographed in his kilt, was himself illegitimate, so he may have been happy to overlook her family's shame. Described as much given to good works, Sarah lived into the twentieth century, dying in 1907 in what sounds like the suffocating respectability of Amberley, The Park, Chislehurst. A photograph taken of her in old age shows a plump, elderly Victorian matron with just the hint of a moustache, her grey hair moulded into the ringlets fashionable in her youth, dressed all in black (she was a widow for nearly forty years) and placidly reading a newspaper.

Bad evidently alternated with good among the siblings. Nevertheless, when it came to their father's will, they seem to have reached an amicable enough solution among themselves. As the oldest male child, Joseph might have inherited the lot, but instead agreed to an arrangement for each of the seven of them to receive £7,000 each, leaving the residue of at least £25,000 for their mother, Sarah. The colliery leases also went to her. There was one proviso: that she should not marry again. This last was probably to ensure that the money ultimately did not leave the family, because a wife's property became her husband's on marriage and a widow aged forty-four in possession of a good fortune might expect to have many suitors. The restriction seems to have meant that she embarked on a number of affairs instead. She gave houseroom and space in her bed on a regular basis to the solicitor Jerry Smith, nearly twenty years her junior, who was later made to squirm in the witness box about their liaison.

Mayhew uncovered her association with another figure, a rascally linen-draper named Duffy, who had departed the vicinity without warning or paying his bills, leaving behind only a portmanteau of dirty clothes and the love letters Mrs Palmer had written to him. Thomas Clewley, the landlord of the Shoulder of Mutton pub in Rugeley, where Duffy had stayed, was prepared to tell reporters about the letters for a small consideration. Clewley, described as a fine-looking man with white hair and "a cherry-red face reminiscent of a trifle at an evening party", said he had found them with the dirty clothes, having opened the case when the smell got too bad:

The letters finished off with loving and kissing. They made appointments to meet at many different places but I was in no way interested in their loves and I never troubled my head about it: it was the women as exposed the whole business – nobody would have seen 'em or known anything about them if it had not been for them. I should have burned them or kept them secret. No, I never charged sixpence a head to see them. I only showed 'em for a lark. The way in which they came to be seen was this – my missus got speaking of 'em and one or two young chaps came here and gammoned the missus to show 'em. They spent one or two shillings in grog to have a look; then come another and another and at last I took 'em away; but the missus got 'em again. There's no keeping the women quiet in such matters. I can't say how many letters there was – they was mixed up with tradesmen's bills and that sort of thing.

"Not one of the sons has, in his own life, purified the name of Palmer to a proper extent in the nostrils of Rugeley," the *Illustrated Times* stated unjustly in its pre-trial supplement. "On the other hand it is to be feared that they had not the advantage of a good mother."

The prospect of each offspring inheriting £7,000 when they reached the age of twenty-one – the equivalent in today's money of about £400,000 – was a considerable benefaction for the younger brothers, and there were those who were quick to tell the gentleman from the *Illustrated Times* that it had spoiled the thirteen-year-old. Previously William's father had kept a stern eye on the boy's behaviour, but now he was allowed to run wild by an indulgent mother for whom he could do no wrong. By this time he had become a pupil at the local grammar school, alongside Sam Cheshire, and opinion was mixed about his nature, at least among those who talked to the journalist. Mayhew bustled assiduously about, probably buying drinks, knocking on doors and carefully noting down the tales of everyone he talked to around Rugeley. A man called Littler who had been a sawyer in Palmer's yard, who knew the whole family and claimed to have nursed William many a time, confided that he was a good boy really:

well, perhaps he was a little sly. You see young men will be young men and William was quieter like! People round about said he was the best of the bunch. I've often carried him through the fields in my arms; we used to play together at marbles. I never saw him in a bad temper. No sir a better tempered or more generous child there never was; he was a very nice young gentleman. When a baby he was very fat and lust – but the family all were . . . he was a capital aim at marbles.

Yes, William Palmer was just as generous when he grew up. He never forgot an old face. Why he never met me but he said "Littler, will you have a glass of something to drink." He gave a deal to the poor, he was very charitable and kind.

At this point Littler probably added, "Yes sir, I don't mind if I do . . . "

Others were more guarded. A man called Sherrit, who had taught singing at the school and was now the parish clerk, said: "I never knew any harm of him. He was a very good boy with me, but then I would not have anybody in the class unless he was; but the boys used to tell tales about him – that he was given to swearing and other tricks." Some spoke of him as a bully and a cheat, defrauding his father's workers out of sixpences, but Mayhew diligently reported both good and bad. Many years later, George Fletcher, a Cambridge graduate and visiting magistrate at Pentonville Prison, obsessed with the Palmer case, tracked down another of the doctor's schoolmates, John Timmis. "He was a thoroughly bad boy and did not mind how he cheated," Timmis told him in 1907. "He would get other boys to write his thesis and many of his exercises. He was not cruel to small boys, but very cruel to animals and sneaking in every detail. He was a great deal too flush with money and could often show three or four sovereigns, which to us boys seemed a fortune. He used to rob his sisters' pockets and his mother's purse and steal any cash lying about." Fletcher noted this all down and two decades later regurgitated it in his book.

William Palmer left school at the age of seventeen and was sent to follow in his older brother Joseph's footsteps to Liverpool, where he was apprenticed to a wholesale chemists' company, Evans & Sons, of Lord Street. Clearly, the Palmers, if not necessarily socially mobile, were rising in the professional classes. "The sons were divided as the sons of the middle class are when there is money enough to start all, into the different professions," wrote Mayhew. In William's case, his career with Evans & Sons did not end well. If, as Mr Timmis alleged, he was already stealing from his family, he appears to have continued the practice after starting with his first employers. Palmer had initially seemed a model worker, diligent and neat, but he was soon caught embezzling money. His duties had included going to the post office every day to collect the firm's mail; but he was caught after he was seen by one of the firm's partners jiggling the envelopes to assess their contents and opening one on the way back to the office to see whether there was any cash inside. The fact that the envelope he had opened and stuffed into his pocket had not in fact contained money probably saved him from prosecution and a conviction that would have incurred a stiff prison sentence, but money from customers had gone missing in the post previously and he was sacked anyway. Palmer's mother repaid the losses to hush things up, and his brother Thomas – the one who would later become a clergyman – was allowed to take his place and complete the apprenticeship to avoid the family name being disgraced. The money William Palmer had previously abstracted seems to have been spent to impress his landlady's red-haired daughter Jane Widnall; also, it was alleged, "not by any means an inconsiderable portion . . . [had been spent] in the society of females of the worst character, with whom, unfortunately Liverpool, like most large seaport towns, abounds." Apparently, he had discovered "the evil habit of gambling", betting on races at Liverpool and Chester. It was probably unfortunate that the Grand National had been run at Aintree for the first time five years before and, by the time Palmer was apprenticed in Liverpool in 1841, had already become a major race in the national sporting calendar.

So Palmer returned to Rugeley and was apprenticed instead to a local surgeon called Edward Tylecote, who lived in the neighbouring village of Great Haywood. Tylecote, who was thirty-five in 1841, had trained in London and already employed a number of young assistants. He lived opposite Mary Ann, Palmer's eldest sister, and took on Palmer as a trainee for five years. If Tylecote was unaware of the young man's previous record, he would quickly find out about him. The young man, outwardly charming and responsible, soon appeared to be slippery where both money and local girls were concerned. Fees paid by patients went missing, and there was also a curious dispute with another of Tylecote's assistants named Peter Smirke, "a young man rather weakly in frame but affecting a fashionable exterior". Smirke found all his clothes ruined with acid and his new pair of dress boots cut up with a penknife after falling out with Palmer, who implausibly denied that he had had anything to do with the vandalism.

Palmer also resumed his relationship with Jane Widnall, who seems to have followed him to Staffordshire when her mother had married a gardener on the Shugborough estate, which borders on the village. At one point William and Jane eloped, but only got as far as Walsall – not necessarily the most romantic of destinations even then – where they had to be rescued from an inn after Palmer was unable to pay the bill. Understandably Tylecote was reluctant to redeem the debt, as was Mary Ann's husband, and eventually his brothers Joseph and George had to go and bail the couple out with Mrs Palmer's money. They found William at the inn cracking walnuts insouciantly and knocking back a bottle of sherry. Jane Widnall seems to have been a particularly persistent girlfriend and he also appears to have found her useful. The story was that he would attend church on a Sunday morning and bribe a local urchin to have him called out in mid-service to attend a supposed medical emergency, which would give him the opportunity to slip away and see Jane while her mother and stepfather were safely out of the way at the service. Palmer would not have been the first to skip church under similar circumstances, nor the last. More disreputably, though, he was said to have discovered that her stepfather, the gardener, whose name was George Vickerstaff, had life savings of £100 – a great sum for a working man – and managed to borrow it after promising to marry Jane. Then the marriage did not take place and the money disappeared. Jane eventually married Peter Smirke and the couple emigrated to Australia, where he set up in practice as a doctor in Sydney. Meanwhile Palmer lost his apprenticeship with the exasperated Dr Tylecote.

In May 1843 Palmer, or more likely his mother, paid five guineas to be enrolled at Stafford Infirmary as a "walking" pupil – one who accompanied and observed doctors on their rounds of patients. It was at this time, it was supposed, that Palmer had first developed an interest in the narcotic properties of medicines and might have been allowed for a time to rummage in the infirmary's medical store and start dispensing them. He may even have taken them home with him. If so, it was a practice that was quickly brought to a stop with new hospital regulations, though whether this was due to Palmer's activities or the result of a more general tightening up of procedures is impossible to know. It was alleged, at any rate, that the new rules had been adopted specifically to keep Palmer out of the dispensary.

The infirmary seems to have been as uncaring of its patients as its successor, the Mid-Staffordshire Trust, became 170 years later. It declined to purchase the new anaesthetics on grounds of cost and employed incompetent nurses. Perhaps the Board of Guardians shared the scepticism of the army's chief medical officer, Dr John Hall, about the efficacy of drugs: "the smart of the knife is a powerful stimulant and it is much better to hear a man bawl lustily than to see him sink silently into the grave." Hospitals were not safe places to be in the 1840s, nor were they likely to cure patients – especially if, as was rumoured, medical students like the teenaged William Palmer were raiding the library looking for books on poisons. The chief requirement of a hospital, said Florence Nightingale echoing the Hippocratic oath, was that it should do the sick no harm, but her ideas on hygiene and administration were considered radical. Hospitals in the 1840s and for years after were for the destitute and poor. If you had money, you would be treated at home by a doctor who visited, not in the squalid and foetid wards, where relatives could watch you die in the midst of smell and squalor.

Within a year or so Palmer had moved on, this time to London, to train at St Bartholomew's Hospital, where once again, it was later said, he wasted his opportunities and squandered his money. It was here, as though tiring of listing Palmer's iniquities, that Mayhew – possibly lacking much information about this period of his life – unleashed his inner misanthropist with a lengthy generalised diatribe against medical students as a breed, rather than just Palmer in particular. Perhaps he had had direct experience of some of them. Medical students clearly had a reputation for riotousness a century before Richard Gordon wrote *Doctor in the House*. They were all drunks, gropers and disturbers of the peace, in the *Illustrated Times*'s estimation:

> The *summum bonum* of human happiness to the medical student's mind seemed to consist in strolling down the Haymarket or Regent Street, clad in the roughest of all overcoats, smoking the strongest of cigars and peering under the bonnet of every female passer-by ... This he would call "a lark". Great was he at

Lullaliety! Three drunken medical students, according to the dyspeptic *Illustrated Times*. This was a stock picture hurriedly chosen to illustrate the paper's narrative.

the bars of public houses ... Boisterous was his merriment too, later in the evening (civilised people call it night) when ... he would walk along with three or four companions, all abreast and arm-in-arm, taking up the entire width of pavement and shouting "Lullaliety!" whatever that may have meant, in a voice that would not only wake the slumbering echoes but the slumbering householders as well and make them wonder what on earth they paid police rates for.

Naturally the intent was to paint Palmer as one such wastrel, possibly even the worst: "*He* ate and drank of the best, spent his days and nights in riotous living and gave but little thought to those severe studies which he was required to surmount to become fitted for his profession." And of course there were racing men and women picked up in theatres around St Martin's Lane and Covent Garden:

> many rustling silks and satins, many feathers, much ochre and bismuth, technically termed "slap", much male mirth and alas! forced female gaiety. This was the sort of company William Palmer delighted in. Here he found men who were well up in the slang of the racing fraternity. Men whom he regularly met on the race courses in the neighbourhood of London – flashy in dress – shallow in intellect – and depraved in morals.

The picture of Palmer was calculated to be an awful warning – to make respectable readers shudder and take heed of where such depravity could lead: to a murder trial which had not yet taken place.

But Palmer may not really have been such a wastrel after all. Nestling in the files of the National Archives at Kew is a book of medical notes he wrote between October 1843 and January 1844, during his days at Bart's, and it gives a very different picture. It is a handsome, blue leather-bound, lined pocket notebook with marbled end-papers, more than a hundred pages long, signed by Palmer inside the front cover and filled with his neat, blotless, copperplate handwriting. It looks as though he was diligently taking down notes verbatim, directly from the lectures he was attending – phrases such as "it is scarcely necessary to add" pepper the pages – and each subject is carefully delineated. There are sections on flowers, fruit and herbs, and their medicinal uses: peaches, roses, "the buckwheat tribe", lobelias, peppers (which "stimulate the stomach"), legumes, even the madder root ("the odour is feeble, the taste bitter and astringent"). There are also notes on common symptoms and remedies: "dinner is the meal after which dyspeptic acidity is, generally, most inconveniently, prevalent and the alkali remedy should be taken an hour before and repeated at bedtime . . . [but] little permanent relief is attained without abstemiousness, regular hours and a proper selection of food." There are certainly references to poisons, but no more than a medical student might be expected to make and none, apparently, to strychnine.

It seems, however, that Mrs Palmer was warned that her son would not pass his examinations, so she engaged a doctor named Stegall to act as a "grinder", or crammer, promising him 50 guineas if he could get her William through to qualification. She later added a further 10 guineas as an incentive, as did Jerry Smith. Stegall did his work and Palmer did indeed pass, though the doctor later had to threaten to go to court before he got his money. Palmer's training – as with many would-be doctors – was fairly vestigial, given the state of medical knowledge at this period, but he qualified in August 1846 and was then able to describe himself – as he later did on the nameplate outside his house in Rugeley – as MRCS: Member of the Royal College of Surgeons. He could not have been completely hopeless as he was immediately appointed a house surgeon at St Bartholomew's Hospital, but he resigned within a month and returned to Rugeley to set up in practice there, among the people he knew and who knew him.

Palmer has usually been described as a doctor and was known as Dr Palmer, but as a surgeon he was of a lower order in the medical profession and in the social hierarchy – a sawbones, not a philosophically and theologically trained gentleman from a good school and a fine old university. Doctors had degrees and status, even if their training rarely included much contact with, or knowledge of, patients and their diseases, nor had many of them much more idea of how to treat them than anyone else. Medical men such as Bamford and Jones, who treated Cook, described themselves as surgeons, and though their social status was much higher, they were little better than manual workers. Their medical training, if they had any, was limited. They would have some knowledge of anatomy and could cut out and cut off things, set broken limbs, help with obstetrics, try to treat venereal diseases, and maybe attempt a little limited trephining and thoracotomy. They would have amputating knives and saws, scalpels, needles and forceps. Theirs was a profession of physical carpentry. They were ignorant of antiseptics, their theories of how diseases spread were wrong-headed (as were those of the university men who taught them), and the first operations with anaesthetics were only conducted in 1846, the year Palmer graduated. A surgeon in a hospital would operate on a patient while still wearing his street clothes and with the silk ligatures to bind the wound together threaded in bunches through the buttonholes of his coat. Even straightforward amputations of legs or arms carried the high risk of gangrene and death from infection. Surgical wards in hospitals such as St Bartholomew's or Stafford would have smelled foul, and those patients who survived the immediate shock of surgery would routinely have a zinc tray placed under their beds to catch the "laudable pus" which seeped from their wounds and was taken as a sign of returning health.

Palmer's training was even more vestigial than the three or four years undergone by many medical students who were to become doctors. Their training included chemistry, midwifery, botany, and – importantly – theology and Latin. Medical knowledge and experience in treating disease was improving all the time: Florence Nightingale was opening her hospital at Scutari during the Crimean War in the last year of Palmer's freedom. But it is doubtful whether he took much notice of the changes – by then, he had more urgent matters on his mind.

In the autumn of 1846, though, he was not only returning to Rugeley to practise his profession, but also to arrange himself a wife. The young woman he chose was called Annie Brookes and her short life was to be intimately interwoven with his. Annie herself had had a chequered background and a difficult childhood. She was three years younger than Palmer, born in 1827, the outcome of a lengthy liaison between a retired Indian army officer named Colonel William Brookes, who had returned to England in 1820 and settled in the middle of Stafford, and his housekeeper Mary Thornton. Brookes apparently declined to marry someone from the servant class – and his friends in turn refused to meet her – but the colonel acknowledged the child as his own and she generally carried his surname. Thornton, seemingly angered by his refusal to make her his wife, was said to have grown cantankerous and belligerent, drinking heavily, indulging in affairs and violently attacking the colonel, at least once with a knife. The pretty young servant maid that she had once been had been replaced by a tall, thin and angular drunken termagant, making his and their daughter's lives a misery, until he removed Annie and placed her in a boarding school run by a Miss Bond in Great Haywood, the village near Rugeley where Dr Tylecote lived. By 1834 the colonel had had enough and, following the example of all four of his brothers, shot himself. Annie, aged seven, was left in the care of two guardians who had been friends of the colonel and was bequeathed his savings of about £8,000, which was enough to give her an annual income of about £250. Her mother was left the nine properties that the colonel had owned in the centre of the town, including a pub called the Noah's Ark (it is still there, but known these days as the Surgery Café Bar), to which the old man used to retreat when she was on the warpath. The properties were expected to go to Annie after her mother's death. Whether it was the money or the prospect of inheriting the properties that first attracted William Palmer to the eligible young woman a decade or so later, or her looks and charm, is unclear. He certainly knew her before he went to London to train as a doctor, perhaps because he had met her in Haywood, though that does not seem to have stopped his elopement to Walsall with Jane Widnall. He also wrote her passionate love letters (though she was not to be the only recipient of those), one of which was read out at his trial:

> My Dearest Annie,
> I snatch a moment from my studies to write to your dear, dear little self. I need scarcely say that the principal inducement I have to work is my desire of getting my studies finished so as to be able to press your dear little form in my arms.
>   With best, best love, believe me, dearest Annie, your own,
> WILLIAM

It was in the interests of the reporters who sought every detail of Palmer's life after his arrest to paint the mother-in-law Mary Thornton as a harridan, in the best traditions of pantomime – not a wicked stepmother, but certainly a wicked matriarch; and at the same time to invest Annie Brookes with the mantle of a saintly and stereotypical paragon. The illustrations accompanying the potted biography of Palmer show a demure and modest beauty, with appropriately downcast eyes, like any number of Dickensian heroines: a Kate Nickleby, perhaps, as written in 1838–9, a Mary Graham from *Martin Chuzzlewit*, or even an Agnes Wickfield from *David Copperfield*. The same illustrations depicted Palmer himself as a tall, slim, romantic figure with curly hair and lavish sideboards, instead of the slightly dumpy, balding, flush-faced man he actually was. In fact these were generic pictures taken from the newspaper's stocks: "nearly the whole of them had done duty in books and periodicals more than once before," Henry Vizetelly, the editor of the *Illustrated Times*, wrote in his memoirs nearly forty years later. "My ingenuity was taxed to assimilate the text with the puzzling pictures which were supposed to illustrate it." Annie may well have been full of all the

This supposedly depicted Palmer's mother-in-law's death but was a highly sentimental stock illustration chosen by the *Illustrated Times*. However Mary Thornton died, it was not like this.

virtues – "proverbial for her simplicity, her kindness and engaging manners . . . the general favourite of the town" – but it is quite hard to discern what she saw in Palmer, apart from his professional status, eventual future prospects – and willingness to marry the illegitimate daughter of a suicidal Indian army officer and a drunken harridan. Certainly, her guardians were wary and tried to warn her off him. Perhaps his charm swept her off her feet; but well before their marriage in 1847 she must have known of his periodic petulance and wandering attention, as two letters which appear to date from September 1846 show. The Mr D referred to is her guardian Charles Dawson, a druggist with whose family she then lived in the village of Abbots Bromley, north of Rugeley:

> Tuesday
> My own dear William,
> Why did you sulk when you bade me goodbye in the park this morning? Mr D is always very kind to me and I should ill requite his goodness by acting directly contrary to his wishes. Come, put on one of your best smiles and write me a real sunshiny

note, for you have made me very unhappy. I shall expect a letter
on Thursday –
Ever yours dearest,
ANNIE BROOKES

Then:

Abbots Bromley, September 13, 1846 – 9am
Dearest William,
I think it was your turn to write and I fancy that if you will
only try and recollect, you will think so too. But never mind,
although I have not written, you know quite well that I am
always thinking of you . . .
   . . . I have got a present for you, but as it is intended as a
surprise, I must not spoil it by telling you what it is. Suppose
instead that I tell you something you will not care to hear half
so well, namely, that I am ever, my very dearest William, your
affectionate,
ANNIE

At some other time, William Palmer wrote to her again, expressing deep
devotion, and, apparently, was still trying to win over Dawson and Annie's
other guardian, a Doctor Knight:

Rugeley, May 16
My Dear Little Annie,
   . . . Oh Annie! You cannot tell how dull I have found the last few
days; I sit and think over my miserable bachelor life and feel so
dull and lonesome, I really cannot explain. I resolved, yesterday,
to write again to Mr D, but you forbid me doing this, so I must
wait the other four months. My dear Annie, I cannot tell you how
much I love you and how I long to call you mine forever,
Yours most affectionately,
WP
Did Dr Knight get the game I sent; did he mention anything
about it?

All these letters were allegedly found interleaved in a book about poisons discovered in Palmer's study after his arrest, and the *Illustrated Times* had no hesitation in publishing them in full. "We have been so fortunate as to procure three unpublished specimens, which we here lay before the reader," it proudly announced. They certainly seem to show passionate affection between the couple, though perhaps slightly more desperation on her part than on his. It also seems that game was Palmer's gift of choice when he wanted to flatter or cajole. The letters must have struck the Victorian public with the thrill of an authentic true-life epistolary novel, the more thrilling because they knew by then how the relationship eventually worked out.

It is possible that the surprise Annie had for Palmer was the revelation of her illegitimacy, though it is equally likely that he knew all about that already. Annie could not escape her origins and was very conscious of them – and, had she ever tried to forget them, she was sure to be constantly reminded by well-meaning Victorian contemporaries. When they married in St Nicholas Church, Abbots Bromley, on 7 October 1847, the register noted – instead of her father's name, which was not mentioned – only that she was called Ann Thornton and was the natural daughter of Mary Thornton. William, who customarily signed his first name as an abbreviation ('Wm'), was told by the vicar to cross it out and write it out in full. George Palmer, the solicitor brother, was one of the witnesses and Mary Knight the other, so it seems that Dr Knight had probably come round to the young doctor after all, or at least raised no absolute objection to him in the end.

Now, with their partnership duly solemnised, the Palmers – William aged twenty-three, Annie just twenty – were free to settle down to respectable lives of peaceful, worthy and comfortable obscurity, ministering to the sick of Rugeley, where they rented the pleasant house in Market Street, opposite the Talbot Arms. They had a carriage – loaned out to Sam Cheshire for his Sunday jaunts with his wife – and later Palmer bought Annie a chaise and pair of ponies: the nineteenth-century equivalent of a little sports car for the doctor's wife. Palmer also enticed the apothecary Ben Thirlby away from his employment with Thomas Salt, a rival surgeon in Upper Brook Street, to come and dispense medicine for his patients instead – maybe this was the reason for Salt's antagonism towards him and his need to visit

Charles Newton, Salt's apprentice, surreptitiously on the day before Cook died. The Palmers would go to the parish church across the road from their house, St Augustine's, where they had their own pew. William was a regular worshipper most weeks and made notes about the sermons in the margins of the Bible given him by his mother. They also subscribed to the Stafford Church Missionary Association. Just over a year after the couple's marriage, their first child, Willie, named after his father, was born, and four more children followed in quick succession. The Palmers might have been a happy family for years to come. But within a decade, all but Willie would be dead.

The reporters who descended on Rugeley following Palmer's arrest found a quiet, small town "about as large as Twickenham" and described it in terms that make it sound like the set of a television classic serial: a straggling place of small houses, "kept very clean and occupied by persons extremely well-to-do in the world". It was a good place for business, with honest folk keeping particularly safe accounts: cottage shops and red-brick houses with large leaden lights and big shutters. There was even a tall maypole "as high as a three-decker's mast" in Brook Street and annual horse and cattle fairs in the summer, but that was about it so far as excitement was concerned. "To those who like bustle and crowded pathways of course the country quietude of the town would be oppressive and saddening," wrote the ubiquitous Mayhew for the *Illustrated Times*'s issue of 2 February 1856:

> But to us there is a certain charm in the deserted thoroughfares when the only persons to be seen are the housewives at the windows, behind the rows of geraniums, plying the needle, whilst the husband is working in the fields . . . Mr Wright's hammer ringing on the anvil . . . the rumbling of bus and cab wheels under our windows . . . the young lady on the hot pony standing on the footway of bricks, close up to the shop door and giving her orders to the baker's wife. Nobody is out walking and yet there are plenty of inhabitants – hard-working people – who are earning their day's hire at Bladen's brass foundry or Hatfield's manufactory.

It is not quite clear how the reporter would have seen window-boxes of geraniums in mid-winter. Perhaps Mayhew was employing imagination and artistic licence, or possibly the plants were inside, obscuring his view as he peered through to spy on the women sewing away within.

Mayhew's opposite number, Edward Whitty, writing for a weekly called the *Leader*, also wrote lyrically, if with metropolitan condescension, about Rugeley as a town surrounded (in the deep mid-winter) by "meadows trim and daisies pied". Reports such as these established a picture of a rural idyll stalked and ripped apart by a rapacious and insidious villain: a cliché of the sort that has been common in newspapers ever since. The town hall had the court-room upstairs and a literary institution and a savings bank on the ground floor, where the cashiers did not seem hard at work, opening at ten o'clock and closing at three. There were "London-looking" shops and country ones: butchers with half sheep carcasses hanging up, women's tailors selling stays and bonnets, gentlemen's outfitters where Palmer bought his clothes, and a thriving bookseller's with a fashionable mahogany and plate-glass window. Outside the Talbot Arms stood old Tom Masters, the landlord, in his drab breeches and a cutaway coat, who had lived there for three-quarters of a century and still rode a brown mare that was itself more than thirty years old: "We make a good bit over a hundred together," he chuckled. Opposite was Palmer's house, empty and shuttered, standing back from the road behind its little front garden, "as if in shame". And further along was the shop of the only person in the area to have benefited from Palmer's activities: Mr Keeyes, the undertaker. Respectable folk, clean-living and doubtless keeping themselves to themselves – had the reporters thought to coin the everlasting cliché of newspaper reporting from the neighbourhoods of great crimes – had nevertheless only one topic of conversation: "Everything in Rugeley is Palmer now. Nothing else is talked of."

All the stories about Palmer's career – the people he cheated, the girls he seduced and deserted – were breathlessly related in the weeks after his arrest, so they may well have been doing the rounds in Rugeley for years, even while Palmer was engaged as an apparently reputable surgeon there. His reputation for untrustworthiness and spite does not seem to have unduly handicapped him in his dealings with patients, or professional colleagues, or the local authorities. Nor did it prevent him from living locally, but the rumours immediately spilled out after his arrest. The stories, of course, are largely unverifiable, though Dr Tylecote was certainly living in Haywood at the time of the 1841 census, as was a thirty-year-old gardener named Vickerstaff, who was living with his sixty-year-old mother. Tales about Palmer clearly grew in the telling: one old man in the village reckoned he had made fourteen local girls pregnant. And all this was published while he was still awaiting trial. Much more seriously, by now rumours of other murders and suspicious deaths were also being circulated and laid at Palmer's door. They would give a sensational national twist to what would otherwise have been a local story for the *Staffordshire Advertiser* and the towns of the Black Country. Was there a mass-murderer in the small Midlands town? And how many had he killed? Was it two, three – or a dozen? Or even more?

6

"If public rumour be worthy of credit"

NOT MANY DAYS HAD PASSED AFTER WILLIAM PALMER'S REMOVAL TO Stafford prison before practically every unexplained or sudden death in the Rugeley area over the previous ten years was being attributed to him – some plausible, some possible, others in every degree unlikely.

The first victim may have been a 27-year-old man named George Abley, who died in October 1846 following a drinking contest with Palmer at the Lamb and Flag, which still stands in the middle of the village of Little Haywood, near Rugeley. The story went that Abley, a plumber and glazier, a thin, pale man in indifferent health, had found himself being offered a brandy by the personable, newly qualified young doctor in the pub one cold autumn night. He refused, saying he had not a head for brandy-drinking, but was teased by Palmer's companion, a man named Timmis.[1] Palmer jocularly bet Timmis three to one in half-sovereigns in front of him that Abley could not knock back a full tumbler of neat brandy. The plumber again refused until Timmis offered him 10 shillings out of the prospective winnings – the equivalent of half a week's wages – if he could do it. They negotiated the price up to 15 shillings and Abley then downed the brandy. Palmer now raised the stakes, betting that he couldn't drink another, and so Abley drank that too, to general merriment in the bar at Palmer's expense. By now the

---

[1] It is impossible to tell whether this was the same Timmis who spoke to Fletcher more than fifty years later about Palmer being thoroughly bad, or even whether he was a relative.

plumber was raring for more, but presently turned green and went outside for fresh air, while the rest of the pub's customers settled down to a joke-telling session. It was not until an hour later that they realised Abley was still missing, and when they went outside to look for him, they found him lying in the stables groaning and clutching his stomach. He was carried home and died later that night. This hardly sounds like murder, more a silly drinking game of the sort Palmer had probably recently been playing with his fellow medical students down in London, and an inquest jury subsequently decided that Abley had died of natural causes. His death certificate, signed by William Ward, the Staffordshire coroner, gave the cause of death as "exhaustion the result of diseased blood vessels of the lung".

Abley lies now in an overgrown corner of nearby Colwich churchyard, under an ornate headstone giving his age and date of death. It must have been quite an expense for a labouring man's family to afford. One hundred and seventy years later the headstone is still just visibly incised with the admonitory fifth verse of Psalm 39: "Behold, thou hast made my days as an handsbreadth and mine age is as nothing before thee: verily every man at his best state is altogether vanity." That might have been an end to the matter, but the inquest jury foreman Edward Jenkinson popped up nearly a decade later, after Palmer's arrest, to say that he had disagreed with the verdict and that Abley had been knocked off because Palmer had fancied Abley's buxom wife. He told this tale around the pubs and to anyone who would listen, but even at the time there were those who said his motive was jealousy at Palmer's success with women.

More plausible as a possible murder was the death of Annie's mother Mary Thornton, who had spent the years following the colonel's suicide getting progressively more crotchety and increasingly sozzled on gin. She did not like Palmer – and he probably didn't like her much either – and accused him of poisoning the cats that swarmed around her house. Thornton periodically passed him sums of money, apparently because she feared what he might do to her otherwise, though that did not stop her swearing at him in public. Finally, after Christmas 1848, she agreed to move in with the Palmers – allegedly saying that if she went she would be dead within a fortnight – and was duly found collapsed and delirious in the street in the first week of January 1849, eventually dying in her bed at their home twelve days later at the age of fifty. The rumour was that she had refused to lend Palmer any more money and that he had wanted to get his hands on her properties in Stafford by fair means or foul. If so, he had miscalculated because there had been a dispute over the colonel's will after his death 15 years earlier, about whether he could legally leave the houses to a woman to whom he was not married, and they had been placed in Chancery, administered by the court for the benefit of Annie and her mother. Now, following Thornton's death, the court awarded the properties to Colonel Brookes's nearest relative, a man named Shallcross, and Palmer not only lost the chance of benefiting from a substantial slice of Stafford, but even lost the money he had spent in renovating them in the expectation that they would come to him through his wife's inheritance. This anyway was the story that circulated following Palmer's arrest seven years later. The *Illustrated Times* related it in its supplement in February 1856, though it glossed over Thornton's drinking habits and ill health, saying merely that she was a person of eccentric habits. The newspaper relished the story that she had feared that she would be dead within a fortnight: "these forebodings proved to be true, for she subsequently went to live with her daughter and four days afterwards [*sic*] she was a corpse" – though it did not confide to whom she had made the remark, or when, or where she had said it. The report went on to claim that Palmer had indeed inherited the properties and "thus became possessed of a respectable income". It was, the report said, a case pregnant with suspicion. The correction, that Palmer had not in fact inherited the houses, only came later with the publication of the newspaper's book about him, after his execution. And by then it was too late.

By the turn of the decade, it seems that Palmer was becoming increasingly addicted to racing and gambling. The next person he would later be accused of murdering was a man called Leonard Bladen, who had just been to Chester races with him. Bladen, who at forty-nine was more than twenty years older than Palmer, worked for the Charrington brewery company in London and had recently received an injury at work when a dray backed into him. It was serious enough to keep him from his job, but evidently not sufficiently painful to prevent him crossing the length of the country to get to the race meeting in the spring of 1850. While there, Bladen seems to have won a considerable amount of money – friends said he had as much as £500 in his money-belt – and at the same time was owed even more by his racing companion, Palmer. He apparently wrote to his wife to say that he would be coming home with £1,000, but meanwhile had accepted an invitation to stay with the doctor's family at Rugeley for three or four days on the way back. Probably he did so to ensure that he got his money, but he was sure that Palmer could be trusted as a good loser and anyway he had been promised some sport with a gun during his visit.

Bladen stayed overnight at Rugeley and then obviously felt well enough the next day to visit his brother Henry at Ashby-de-la-Zouch thirty miles away. He was driven over and back by Jerry Smith. Henry was a shoemaker, so Bladen ordered some boots from him and then returned to the Palmers'. There, he fell ill – no shooting occurred – and took to his bed, where his condition rapidly deteriorated despite the best efforts of Palmer, Thirlby and old Dr Bamford, who prescribed what was called "a mixture" for him. Palmer seems to have been the doctor mainly in attendance, bringing him his food and medicine. Whether Bladen asked him not to tell his wife, because she disapproved of his race-going, or Palmer decided she did not need to be told, Mrs Bladen down in London only found out that her husband was ill from another friend who had stopped off to see him in Rugeley on his way home to the capital. By the time she got to his bedside, her husband was delirious and no longer recognised her. He died a short time later. When the bereaved woman counted up her husband's money, she was surprised to find that, far from having £500 or £1,000, there was only £15 left. His betting book was missing, and instead of Palmer owing him £600, he insisted that he himself had actually been owed £60 by her late husband. He told her that Bladen had been gambling heavily and must have lost the rest. Magnanimously he promised not to enforce the debt. Not wishing to create a scene and grateful to the Palmers for looking after him, Mrs Bladen left and the family subsequently let the matter drop. The *Illustrated Times* published a letter it said she had written to some friends a month later, saying that Palmer had originally asked her to sign a paper acknowledging the debt:

> The gratitude I felt for the kind treatment Bladen had, I thought, received from them, would have induced me to have signed it in a moment, could I have done so without distressing myself; but knowing the embarrassed state of my affairs, which I candidly informed them of, still Mr Palmer insisted on my signing

the paper, urging if it was not in my power to pay, he would not compel me to do so; and I think I should have been induced to do so had he not said he had never borrowed a farthing of Mr Bladen in his life. I knew in that he told a falsehood as I had seen a letter in which he acknowledged £100 and told him so. From that moment he ceased to insist on my signing the paper, telling me he would make me a present of it; and on Mrs Palmer coming into the room . . . he told her to throw the paper into the fire . . . That Mr Palmer has acted unjustly in money matters I have good reason to believe; his letters I have placed in the hands of the Brewery firm and if they think proper and that there are sufficient grounds they will, no doubt, investigate the matter.

No investigation seems to have been carried out, either by the police or by the brewery, and Mrs Bladen's letter adds that she had no suspicions over her husband's demise. Bladen's certificate gave the cause of death as "injury of the hip joint 5 or 6 months; abscess in the pelvis 12 days certified". He lies buried under a tablet slab by the wall in Rugeley churchyard a few yards away from where Cook would also be interred five years later. Bladen's relatives turned up after Palmer's arrest hoping to get Leonard's body exhumed and added to the list for post-mortems, but were unsuccessful. How much could have been established, given the state of contemporary pathology, must have been doubtful, and in any case those wishing to prosecute Palmer had better, more recent cases to pursue.

After Palmer's arrest his name became attached in newspapers and folk-tales to a number of other murders or suspicious deaths across the country, many of them bearing similar features: a victim owed money, suspicious illness, a solicitous doctor, then death followed by Palmer's insistence that he was owed money by the dead person. The details are mainly elusive, and some of the stories seem to be little more than myths. There was, for instance, a story about a man called Bly, from Beccles in Suffolk, who was supposed to have been a racing companion of Palmer even though they lived 180 miles apart. Bly's death was already doing the rounds before Palmer's trial and was first published in the *Norfolk Chronicle* in a story missing many crucial details, including Bly's Christian name, the date of his supposed poisoning, the location where it happened and precisely how Palmer was involved in his fateful treatment. Mayhew hazarded a guess that it was "either at Rugeley, or at some town adjacent to a racecourse, by many said to be Leicester". Just like Mrs Bladen, Mrs Bly was said to have hurried to her husband's bedside, where Palmer tried to shoo her away, but she had been admitted to see him before he died, and in an affecting interview he had expressed contrition for his ill-spent life (an authentic Victorian moral touch) and told her that Palmer owed him £800. He then died, but when she mentioned the money to Palmer, he had suavely informed her that her husband had been confused and that actually Bly had owed him the money, not the other way round. Nothing further seems to have happened, though a book entitled *The Diary of a Norwich Medical Student from 1858 to 1860*, by a man named Shephard T. Taylor and published in the 1860s, mentions *en passant* that Palmer had murdered a relative of the author. The reference occurs in a paragraph about a lecture the student attended about strychnine in relation to the Palmer case and it then adds: "Palmer undoubtedly poisoned a cousin of my mother's named Blyth ten years ago, but the evidence was not considered strong enough to justify taking legal proceedings against him." It does not say who investigated the death or who took the decision not to prosecute. And of course Blyth is not necessarily Bly.

Other stories also seem apocryphal. Palmer was said to have poisoned a wealthy if disreputable uncle of his wife, Joseph "Beau" Bentley, supposedly after a brandy-drinking bout, very similar to the one with Abley exactly six years earlier. You might have thought that, in the light of the earlier experience, Palmer would have avoided brandy-drinking contests, but supposedly he had some hopes of an inheritance: "it is the general opinion," remarked the *Illustrated Times* blandly, "that Palmer wanted his uncle out of the way." Bentley's death certificate in October 1852 stated that he had died, aged sixty-two, of a malignant disease of the stomach. Then there was the tale of a sick Bentley aunt whose suspicion of Palmer's treatment practices meant that she quietly threw the tablets he prescribed for her out of the window rather than taking them – and the next morning the chickens in the yard below were all found to have died. And, of course, there were allegedly a number of abortions of illegitimate babies that Palmer had sired with serving maids around rural Staffordshire too – though it may be that only his mistress Jane, who was blackmailing him at the time of Cook's death, had an abortion, carried out not by Palmer but by a chemist in Stafford.

Nor were Palmer's murders said to be confined to cronies and relatives. The Tory politician Lord George Bentinck, who had pursued a keen and vengeful interest in rooting out some of the corruption in horse-racing, died suddenly in 1848, a death ascribed by some to Palmer's long-distance malignity. The rumour was quickly in circulation once Palmer's enthusiasm for horse-racing became known, and was reported in newspapers such as the *Morning Chronicle* in January 1856, long before his trial. Bentinck, immensely wealthy and the brother of a duke, was one of the Tory backbenchers who had harried Sir Robert Peel out of office over his government's repeal of the Corn Laws in 1846, but he died aged forty-six two years later while out for a country walk on his Nottinghamshire estate. The *Morning Chronicle* was a Peelite paper and maintained that the rumour about its hero's old enemy was unfounded, though that did not stop it reporting the matter. But, unfortunately for the conspiracists, Bentinck's campaign against horse-nobbling took place while Palmer was still a medical student in London and he had given up his active interest in the turf in favour of politics some time before his death. The circumstances of his subsequent demise a few months later bore all the symptoms of a heart attack – and that was certainly what Bentinck's biographer Benjamin Disraeli believed.

Nevertheless, death was coming too regularly to Market Street and Annie Palmer seems to have felt it after Bladen's end. She was said to have exclaimed: "My poor mother died when on a visit here last year – and now this man. What will people say?" But whatever people may have said privately, they did nothing. The *Illustrated Times* hedged its bets too: its account of the stories surrounding Palmer is littered with phrases such as "if public rumour be worthy of credit" and "rumour goes on to say that".

Following the birth of their eldest child, William junior, in October 1848, another four children were born to the Palmers in the succeeding five years and none lived for more than a couple of months. Elizabeth, the second child, died aged ten weeks on 6 January 1851. Henry died on the same date a year later aged one month. Eleven months later, on 19 December 1852, another son, Frank, died after just seven hours. Then, on 27 January 1854, their last baby, John Palmer, died when he was four days old. Each was certified in turn as having died of convulsions. Only William, known by his father as Little Willie, lived to grow old.

Such a catalogue of tragedy might have been expected to unhinge not only the parents but also those around them. It may have had that effect on Matilda Bradshaw, the family's nurse and cleaning woman, who after John's death was said to have run to the Bell – the pub next door to the Palmer's house in Market Street – crying that she would never go back there again and that her employer had "done away with" another baby. She claimed that she had been looking after the child upstairs when Palmer came in and insisted that he would take over. No sooner had she gone downstairs than she heard John screaming, and by the time she got back he was dead. Bradshaw would later claim that she had heard Palmer say that the babies had imposed a financial burden and that he could not altogether blame providence for their deaths. She alleged that he would dip his finger in poison, then sugar or honey, and allow the babies to suck on it, though Bradshaw admitted that she had never actually seen him do it: "No, but I know it in my heart to be true," she said. If so, she does not seem to have expressed her fears to anyone in authority beyond the pub and she was never questioned about the allegations after Palmer's arrest. Meanwhile, the town watched another melancholy procession following a tiny coffin to the churchyard.

At this distance, it is impossible to tell what killed the babies, since no examination was carried out at the time. Infant mortality was high and not unexpected. It was not uncommon for successions of babies in a family to die: many graveyards bear testimony to this, though usually they were carried off by epidemics or childhood diseases that could not at that stage be cured. It was not even unknown for parents, or guardians, or baby-minders to do away with infants for financial, or other, reasons. Nor was it especially remarked upon unless the deaths became particularly egregious. Amelia Dyer, the Reading baby farmer who was eventually hanged in 1896, may have done away with several hundred babies in the course of a twenty-year career, accepting money to adopt them from guilty, unmarried servant girls and then strangling them and dumping their bodies in the Thames shortly after their mothers had left. Dyer was not alone in her ghastly enterprise; she was not even the only Amelia who was a serial killer of babies: Amelia Such would be hanged for similar, though less prolific, crimes in 1903, seven years after Dyer.

If it was less common for the children of middle-class or professional parents such as the Palmers to die in such numbers, it was not unknown. It is possible, for instance, that the children inherited some sort of genetic defect or haemolytic disorder such as Kell syndrome, caused by a mismatch of William and Annie's antigens. In this, the first child survives in good health, but subsequent babies' blood supplies are contaminated and react against the mother's antigens in the womb: about 91 per cent of the population are $Kell_1$ antigen negative and 9 per cent $Kell_1$ positive, and if the mother is negative and the father positive, the syndrome occurs. The mother develops antibodies after being exposed to red blood cells that are positive during her pregnancy with the first child, and this affects subsequent pregnancies. (It is thought that Henry VIII and Catherine of Aragon, in light of her repeated miscarriages, may have had this problem.) It is a condition that is now routinely tested for and treatable during pregnancy. If Palmer was indeed the murderer of his own children, it is possible that he was aware of the syndrome, though he would not have known its cause. It would be rare, though possible, for such babies to survive so long after birth, so it may have been that they had other congenital diseases. Such evidence as there is suggests that Palmer was a loving parent to Willie and protective of him. He could not have benefited financially, spiritually or emotionally from the babies' deaths – except that they no longer cost him anything – and he must have been aware of the effect their deaths were having on his wife's health. But perhaps by that stage he was growing both reckless and desperate.

Did Annie herself have fears for her own safety when her husband was about? If she did, it did not stop her clinging to him. She would have been conscious of the dim view Victorian society took of wives abandoning their husbands – though his brother Walter's wife had done so – and the lack of legal redress and protection they received if they did. Annie would also have been aware of her precarious social position as an illegitimate child. Still, it must have been an ominous household after so much misfortune, so many deaths in quick succession – heavy with lurking dread, grief and mourning. She must have consoled herself with her husband's affection, but she was the next to die. By this time William Palmer's debts were spiralling out of control. He may have thought, when he insured Annie's life for £13,000 in April 1854, that he had found a way out of his financial difficulties. It was an immense and notable sum for a country doctor to take out on his wife – the Prince of Wales Insurance Office offloaded some of the risk onto the Scottish Equitable and the Sun insurance companies – and the first premium, of £760, was a very large amount too, especially in Palmer's circumstances. To secure the policy, he had claimed that it was necessary if she died to cover the potential loss of income from her inherited property in Stafford. As it was, though, it was the only premium that Palmer ever needed to pay.

In September 1854, nine months after little John's death, Annie went up to Liverpool to stay with her sister-in-law Sarah Palmer – two respectable ladies, both devoted to good works – and while she was there, they went to a concert in St George's Hall. Annie wore only a light summer dress, and by the time she returned to Rugeley on the train the following afternoon, she was nursing a chill and went straight to bed. The next morning her dutiful husband took her a breakfast of tea, sugared but without milk, and dry toast, and shortly after that she started vomiting. By the weekend, four days later, Dr Bamford had been called in and diagnosed English cholera, prescribing pills of calomel and colocynth and what was called an "opening drought" to void her bowels. Next to visit was Annie's guardian Dr Edward Knight, the man who had been reluctant to let her marry Palmer seven years earlier, who was deaf and nearly as old as Bamford. Benjamin Thirlby, Palmer's chemist assistant, also weighed in with the suggestion of arrowroot and brandy, but by then Annie was sinking and not able to speak. Palmer appears to have ordered a dose of prussic acid, which apparently was meant to stop retching. She also drank some glasses of clean water with effervescing solutions administered by his hand and said they did her good. In any case, Annie was unable by now to take any pills at all. By the following Friday, she was dead and Palmer was distraught. He wrote in his diary (according to the *Illustrated Times*): "My poor dear Anne expired at 10 past 1"; and (according to George Fletcher in his book seventy years later): "My darling Annie was called today by her God to the home of bliss so well deserved." On the day of her funeral at St Augustine's parish church in Rugeley, he was overcome with grief and heard to cry: "Take me, O God, take me with my darling treasure."

If that was so, it did not stop the local gossip that Palmer sought direct personal consolation with the family's maid Eliza Tharme, who would subsequently become pregnant. Annie Palmer died on 29 September 1854 and

Eliza's son Alfred was born in the house in Market Street on 26 June 1855. Palmer was away at the time – she was attended by his assistant Thirlby – but he recorded the event in his diary for that day in a note accompanied by seven crosses: "Eliza confined of a little boy at 9 o'clock at night." The birth was recorded in the parish register, with no father named.

It was more than gossip that Eliza had been Palmer's mistress. She was "a good-looking young woman", according to a legal opinion produced for the trial, discussing whether she should be called to give evidence. Tharme was not called, but her own statement said:

> Mr Palmer would have been familiar with me before his wife's death, but I had not given him consent, not for a few days after. He had offered to take liberties with me before Mrs Palmer went to Liverpool. Mr Palmer promised to marry me and I consented to his liberties, that was a very few days after his wife's death. I was confined in Mr Palmer's house on the 26th June 1855. He was the father of my child.

Against the statement, someone – presumably a prosecution lawyer – added a note saying:

> This young woman continued to live with him down to the time of his arrest and she was the only person he expressed any great anxiety to see prior to his removal to Stafford gaol. His parting from her betrayed the only little bit of feeling he has ever shewn and a few days before he gave her a £50 Bank of England note for her wages.

On another copy of the statement in the archives a neat, lawyerly hand has written: "This woman is a very unwilling witness. She cohabited with the prisoner and had a child by him nine months and 14 days after his wife's death. Nothing further can be learnt of her." Tharme did not appear as a witness in court and disappears from history thereafter.

The death certificate signified the cause of Annie's death as English cholera and it was signed by Bamford and her former guardian Edward Knight. Nor was it necessarily a suspicious or inherently unlikely diagnosis:

English cholera was what is now called dysentery and was common enough in the industrial cities of Britain, particularly in the summer and especially near ports and rivers with heavily polluted water supplies. Dysentery was no respecter of class: it would kill the rich as easily and quickly as the poor. Cities such as Liverpool had appalling death rates and severely truncated life expectancy. The city was expanding in population by 7 per cent a year throughout the first half of the nineteenth century: 82,000 in 1801 had become 376,000 fifty years later. Its growth was far too rapid for its infrastructure to cope with. The average life expectancy of a labourer in Liverpool was in the teens and a professional man might live only into his thirties. Only half the children born in such a place at this time would survive until the age of five. The newly built St George's Hall, where Annie attended the concert, was (and is) a great Athenian-style, pillared monument to civic pride and burgeoning mercantile self-confidence, but there were workers' hovels close by of nearly indescribable squalor and non-existent sanitation. In the 1850s, too, there was an even more lethal and highly infectious strain of cholera, which had spread from India in pandemic waves over the previous twenty years and regularly wiped out thousands in Europe and America. The causes of cholera were misunderstood. It was still widely thought by doctors to be caused by a malign miasma in the air, rather than infected, germ-laden water supplies – and the medical treatment for it was accordingly underdeveloped. In the circumstances, pills and prussic acid were probably the last things Annie needed: if it was dysentery, she would have urgently required something to prevent dehydration, so the draughts of clean water with effervescing powder may have done her good, depending on what was in the powder. No wonder she had difficulty swallowing Bamford's pills. Annie might have been poisoned, but she also had the symptoms of dysentery.

What Palmer had from her death was the benefit of the life insurance policy so recently and fortuitously taken out. The insurance companies grumbled but paid up, as Annie's death certificate had after all been signed by three doctors, including her guardian. They also, of course, made a note of what had happened because it was a huge loss to them. Then, a few months later, Palmer tried again. This time, it was his older brother's life that Palmer wanted to insure. Walter was a year older than William and, aged thirty-one, was a hopeless alcoholic. He had tried his hand as a corn merchant, married and lived on the Isle of Man for a while, but by 1855 he was back in Stafford, a bankrupt as well as a drunk.

He was described as a great heavy drunken man, very simple-hearted, and was known to his cronies as Watty. He had married Agnes Milcrest from Liverpool, the sister of his older brother Joseph's wife, and she had brought with her an income of £450 a year, but that was not enough, for he gambled too. By the early 1850s he was having bouts of delirium tremens, he had separated from his wife, who had gone back to Liverpool, and he was incapable of work. Walter was not on the face of it a very good risk for life insurance, but William apparently offered him £400 if he would let him insure his life, on the basis that he, Walter, was not likely to live ten years anyway and meanwhile could use the money for drink. So, less than four months after his wife had died, William now tried to get a life policy on Walter for the staggering sum of £84,000, through policies with six different companies, which would have required an annual premium of £4,000 – William, of course, being the beneficiary, not Walter's wife Agnes. William went to Thomas Pratt, the London money-lending solicitor, to see if he could arrange a policy for him. Pratt told him that he could manage to raise insurance of no more than £13,000 and advised him not to try for any more, so soon after his wife's payout. It seems that Pratt may even have paid the first premium – £710, which included a £106 commission for himself – with, astonishingly, the Prince of Wales Insurance Office again. Within a few months, in June 1855, Palmer was trying to take out another policy on Walter, for an extra £10,000, with the Gresham company. They imposed a condition: they would not pay out if his brother died within five years. "Oh," Palmer allegedly said insouciantly. "That would not suit my book at all."

Nevertheless, Pratt did manage to organise a policy for Walter. What happened was outlined in an article in the *Post and Insurance Monitor*, the weekly publication of the trade, in early January 1856, the week of Walter and Annie Palmer's inquests:

> Mr Pratt one day in June last year met in Sackville Street, Piccadilly, Colonel Addison, manager of the Phoenix Life Insurance Office and stated he was in some little perplexity from not being able to get a particular life insured for £13,000 though he was

willing to pay an extra premium, the life being risky. Colonel
Addison did not seem disposed to have anything to do with
risky lives himself but told Mr Pratt he thought he could get the
thing done for him if he was prepared to pay a 'declined rate'.
On turning into the Quadrant they accidentally met Mr
Hornby, secretary of the Prince of Wales company, who seems
to have been a much bolder man than the colonel, for the matter
having been gone into and the risky rate determined upon, the
Prince of Wales granted a policy for the entire £13,000. Subsequently and without much loss of time it may be supposed
the Prince of Wales effected a reassignment for £12,500 with the
Athenaeum Life office which, after retaining £2,000 for its share,
parcelled out the remainder of the risk.

What had persuaded Hornby to agree to the policy on Walter's life was
the assurance on the application that he was unmarried and in good
health, neither of which was strictly true – though evidently he really knew
better since the additional premium was imposed. Walter was kept sober
long enough to sign the forms and to pass a medical signed by a surgeon
named Cornelius Waddell from Stafford, which stated that he was
"healthy, robust and temperate", none of which was true either. Waddell
did allegedly add a confidential coda for one of the insurance companies
that employed him: "I am told he drinks – be cautious", but perhaps the
Prince of Wales Office pretended that it had not seen this note before it
agreed to the policy, or assumed the risk was worth it. Actually, what persuaded the company's agent to insure Walter's life – on a premium that
would normally have been levied on a man of fifty-five (an age towards
the end of an average Victorian lifespan) rather than one, like Walter, in
his early thirties – was the prospect of the commission. Life insurance was
expanding rapidly in this period as increasing numbers of middle-class
Victorians insured themselves and their families. Exotically named, inadequately capitalised companies were sprouting up to take advantage of
the market: launching with big advertising budgets and tempting offers,
failing, merging and being amalgamated and swallowed up. Most have
long since disappeared without trace, but some survived and grew rich,
with names still recognisable today: Prudential, Britannia, Equitable Life,

Phoenix, all with sufficient reserves and caution to meet the demands placed on them. The Prudential, in particular, was an early and aggressive advertiser of its products, with posters at all railway terminals just to remind travellers of the risks they were taking by going by train. These companies were the canny ones, cautious of risk and reluctant to pay out on policies: when the relatives of a convict tried to claim on his life insurance after the prison ship transporting him to Australia sank, they were refused on the grounds that he had left the country without the insurer's permission. Meanwhile, freelance insurance agents, selling on commission, were in fierce competition, often insuring the same life several times with different companies and receiving fees from each. The life insurance market, which had been valued at £10 million a year in 1800, was by 1850 worth £150 million and in 1870 would reach £270 million.

No one was uninsurable, not even Walter. The Prince of Wales Office spread the risk on the policy across twenty other insurance companies. It retained £2,500 for itself and passed the rest onto the Athenaeum company, which in turn offloaded portions onto the Magnet (£750), the Beacon (£750), the Observer (£250) and many others for greater or lesser amounts. But, as the *Post and Insurance* pointed out, the companies' seeming independence was an illusion: most of them were linked to the Athenaeum; they were all connected to each other by ties of consanguinity; and many had the same board members. A clergyman called the Rev. J. Bartlett was a director of no fewer than six; as the *Post* reported, "The reverend gentleman was required by his brother directors to resign in consequence of his connection with so many offices", though whether that occurred only once his directorships became publicly known is not clear. Presumably he was on the company boards to give them an air of respectability and his multiple memberships would have been known to his brother directors, if only because so many of them were on the same boards themselves.

Colonel Addison of the Phoenix Life, having declined Walter's application, took a few days off in the country and came back to find out that one of his colleagues had nevertheless agreed to take a £500 share of the policy for his company anyway. "It is rather singular," the *Post and Insurance* commented, "On his return he was congratulated by the secretary for the amount of business that had been done in his absence, among other matters, a policy having been granted on the life of Walter Palmer."

The *Post and Insurance* was severe in its editorialising about what it aptly described as the Palmer lottery: "The manner in which the ongoing risk was taken and the curious batch of offices . . . afford a tolerable specimen of what is taking place among a class of companies whose existence depends on the Sir Pertinax maxim: 'get money'." It had little sympathy with the companies, now that Walter had died within a few months of the life insurance being taken out:

> Unless it can be shewn that Walter Palmer in effecting the assurance was aware he was going to be poisoned by somebody for the benefit of those who were to receive the amount of the policy, how can payment be legally refused? Now, we ask, upon what ground the Prince of Wales office for the sake of a premium of £500 should have taken upon itself the enormous collateral risk of £12,500 in which it could have no possible beneficial interest beyond whatever commission may have been paid by the Athenaeum for the transfer.

Of course, ultimately the policy did not pay out, so the insurance agents got away with it and their commissions. It would be another fifteen years before company regulations would be tightened up in legislation.

Earlier, in February 1855, Walter had moved in with a man called Tom Walkenden, who was instructed by William Palmer to look after him and allow him to drink, which he did so efficiently that in the following five months he purchased 19 gallons of gin for him, with money supplied by William. Walkenden said later:

> He repeatedly begged of me, in case I saw he was likely to have another attack of delirium tremens, not to take his gin from him . . . for he said: "If I had only had my gin then when I wanted it, I should not have been half as bad as I was." When he had the delirium, I would not give him any gin, because Dr Waddell said he was only to have two or three small glasses a day. But I used to see that he was sinking and perhaps I would give him a glass

or two more than Dr Waddell directed when I saw there was any necessity. But what was I to do? The poor fellow used to beg and cry for it as if it was his life. He would be cunning to get gin. One morning . . . I thought he was so ill that he could not possibly leave his bed [and] while I was eating a little breakfast, I heard a noise overhead. I ran upstairs and found him crawling on his hands and knees and searching for something under the dressing table, in the same place where formally he used to hide his gin . . . he used to hide his gin bottle in all sorts of places – under his bed head, or under his mattress, or in his boots, or anywhere.

By the summer, Walter was sinking. In early August, he managed a trip to Liverpool to see his wife. Then, a few days later, he wrote her an affectionate last letter, including the words: "Drink is always at my elbow." There was also a trip to the races at Wolverhampton. William was a frequent visitor and the landlord of the nearby Junction Hotel in Stafford claimed later to have seen him mixing something in a small bottle in the stables before one of his visits to see Walter. "Taking his drink away from him and giving him medicine will not do for a person who has been in the habit of drinking and I hope this will do him good," Palmer had said to him. The landlord, a man named Lloyd, alleged that William also bought a bottle of very best brandy for his brother and told him that if Walter wanted any more, he was to supply it and charge it to him.

Now Walter was drinking continuously, and on 16 August William came to visit. Walkenden graphically described what happened that day:

He was certainly not sober when he got up. It was his general habit to say when he got up of a morning, "come let us have another tot" and I used to replenish his glass. He was taken unwell when sitting in an easy chair in the front room. He said to me: "Help me to the sofa for I feel very ill," which I did . . . I think I was with him the whole of the time that his brother was present except when, on his being sick, I went to the kitchen to fetch a basin and I was not more than a minute absent . . . After he was attacked his face became very black; the perspiration stood on his countenance like peas and his head hung over the head of the sofa. I ran to the kitchen for William Palmer immediately and told him to come and see the state of his brother.

Walter died a few minutes later with William and Walkenden at his side. Walter never had received the £400 he had been promised, just £60 and the pledge that William would pay all his bills for drink. It was another promise reneged upon.

Shortly after this harrowing scene, William Palmer went out and found the boots at the Junction Hotel to ask him to take a message to the railway station and have it transmitted by telegraph. It was not to let Walter's wife know of his death, but to lay a £50 bet on his horse Lurley, which was running in the next race at Ludlow that afternoon. He had been told by Jerry Smith that it was a sure thing to win, but it wasn't. Palmer lost again. On the same afternoon, within an hour of Walter's death, he also ordered a strong oak coffin to be encased in a lead one. The following day, Friday 17 August, Palmer went up to Liverpool to see Walter's wife with the news, which came as a considerable shock to her as he had written only a few days earlier, but when she asked to see his body one last time, she was told that it was too late and the coffin had already been sealed. Mr Vittie, the Stafford undertaker, told Walter's inquest a few months later that there had been no need to embalm him because "there be enough gin saturated in the flesh to preserve him for a year". The funeral took place in Rugeley the following Monday.

On the night of his brother's death Palmer wrote in his diary: "Went to see Walter who was very ill." Then he added: "Walter Palmer died at half-past two pm." The cause on the death certificate was given as: "General visceral disease and apoplexy."

Three months later Eliza Tharme's baby, Palmer's illegitimate son Alfred, also died. He had been sent away to be looked after by a wet nurse in the nearby village of Armitage, and his life ended there five months after his birth, on 17 November, the Saturday of Cook's illness at the Talbot Arms. Unlike his birth, the baby's death was not recorded in Palmer's diary. The *Illustrated Times*'s account a couple of months later stated baldly that the baby had been brought to Rugeley to be shown to his father and "the reader will guess the result, the child was seized with convulsions while going home and died shortly after". But the cause of death was recorded as erysipelas – St Anthony's Fire – which is actually a bacterial infection which causes a livid red rash and can easily be fatal, particularly in babies (Queen Anne and John Dryden also died from it). It is now treated with antibiotics and its symptoms are not those of poisoning, nor is it marked by the convulsions that characterized the deaths of Palmer's other infant children. Ben Thirlby had been present at Alfred's death as well as his birth, and so presumably would have noticed what caused it.

Already two deaths – Walter and now little Alfred Tharme – around Palmer in 1855, to add to the deaths of his wife and baby the previous year and three other babies before that. And within a week there would be the last: John Parsons Cook.

The boots at the Grand Junction Hotel, Stafford who claimed to have been sent to place a bet by Palmer within minutes of Walter's death.

7

"On – on! Like the
rushing whirlwind"

WILLIAM PALMER'S DOWNFALL WAS UNDOUBTEDLY CAUSED BY HIS
passion for horse-racing in the last three years of his freedom. He
may have been in financial difficulties before, but it was the cost
of keeping a string of largely unsuccessful but inevitably expensive thor-
oughbred horses and the fact that they kept losing at critical moments that
cast him deeper and deeper into the clutches of moneylenders, causing him
to sink ever further into a vortex of debt and to cast around increasingly
desperately for a means of paying off his creditors. The figures – more than
£24,000 owed and usurious interest of £1,000 a month – seem bad enough
now, but in the 1850s they were truly devastating: the equivalent perhaps
of more than £1 million and £60,000 interest to find each month.

His aspirations were nevertheless not wholly unrealistic: a good victory
at long odds could net an owner, or a betting man, tens of thousands of
pounds in one go. Reputedly, John Gully, the MP and former boxer, and his
associate Robert Ridsdale won £60,000 when their horse St Giles took the
Derby in 1832. Lord George Bentinck, who boasted he kept horses in three
counties, won £10,000 in bets on his horse Crucifix, which he had bought
for 54 guineas. Abraham Goodman, a swindler who ran a ringer called Running Rein which won the notorious 1844 Derby when it was actually an in-
eligible four-year-old called Maccabeus, escaped to France leaving behind
£50,000 in what would have been winnings if he had not been found out. A
man might make a good living out of racing and come out rich. Joe Pickers-
gill, originally a Leeds butcher's boy, died much later in the century worth

£746,000; Nat Flatman, a jockey who rode occasionally for William Palmer, left £11,000 when he died; and George Herring, the agent Palmer used to collect Cook's winnings, became a millionaire, having invested his gains from racing in a career in the City of London. But you had to be canny, careful, lucky, perhaps even occasionally corrupt, to be successful. Many, perhaps most, owners lost money on their horses and many trainers and jockeys ended up destitute. It was a gruelling and often short life for jockeys in the 1850s. They would be entered for rides sometimes when they were still young children, not strong enough to control their powerful horses: George Fordham, one of the great Victorian jockeys, won his first race at the age of fourteen, weighing less than four stone. There was arduous travelling between courses, small and inadequate pay at the hands of miserly and sometimes welshing owners, no compensation for injury or wages while injured, constant battles to keep weight down, little social status, future career prospects only as stable lads and, not infrequently, an early death from tuberculosis.

Racing was extremely popular with all classes – evangelical attempts to get it banned were largely unsuccessful – but it was under-regulated in the 1850s and deeply murky. Races were fixed – the 1844 Derby was notorious only because it was successfully exposed. Horses were nobbled; jockeys, stable boys and trainers were bribed; owners sometimes fixed the odds and not infrequently the handicaps on their horses; and the track authorities were reluctant to take action against abuses. While some clergymen preached, as the Dean of Carlisle did, against "a kind of pleasure which seems to be an unmitigated evil", the clerks of some courses even allowed known card-sharps and other fraudsters in, just so long as they paid an extra fee for access to the punters. Above all, race meetings were largely unregulated by the Jockey Club, or by any other national body. There were many small country courses, running races according to their own local rules; there were three in the Rugeley area alone, and nearby Hednesford, just across Cannock Chase, was the location of significant racing stables. Many courses were used only once a year, for one day's racing. In 1848 there were 117 race meetings in Britain, but sixty-one of those were held on a single day and only thirteen of the courses in the country had more than one meeting a year.

In the days before photography or regular veterinary testing, the true identity of horses, or even their ages, was often unclear. In the 1844 Derby Running Rein kicked one of the other contenders, named Leander, which broke its leg as a result and had to be destroyed. Leander turned out to have been a ringer too, but when its body was dug up later during inquiries into the race, it was found that its jaw had been sawn off so that its teeth could not be checked to determine its real age. Horses could be nobbled at any stage, by breaking into the stable yard or even on the course; a groom named Daniel Dawson was hanged in 1811 for poisoning the horses of rival owners, though that did not stop the practice and the bookies who had induced him to do it went unpunished. Horses might be fed anything from arsenic in their water trough – the method that did for Dawson – to opium balls or lead shot to slow them down. Conversely, to make a horse run faster, it was not illegal to dose it with stimulants such as cocaine. And owners could rig the odds, pretending their horses were more or less successful or fit than they really were, or bribe jockeys and trainers – their own, or their rivals – not to race flat out. False starts could be staged to wind a competitor and extra weights inserted under saddles. Innovations, only just being brought in following Bentinck's initiative in the 1840s, included the identification of jockeys and their mounts by the "silk, velvet or satin" jackets they wore, the introduction of a dual flag system to limit wayward starts, and an insistence that horses must be saddled and mounted in full view in the paddock. But even so, cheating was widespread and probably largely undetected. Horse-nobbling was one of the many ancillary crimes levelled against William Palmer, seemingly on the basis that everyone in racing was doing it, but despite the insinuations there seems to have been no substance or proof to the charge. Racing for him was anyway clearly a particularly risky business.

Despite its reputation many members of the aristocracy were associated with horse-racing, giving it an air of respectability as "the premier sport of Englishmen". Prince Albert had racehorses and even the queen attended Royal Ascot, though she went to the Derby only once and it is doubtful that she was enthralled. Victoria once asked the owner of a Derby winner whether his horse had ever taken part in the race before (as the Derby is only open to three-year-olds, horses only get one chance, though in the light of the Running Rein scandal her question may not have been entirely inapposite). The big race meetings drew increasingly large crowds. The Derby on Epsom Downs in late May each year was traditionally a time of holiday, jollity and debauchery for tens of thousands of Londoners: a day to hurry out of town by excursion train, pony and trap or even on foot, to lose

money, get drunk and have fun, and then to riot on the way home. Dickens himself was appalled after he attended the race in 1843 to see the road back to London littered with dead horses, animals which had not survived the rigours of pulling overloaded carts full of drunken revellers back into town. Even Parliament was adjourned for the day each year, and it was generally regarded as the one occasion when all social classes could mingle in what the *Illustrated London News* called

a temporary saturnalia of social equality . . . [when people were prepared] to positively hob and nob with those palpably inferior to them in station . . . Liberty, equality and fraternity being qualities very strongly insisted upon on the Derby Day . . . the day when poverty elbows pride and wretchedness stalks cheek-by-

A study for William Powell Frith's famous painting of Derby Day 1857.
The original hangs in the Tate Gallery's collection in London.

jowl with wealth . . . the snob pushes by the gentleman and the
cad insinuates himself among the cream of the land.

As an article in Dickens's *Household Words* stated in 1853: "We have hardly
a real holiday in England. Executions and races make the nearest approach
to one."

The fashionable painter William Powell Frith's enormous panoramic
painting *The Derby Day* captures the scene very well in all its mid-Victorian
variety and rackety raucousness. It may be the single most popular British
painting of the entire period. Frith visited the Derby in 1857. The previous
year's race was held by coincidence on the day after Palmer's conviction at
the Old Bailey; but Frith's painting captured a scene that the Rugeley surgeon would have recognised very well – and indeed Palmer had attended

the Derby in 1855 and probably in earlier years too. Frith was not interested in the racing, so his picture concentrates on the crowd – jockeys and their horses are only dimly visible in the background – and it depicts ninety direct portraits and nearly a hundred distinct social types. On the left, near the Reform Club's tent, there are rich city gents in top hats and riding boots watching a thimble-rigger who is in the process of cheating the gullible out of their money; nearby stands a stunned youth, hands in pockets, who has gambled away his pocket-watch and all his money. Just across the way a young country woman is trying to dissuade her besmocked yokel husband from joining the game. In the centre of the painting there is a little group of desperate street entertainers being idly watched by a crowd including soldiers and Londoners as an acrobat tries vainly to get the attention of his small child so that they can start their performance. The child's attention has been riveted by the picnic being laid out near their feet by a uniformed coachman in readiness for his employers. Behind in two carriages sits a crowd of young women – are they fashionable and successful prostitutes, or just out for a spree? – who are being paid court by two fashionable young men, one of whom appears to be marking their race-cards for them. Then on the right, in a smart, open-topped, high-sprung barouche carriage – the nineteenth-century equivalent of a sports car – another young woman, shaded by her parasol, tosses her head away from an old gypsy woman who is trying to read her fortune, while her bored lover leans negligently against the side, gazing contemptuously at a young, barefoot girl who is attempting to sell him a sprig of lucky white heather.

There are thieves and pick-pockets, prostitutes and beggars, musicians and street vendors, cads and City types. Frith believed rightly that they could be distinguished by their clothes and bearing, but also by their physiognomies, which would show their degree of refinement, character and social position. All human life is there. The painting, which is more than seven feet wide and half that in height, teems with incidents and faces, what Frith called "the kaleidoscopic aspect of the crowd". The artist sketched many of those he saw and commissioned photographs of others from the young photographer Robert Howlett – the man who took the famous picture of Isambard Kingdom Brunel in front of the *Great Eastern*'s launching chains – so it is likely that his subjects were people whom William Palmer knew. The painting caused a sensation when it was exhibited at the Royal Academy in 1858: the police had to be called in to guard it and a protective iron railing was erected to keep the crowds at a safe distance. Later it would be displayed across the country and exhibited in the United States and Australia. It was a recognisably accurate depiction, as far as ordinary spectators were concerned, of the sort of people who were visible all around race meetings, even if, as Frith sneered, its "invidious distinction" made "thirteen elderly Academicians [take] to their beds in fits of bile and envy". He could afford to mock them – his paintings had made him rich.

The weather for the Derby in 1856 was fine and sunny – just as it is in Frith's picture – though the ground was soft, and the crowds were as excitable and raucous as ever. They watched Admiral Harcourt's horse Ellington romp home by a length – "a most exciting race" – at twenty to one in the slowest Derby ever run. It beat the favourite into fourth place, news that must have caused a flutter of excitement to William Palmer in his jail cell back at Stafford and probably a pang at the thought that he had been at Epsom only the previous year. On the day after the race his trial was still taking up most newspaper space, but there was room in the *Morning Chronicle* to recount a small incident of the day which indicated just how turbulent the crowds flocking to Epsom were. One man, the paper said, had been late and, rushing to get on board the one o'clock train as it was leaving, had seized the handle of a carriage door, but the door had slammed and he had fallen under the wheels of the moving train and been killed instantly. It added drily: "Appalling as was this accident, so great was the excitement that no one stopped, but eagerly crowded into the carriages without pausing to reflect on the sad catastrophe." The paper itself thought the incident only worthy of a couple of paragraphs.

The railways were bringing spectators to meetings – special excursion trains had been laid on since the early 1830s – and they enabled owners, trainers and especially jockeys and horses to criss-cross the country. Previously horses had had to be walked to meetings and might arrive exhausted if they had had a journey of several hundred miles, while jockeys had to clamber aboard stage-coaches. Now they could travel hundreds of miles overnight and so could spectators if they followed the turf. But apart from the great meetings in the racing calendar – the Grand National at Aintree, the Derby at Epsom and the St Leger at Doncaster – most meetings had local crowds and localised races. The working classes would trudge to nearby meetings if they could afford the time off work, for races were held midweek, not at weekends, and the middle classes would also attend, "always putting the best face on things and most agreeably sober", as it was said at Doncaster. Local meetings would be big and noteworthy annual events. They might be denounced from evangelical pulpits (though sporting clergymen were known to own racehorses too) and yet still be attended by all the worthies of the district. As Hugh Shimmin, a Liverpool journalist and anti-racing campaigner, wrote of the local meeting in the 1850s, there were vicious practices and questionable pursuits on the course: "more respectable people, merchants who on the Exchange and at home pass for gentlemen engage in indecorous and unbecoming dalliances in a brothel-keeper's booth", while "members of Parliament, magistrates, aldermen, town councillors, merchants, brokers, publicans, businessmen of every grade and many men of questionable character" could be found betting in the ring. Brewers, lawyers – and doctors – seem to have been among the professions most associated with racing, because it was in their financial and social interest to be so. Races were places to be seen as well as to have a good time.

There were fitful attempts to clean up racing – most notably by Lord George Bentinck in the 1840s, though he was not above a bit of sharp practice and the gaining of unfair advantage himself – but the sport lent itself to secrecy. There was every incentive to fix races, with so much money at stake. By and large the sanctions against crookedness were moral ones: being warning off the course, for instance, or excluded from Tattersall's, as Palmer was, so making it harder to place bets and collect winnings. Worst of all was to gain a reputation as a welsher on bets. Bets were not recoverable in law – Palmer was being economical with the truth when he told Stephens that Cook's bets had died with him, since they would only have been null if he had died before the race instead of after it – but they were debts of honour. Even so, it was thought that as many as 20 per cent of bets were never collected. But for a gentleman, or someone with pretentions to be so, to gain a reputation for not settling up was socially devastating. As Squire George Osbaldeston, a famous sporting figure, former jockey, cricketer, crack shot and betting man, once said: "We must pay at Tattersall's or our character and credit will be gone." Even so, standards were slipping. As the sporting newspaper *Bell's Life* noted in 1853: "Some years back if a man was a defaulter he dare not show his face at Tattersall's, or at any place where betting men were in the habit of meeting, but now defaulters obtrude themselves with blushing effrontery." When the outcome of the 1844 Derby finally came before the courts, the judge Baron Alderson – who would also be one of the judges at Palmer's trial – pronounced crustily: "If gentlemen would associate with gentlemen and race with gentlemen, we should have no such practices. But if gentlemen will condescend to race with blackguards, they must expect to be cheated."

There was plenty at stake for William Palmer if he failed to pay his debts. He would lose not only his horses, but also his honour and his good name with bookmakers, owners, trainers and jockeys. He might be warned off courses and was already barred from going to Tattersall's ring near Hyde Park Corner on Mondays, when the previous week's bets were always settled, which is why he had to get intermediaries to do it for him. And, if he was a defaulter, he would also find difficulty making a bet. Bookmakers would not want to do business, in the words of a parliamentary select committee report of 1843, "with men of whose honour and solvency they have not sufficient knowledge". Horse-racing was now the prime focus of sports betting too, cock-fighting having finally been outlawed by the Cruelty to Animals Act of 1849.

The screw was also tightening on betting practices with the passage of the 1853 Betting House Act, another of the periodic parliamentary attempts to improve the morals of the working and racing classes and also perhaps to register disapproval of gambling more widely – in business speculation, stock-market bubbles and the operation of life insurance. *The Times*'s strictures of March 1854 expressed a moral panic and could, perhaps, have been written at any time in the last 150 years:

> we gamble in the Mart and on the Exchange . . . the country parson, the schoolmaster, the hard-working, self-denying small tradesman, risks the savings of his life and the fortunes of his children on an undertaking of which he knows no more than the next turn of a die and brings his family to poverty and degradation.

Palmer might have winced to read it – but then, he was desperately hoping to come out ahead. The Act outlawed off-course betting for money and was supposed to close down places where bets could be placed, thereby limiting opportunities for gambling. Sir Alexander Cockburn, the attorney general and the man who would prosecute Palmer at his trial two years later, told the Commons:

> The mischief arising from the existence of these betting shops [is] perfectly notorious. Servants, apprentices and working men, induced by the temptation of receiving a large sum for a small one, [take] their few shillings to these places and the first effect of their losing [is] to tempt them to go on spending their money in the hope of retrieving their losses and for this purpose it not infrequently happens that they are driven into robbing their masters and employers.

It did not work, of course, though it remained on the statute largely ignored for more than a century. The effect of the legislation, which passed with virtually no debate or discussion, was to drive betting underground – men would now make use of bookies' runners to place their bets clandestinely with off-course bookmakers. Before the legislation there had been at least 150 betting houses in London, but now only private gentlemen's clubs, such as Tattersall's, were excluded from the legislation. Gambling, Lord Brougham had argued in 1843, "had much more fatal consequences and was far more injurious to morals among the inferior classes than among the superior", which was another reason for Palmer not to default if he could possibly avoid it.

William Palmer would have been around horses all his life. Rugeley had a famous annual horse-fair and race meetings, and Hednesford, a few miles away on the other side of Cannock Chase, was a well-known training centre. Palmer had probably been betting from an early age. An anonymous broadsheet published in Stafford at the time of his trial said he had caught the habit after winning £5 on the Derby: "but not contenting himself with gambling in a small way we find him aspiring to be owner of a stud, although without sufficient means to defray the necessary expenditure and he plunged recklessly into the gulph where the future of so many have [sic] been entombed." It went on to add that he had bought his first horse, ominously named Doubt, from John Meeson, the landlord of The Swan inn in

Stafford, though it gives no date for this. Doubt won the Leamington Stakes in 1848, "realising the sum of £1,000 with which it is said he paid for the mare". Certainly it was one of the horses sold at auction at Tattersall's after Palmer's arrest.

Had he stuck with one horse, he might have been all right, but by the spring of 1852 he was actively involved in the racing game on an ever greater scale, "like a country gentleman should", it was said – and if those remarks were his, it says something about his desire for social status. Clearly owning and racing horses quickly became a mania. His medical practice in Rugeley was handed over to the chemist Ben Thirlby to look after, and instead he plunged himself deep into the affairs of the turf. Palmer had seventeen horses by the time of Cook's death, though some of them were just foals or yearlings, and they would have been costing him about £2 a week each for boarding at Hednesford with his trainer William Saunders: about £140 a month, or just over £400 quarterly, which was when most such bills were settled. That was before other costs: fodder, hay and straw, shoeing, entry stakes for races – £20.12s.6d for the Liverpool Chase in March, £50.12s.6d for the Oaks in May – transport to courses and fees to jockeys. Palmer's diary for 1855 was published in one of the quickie books after his trial, and because he was meticulous in listing his expenses, it shows just how much he was spending and how much of his life racing was taking up: in January £450 to Saunders alone; in February £12 to Samuel Cope for oats, £17.14s to Salisbury for straw, £9.14s 2d to the blacksmith Wright for shoeing; and so it goes on through the year. There were journeys to see horses and to buy and sell them and frequent trips to London to settle accounts and see the moneylenders. That year, between May and November, he also attended fourteen race meetings, from Newcastle in the north to Brighton in the south, taking in the Derby at Epsom, a disastrous Ascot week in June, Glorious Goodwood in July, the Doncaster meeting in September, Newmarket and Chester in October, then finally Liverpool and the fateful meeting at Shrewsbury the following month. Time and again, there is a terse note: '1st May Wm. Saunders lost at Chester'; '10th May Wm. Saunders lost at Shrewsbury'; '23rd May Wm. Saunders lost at Epsom, three times'; '5th June Wm. Saunders lost at Ascot'; '30th July Wm. Saunders lost at Goodwood, twice'; '7th September Wm Saunders lost at Derby'; '11th September Wm. Saunders lost at Doncaster, twice'; and so on the next day and the day after that.

Only very occasionally is there a break in the clouds: '13th June at Newton, won the gold cup' and then the next day, 'won the Newton cup.'

Yet Palmer's horses were not bad ones. One would be bought by Major Grove, "commissioner for the royal paddocks", on behalf of Prince Albert when they were sold at Tattersall's the following January, and his associates in the racing world included some of the best-known names of the Victorian turf. John Porter, who would go on to train 961 winners himself, worked in Saunders's stables at Hednesford at that time and rode Palmer's horses in training. George Fordham – a notably honest rider of more than 2,000 winners – raced at least twice for Palmer as a teenager at the start of his career, as did John Wells, later the winner of the 1868 Derby, and Nat Flatman. Palmer's horse Goldfinder won the Tradesmen's Plate at Chester and the Queen's Plate at Shrewsbury in 1853, but nothing thereafter. The Chicken won twice at the same meeting at Durham in August 1854, followed by the Eglinton Stakes at York, then the Craven Stakes at Epsom at six to four on, before coming fourth in the Ascot Gold Vase and later winning the Mostyn Plate at the Chester autumn meeting and the Handicap Plate at Newmarket at seven to one. Lurley, another of his horses, was the mount that won twice at the Newton summer meeting in 1855, though it lost at Ludlow on the day of Walter Palmer's death. Meanwhile, Cook's Polestar, the horse that Palmer told Pratt that he must have in the letter written on the day of Cook's death, won five races in 1854 and five more in 1855, twice with Fordham up. Polestar's brother Morning Star, owned by Palmer, was less successful but won twice in 1853, was placed in five races without winning in 1854, but then won the Portland Plate at Mansfield and the Welter Cup – by twenty lengths – at Ludlow in 1855. Doubt itself won two races – one at five to one – in 1853 and 1854.

And then there was Nettle, which was running second in the Oaks in 1855 before she suddenly veered off the course, plunged over the chain fence alongside, threw her jockey Charlie Marlow, breaking his thigh in the process, and galloped off into some furze bushes. Marlow would not have been best pleased: such an injury would keep him out for months, unpaid, if it did not end his career. Nettle had been the favourite, running at two to one, and Palmer had backed her heavily. When a crony sympathised, he merely smiled, as though indifferent, and said: "It *is* a bore though, isn't it?" It was important to be a good loser. There were those who said Palmer's money troubles started from that disaster: had Nettle won, he would have netted £10,000 and cleared his debts. As it was, he lost his shirt.

After his arrest newspapers tried hard to paint Palmer as a racing cheat and horse-nobbler, to add to his other crimes, but never quite succeeded. There were dark hints of shady meetings with trainers and of carrots laced with arsenic being fed to horses. After all, it was written,

> scarcely a race is run at which some case or other does not occur ... it is said that Palmer was his own "nobbler" and this, if true, will at once account for nine grains of strychnia known to have been purchased at Apothecaries' Hall fifteen months ago by Palmer and Cook under a certificate from a London surgeon. "Nobbling" is a crime necessarily so mysterious that but few records of it are obtainable.

Note the "if true". There is no further mention in the case of nine grains of strychnia purchased at Apothecaries' Hall, so that can have been no more than gossip and rumour.

What is as likely is that Palmer was caught up by the thrill of the sport with the added excitement of betting on the outcome, which would certainly have appealed to his gambler's instincts. Gus Mayhew's account catches a thrill that persists today:

> "They're off!" sounds on the course, the same two syllables cried simultaneously by thousands of voices, while the crowds press against the ropes so closely that it seems impossible for them to move an inch, yet do accomplish the seeming impossibility and are compressed into one half the space as every eye is strained and every neck out-stretched to catch a glimpse of the flying steeds. On – on! Like arrows from a bow; on, on! Like the rushing whirlwind. But all these similes are trite. On come the horses through a long line of intently gazing eyes – of wildly-cheering throats – of frantically gesticulating arms – of madly waving hats! On, on! While amongst all those thousands of spectators every one screams out encouragingly the horse's name, on whose success his gains depend, or yells indignantly if he beholds his

horse behind the rest. On, on! While every faculty is absorbed in the intense excitement, every nerve strung up to the extreme point of tension! for something like two minutes and a half and then the race is won – and lost!

Too often in Palmer's case it was lost. Perhaps more wins would have gained him more acceptance, for Palmer was not quite a gentleman as far as the circuit was concerned. Journalists found racing men quickly distancing themselves from him as soon as he got into trouble. "I knew him, sir. I have done business with him," one told the *Illustrated Times*. "I had a great difficulty in getting my money – he was a bad pay, sir. He was not admitted as a member at Tattersall's, nor was he received by the first class betting men. I've seen him over and over again take his place in a sort of corner immediately under the grandstand just with two or three and, amongst them, a little dwarf of a man, name of Dyke, who used to stick pretty close to him – but none of the nobs went near him."

A groom at Saunders's stables told the same reporter:

He bought a good many [horses] and gave very large prices for them. He used to sell them for most curious prices. He sold two for £10. He wanted money I suppose but they were worth a great deal more than that, you may depend. He bred some good horses, I can assure you, sir. He always seemed to sell his horses for a great deal less and buy them for a great deal more than they were worth. I don't think he betted well; he lost large sums of money. He was a very singular man. He never changed countenance whatever happened. We used to notice it as he passed by. We never could tell whether he had won or lost.

A good loser, then, but probably privately terrified of losing his place and his status, in thrall to sharper men used to dealing with gambling debtors. Palmer would have had no alternative means of raising money than to go to such men and they exacted a heavy price from him. Henry Padwick, one of the moneylenders, was a horse-owner himself; Thomas Pratt, another, held first call on Polestar and on the insurance policies; and a third, Edwin Wright, a Birmingham moneylender, held the deeds of Palmer's properties.

Padwick kept a lower profile than Pratt, or perhaps his correspondence has just not survived: he was certainly cannier and in much less deep – about £2,000 to Pratt's £12,500 and Wright's £10,000 – and although he lost money on Palmer, he was an increasingly wealthy man in his own right. A photograph of Padwick, taken later in his life and in the possession of Horsham Museum (see page 159), shows a cold, calculating man with suspicious, narrowed eyes and a wry, humourless smile. He was a Sussex countryman to start with and had trained as a solicitor before giving that up after finding moneylending more profitable. He kept an office not far from Pratt, in Berkeley Square, convenient for aristocratic young gentlemen who had lost their money at the gaming tables of the West End, and it is said that he entertained them lavishly – he kept a chef and had fine wines. Sometimes he even took their horses as security, or in payment of their debts. In 1855 he had moved to a country estate at Findon, near Worthing, where he kept a string of racehorses in training. He was not the sort of man to be unduly sympathetic to debtors such as William Palmer.

Both Pratt and Padwick would be remorseless in pursuing him, as they had every right to do. The correspondence between Palmer and Pratt in the National Archive files at Kew shows the icy politeness between the two men, Palmer's growing panic, and the increasingly threatening tone of Pratt's letters – "My Dear Sir" and "Yours very truly" notwithstanding – during the summer of 1855.

A court-room artist's sketch of Thomas Pratt shows a fat, prosperous, sleekly dressed man with luxuriantly fashionable sideburns meeting almost under his chin. He was said to have the face of a small boy with "a low weak voice like a retiring female" and was clearly disconcerted by his sudden, unwonted celebrity – and desperate to avoid contamination with Palmer. In his evidence, he comes across as wheedling, and he had to be dragged to appear at Walter's inquest in January 1856, after a request to hear from him by the jury, not the coroner. He admitted that he held Walter's insurance policy and suddenly burst out: "I have lost about £4,000 by my transactions with Mr William Palmer!" When asked by Coroner Ward whether he would still sustain a loss if the insurance paid up on Walter, Pratt, who must have been overwrought, broke down completely, crying: "Oh, do not ask me that question! I am a young professional man with a wife and three children and I have been nearly ruined by this man. How can you ask me such a question?" At this point Pratt's solicitor stepped in and insisted no more questions should be asked because the inquest was concerned with Walter Palmer's death, not his brother's insurance transactions, though he said his client would be perfectly happy to deal fully with those in due course. The coroner agreed to this and Pratt stood down.

It is difficult to feel too sorry for Pratt. As a prosperous solicitor in Queen's Street, Mayfair, used to a little moneylending on the side at 60 per cent interest per annum, he was obviously making a reasonable living from his shady business and had been only too willing to accommodate William Palmer, a man he must have known was getting ever deeper into the toils of debt with every month that passed in 1855.

Their dealings were labyrinthine. According to Pratt, they started at the end of November 1853 (though he had earlier claimed to have known him only since early 1854) with a loan of £1,000, which was repaid. Then things began to get complicated, the more so because Pratt never divulged all their transactions and because Palmer paid off parts of the loans in various amounts whenever he had the money to do so, while taking out further loans at the same time. It is almost impossible to know how much he repaid on what and exactly how much he owed to whom as his debts mounted. There may have been other creditors as well, of whom his mother Sarah would have been one. An additional complication was that some of the debts to Pratt and Padwick were taken out in the name of Sarah Palmer, who had no need of loans herself and almost certainly knew nothing about them – Padwick would unsuccessfully sue her to repay a £4,000 loan taken out by her son on a forged signature. The sums Pratt admitted receiving included £8,000 from the life insurances on Anne Palmer, which had gone to settle three outstanding debts amounting to about £4,000, the residue going to Palmer to pay off debts on other loans. Then in April 1855 Pratt had arranged a £2,000 loan, drawn on the security of Sarah Palmer. By the time of Cook's death there were eight bills totalling £12,500 outstanding on loans made by Pratt and others, but then there were also two other bills, each for a further £2,000, which were also overdue, and bills for £500 and £1,000 which were being deferred and incurring interest from month to month. From Pratt's accounting and his denial of detailed knowledge of some bills, together with Palmer's haphazard repayments of £250, £200 and £50 from time to time, it is never clear which debts he was paying off. It is obvious, however, that Pratt blithely accepted assurances in the name of Sarah Palmer even though he said he had never met her and had never received a reply to his letters to her, because Palmer, probably with the help of Sam Cheshire, the postmaster, always intercepted them. When he turned up in Rugeley to see her, Pratt said, he was told she was ill, so he went away again.

The letters in the National Archive, from Pratt to Palmer from the spring of 1855 onwards, give a flavour of their transactions. After a while, reading the sequence, Pratt's scrawling, urgent, black-inked missives, with their flamboyant signature 'Thos Pratt', become as familiar as they must have been to Palmer as he received them with sinking heart every few days. This is Pratt, writing from his address at 5 Queen Street, Mayfair, on 9 April, about his difficulties getting cover for Walter's life:

> My dear Sir,
> Insurance: I have begged that the acceptance may be sent to me. If the Secretary is such a fool as not to take my instructions I cannot help it. With respect to the £300 premium I think that the best plan will be for you to get an acceptance from your mother to cover the amount which should be about say at least £1,500 and you must recollect there is £1,500 due on the 5th May and £1,300 due the 25th of this month: the £1,350 *must* be paid off . . . it must be repaid. You must prepare for it.
> > Yours truly,
> > Thos Pratt

Then, on 12 May:

> My dear Sir,
> I send you the cheque as desiring £350, the rest as you wish. When shall you . . . make arrangements about ye [*sic*] £1,350 on 6th June?
> Yours truly,
> Thos Pratt

Then, still more money on 11 July:

> My Dear Sir,
> I now herewith send you £400 in notes. I could not get the £500 today. Acknowledge the enclosed . . .

Two days later, Pratt was clearly stretching his own resources – or saying he was – but still prepared to lend more:

> My dear Sir,
> I could not get the promise of the money on the bill at all until Monday 16th and in order to meet your wishes I have drawn on my own resources and the only means I have to help you is to send you the enclosed cheque for £450 which with the £400 acknowledged today draws me quite close.
> I shall no doubt be in receipt of [your] money on Monday and if they doubt you or it let them hold the deeds till it is paid. I've done my best. As I once told you you've a notion that I have an inexhaustible pump to draw upon and make your arrangements . . .

In the autumn Pratt's letters to Palmer grew increasingly pressing. Thus, on 24 September:

> You are aware there are three bills of £2,000 each, accepted by your mother Mrs Sarah Palmer, falling due in a day or two . . . it will be necessary that those bills should be renewed; I will therefore thank you to send me up three new acceptances to meet those coming due . . . I presume the money will be ready to meet, which will amount to £1,500 more than your mother has given acceptances for . . .

2nd October:

> I must request that you make preparations for meeting the two bills due at the end of this month . . . In any event bear in mind that you must be prepared to cover your mother's acceptances for the £4,000 due at the end of the month.

Thomas Pratt, the Mayfair solicitor and moneylender
whose threats made Palmer desperate

Four days later:

> I have your note acknowledging receipt by your mother of the
> £2,000 acceptance, due 2nd October. Why not let her acknowl-
> edge it herself? You really must not fail to come up at once if it
> be for the purpose of arranging for the payment of the two bills
> at the end of the month. Remember, I can make no terms for
> their renewal and they must be paid.

Four days later:

> However, not to repeat what I said in my last but with the view
> of pressing on you the remembrance that the two bills due at
> the end of this month, 26th and 27th, must be met, I say no
> more . . .

A week later:

> . . . it shows how important it is that you or your mother should
> prepare for payment of the £4,000 due in a few days. I cannot
> now obtain delay on the same ground I did the others . . .

By now writs were being prepared and exposure was imminent. Palmer had
managed to scrape together £250 and was promising the same again:

> I will send you the £250 from Worcester on Tuesday as arranged.
> For goodness sake do not think of writs; only let me know that
> such steps are going to be taken and I will get you the money,
> even if I pay £1,000 for it; only give me a fair chance and you
> shall be paid the whole of the money . . .

One cannot fail to be impressed by the efficiency of the Victorian postal service
in all this. The letters flew back and forth with answers received by return.
Palmer could write to Pratt on a Saturday to tell him he would visit him in
London on the following Monday, confident that his message would be delivered in time to let him know. Huge cheques and money orders, maybe even
banknotes, were consigned to the post without seemingly ever going astray –
Palmer never seems to have used that as an excuse for a non-payment.

On 6 November Pratt issued writs against Palmer and his mother for
£4,000. Four days later Palmer went to see him in London and paid him
£300: so £800 had now been paid, including the previous two £250 payments, from which Pratt immediately took £200 as interest. Pratt said he
wanted another £1,000 by the end of the week. This was the week of the
fateful Shrewsbury races. Palmer managed to get him £200 by the Saturday,
paid to Pratt by Ismael Fisher, the London wine merchant who had been
one of those at Shrewsbury. Two days later, on Monday 19 November, the
day when Palmer left Cook at the Talbot Arms and went down to London
to settle bills, the two men met in the afternoon and Palmer signed a letter
drawn up for him in Pratt's handwriting:

> Dear Sir,
> You will place the £50 I have just paid you and the £450 you
> will receive by Mr Herring – together £500 – and the £200 you

received on Saturday towards payment of my mother's acceptance for £2,000 due 25th October making paid to this day the
sum of £1,300.
Yours,
Wm. Palmer

On the following night Cook died, and the next day Palmer sat down and
wrote the letter (referred to above, page 35) in which he reports his friend's
death and then adds that he wants to acquire Cook's successful racehorse
Polestar. Pratt was ruthlessly unsympathetic in his reply the following day:

> I have your note and am greatly disappointed at the non-receipt
> of the money as promised and at the vague assurances as to any
> money. I can understand 'tis true that your being detained by
> the illness of your friend has been the cause of not sending up
> the larger amount, but the smaller sum you ought to have sent.
> If anything unpleasant occurs, you must thank yourself. The
> death of Mr Cook will now compel you to look about as to the
> payment of the bill for £500 on the 2nd December.

Two days later, on 24 November, the Saturday on which Palmer went down
to London in the morning before meeting William Stephens on the train
coming back, there is another letter in Pratt's handwriting, signed by his client:

> Dear Sir,
> I have paid you this day £1,000. One hundred pounds: £75 you
> will pay for renewal of £1,500 due 9th Nov for one month and
> of £25 on account of £2,000 due 25th Oct, making £1,325 paid
> on that account.
> Yours,
> Wm. Palmer

Following his meetings with Stephens over the weekend, Palmer knew that
the old man was not going to drop his search for his stepson's missing
money and betting book, so on the Monday he wrote to Pratt again, marking his letter 'Strictly Private and Confidential':

My dear Sir,
Should any of Cook's friends call upon you to know what
money Cook ever had from you, pray don't answer that ques-
tion or any other about money matters until I have seen you.
And oblige yours faithfully,
Wm. Palmer

On 7 January 1856 Pratt wrote a letter to the *Morning Post*, trying to clear
his reputation and to distance himself from Palmer. It is impossible to read
it as anything other than a desperate attempt to salvage his good name, and
some of it is clearly false: his letters to Palmer, for instance, make it obvious
that he had already realised that Sarah Palmer knew nothing about the
transactions. In the letter he writes:

It is beyond a doubt that I am not a townsman of William
Palmer as I was born abroad, that I have no connection with
Rugeley beyond the accidental fact that a relative of mine by
marriage is settled there. I never saw or had any communication
direct or indirect with any member of William Palmer's family
with the exception of himself and his mother and the latter only
by letter ... My first communication with William Palmer took
place about the beginning of 1854. I never was in Rugeley until
Sunday 22nd October 1854 and only for an hour or two. The
insurance on his wife's life I knew nothing of (they were effected
by agents of offices of the Sun and Norwich in Rugeley) until
he came to town and entrusted them to me to prefer the claim
on the two offices Sun and Norwich Union for £8,000 together.
This was the first matter of business I ever transacted for
William Palmer as a solicitor. I required to be furnished with
proof of his pecuniary interest in his wife's life and this was subsequently furnished by found copies of his wife's father's will
and their marriage settlement. I never knew of any objection to
pay the amount insured except on grounds of pecuniary interest
in his wife's life ...
    Walter Palmer was examined at the Prince of Wales office
on 16th January 1855 and acceptance with charge of 20 years ad-

ditional premium on account of delirium tremens. I was paid the commission as is usual to solicitors on completing the matter. I left it to the Solicitors and General Office to inquire about George Bates as I knew nothing of the party intending to insure. With respect to the advances to William Palmer it is true they were made on bills purporting to be accepted by his mother but the moneys were to a large amount secured by deposit of deeds of lands purchased by him in the neighbourhood of Rugeley, some of which have been and are now in my custody and others ought to be. If [his] bills are forgeries and my letters to Mrs Palmer never reached her the deception practiced on me is complete.

I write under feelings of strong excitement and hastily on the spur of the moment . . . but I feel positive that those who know me will credit my assertions and the inferences to be drawn from my explanations, substantiated as I know they can be by documents.

It is not clear what happened to Thomas Pratt after he gave evidence at Palmer's trial. Some accounts say he was committed to an asylum and died soon afterwards. Padwick himself died a rich man on his Sussex estate in 1879.

8

"The man is as silent as death"

DESPITE HIS GROWING MONEY WORRIES, HIS DALLIANCE WITH ELIZA THARME, the death of her baby, the poor form of his horses, arranging the insurance policies for Walter and watching his brother slowly die of alcoholism, William Palmer had something else on his mind all that summer. He had a burgeoning relationship with a woman named Jane.

We don't know exactly who Jane was – there are several possible candidates – but the story of their relationship is told, like an epistolary novel, in a sequence of thirty-four letters written by Palmer, which now reside in a manila folder in the William Salt Library in a backstreet in Stafford. All are written on good-quality notepaper, each of the same size: approximately half an A4 sheet, neatly folded and without envelopes. Jane's surname is never given, but Palmer signs all of them, usually 'WP' but also sometimes 'Wm. Palmer' – just as he had originally signed the marriage register at Abbots Bromley when he married Annie. The handwriting is well formed and characteristic, and the style is literate and direct. From surviving authentic copies of his signature and writing, the letters were all obviously written by him. The longest letter is only nine sentences long and many of the rest are little more than single-line notes – today they would have been texted, or even tweeted. For many years they were thought too disgusting to be printed and have not generally featured in Palmer's story. They were meant to have been destroyed, but never were, and they trace the arc of Palmer and Jane's relationship from its beginning, through infatuation, to crisis, blackmail, bribery and final parting, just before his arrest. A few are actually dated, and from references in others it is possible to tell precisely when they were written: across the summer months and into the autumn of 1855. It was a time when Palmer's housemaid Eliza Tharme was pregnant with and giving birth to his child and when he might also still have been grieving for his lost wife, his poor dear Annie, "called to the home of bliss so well deserved". But evidently he was not.

As some of the letters are undated, the sequence is not entirely certain, but the following is the order in which they appear in the archive and that seems logical enough. The first letter, using the same opening salutation as all the rest, reads:

> My dear Jane,
> I shall not be able to meet you at the Station but if you come straight to the back of the Grand Stand I will meet you *accidentally* and will take care that you have a pleasant day.
> Yours faithfully,
> Wm. Palmer
> Rugeley, Tuesday morning.

If Jane wrote back to him, it is not known as he did not keep any of her letters. By the time of his next letter, though, he was bursting into poetry:

> My dear Jane,
> How are you this morning? I shall see you this afternoon and then – "As soon as night shall fix her seal upon the eyes and lips of men, oh dearest! I shall panting steal to nestle in thine arms again."
> Yours,
> Wm. Palmer

Now there was an assignation:

> My dear Jane,
> I cannot possibly be with you on Tuesday but you may expect me on Wednesday evening. Will that do for you?
> Yours,
> Wm. Palmer

And increasing, if discreet, urgency:

> My dear Jane,
> Break your journey on Saturday – book – to Rugeley – come to
> my surgery with your handkerchief to your face – no one will
> be in but *myself*. I will perform an *operation* on you and you can
> have a snack and go on by the next train.
> Yours,
> Wm. Palmer

And wooing with more than just a snack, bought from one of Stafford's
grocers:

> My dear Jane,
> Send the enclosed note to Frantz by an errand lad, he will bring
> back a lobster, etc. I am coming tonight to help you eat it.
> Yours,
> Wm. Palmer

Maybe people were beginning to notice:

> My dear Jane,
> If Mrs K calls on you or sends anybody poking into your affairs
> you will know what to do.
>   Mum's the word.
> Yours,
> W.P.

Then:

> My dear Jane,
> I can't today, will try tomorrow.
> Is your cold better?
> Yours,
> Wm Palmer

And:

> My dear Jane,
> I missed you – were you there? I shall be at Shrewsbury on Friday.
> Drop me a line.
> Yours,
> W.P.

> My dear Jane,
> No note for me at Shrewsbury. I hope you are well. I shall call
> on Monday.
> Yours,
> Wm. Palmer

Back on track:

> My dear Jane,
> Will you send the enclosed note to Frantz and give me my sup-
> per tonight.
> Yours, W.P.

> My dear Jane,
> I meant to have called before leaving the town to ask you to meet
> me at Lichfield next week. Will you?
> Write by return.
> Yours,
> W.P.

> My dear Jane,
> You are the right sort. Be near the west door of the Cathedral at
> 11 o'clock on Wednesday – and leave the rest to me.
> Yours,
> W.P.

> My dear Jane,
> How do you feel today? Hope you slept well last night.
> Yours,
> W.P.
> Thursday morning

Dr Cornelius Waddell of Tipping Street, Stafford, the man called in to testify to Walter's health for the insurance company, is mentioned in the next letter, which raises the question whether Palmer ever discussed insuring Jane's life as well. It seems that he did, for Waddell examined Jane, as a letter later in the series makes clear – though that might have been for something else.

> My dear Jane,
> Don't see Waddell until I have seen <u>you</u> which will be in the course of a few days.
> Yours,
> W.P.

What that something else might have been becomes clear in the next letter. It is evident that she was, or thought she was, pregnant. For the first time this note has the instruction "Burn this" underlined three times in the top corner. Jane didn't.

> My dear Jane,   <u>Burn this</u>
> Don't trouble yourself – we can wait a couple of months <u>and</u>
> <u>see</u>. All can be made <u>right easily</u>. And I can drop in at <u>any</u> time?
> I shall be over on Saturday.
> Yours,
> · W.P.

The "any" in the last line was underlined four times.

The next letter was evidently opened and read in the rain: it is covered with watery blots and spots causing the ink to smudge. It is written urgently, as if to coordinate a story that Jane can tell the women who have just seen Palmer and are on their way to her:

> My dear Jane,
> I ran against Mrs. W. and Mrs T. just now – they said they were
> going to call on you and had I seen you lately? Yes, I had just left
> you – <u>I had been to ask you for slips of pansies for my mother</u>.
> You will get this before they arrive – hadn't you better tell
> them where I passed the night?
> Yours,
> Wm. Palmer

By the date of the next letter, she had seen Waddell. "Burn this" is under-lined twice. The court-room drawing of Waddell shows a bald, middle-aged man, with lavish sideboards reaching round to his chin and the hair around his ears swept upwards like little horns, as if in a vain attempt to cover his baldness. He does not look particularly like a potential Lothario, but his eyes are beady. Maybe he was the sort of doctor who would grope his female patients. Or maybe Palmer was just being lubricious:

> My dear Jane,   Burn this
> I knew Waddell would find you alright. Of course he did not discover anything. Did he ask for a kiss? Or did he take one without asking?
> Yours,
> W.P.
> Sunday morning.

Waddell was asked for clearance for an insurance proposal, but warned Jane against it. Was this following his experience with Walter? Did he have sus-picions about William Palmer? Had he spotted something? Whatever it was, he seems to have frustrated Palmer's plans again.

> My dear Jane,   Burn this
> I think the Devil is in it. Waddell says you had better not propose – that means he will report unfavourably – so there will be a dif-ficulty raising the needful for you as intended – though I am pressed you shall not suffer.
> Yours,
> W.P.

The next letter is roguish. You can certainly tell exactly what he means. Unfolding the letter, holding it and reading the contents in the Salt Library feels – as it is – like intruding on a very breathless, intimate and immediate affair, though it took place between two people nearly 160 years ago.

> My dear Jane,
> A lady asked me just now how I liked last night's concert. I said very well but I preferred a duet which followed.
>   So I did – rather – did you?
> Yours,
> W.P.

The following letter suggests the affair was starting to go sour. Perhaps Jane was testing the authenticity of Palmer's affections. If she was indeed pregnant, she must have needed to know urgently what his intentions were and what his commitment to their relationship was. He clearly did not want to put it in writing. He probably wanted to exercise his charm on her in person.

> My dear Jane,
> I do not know what to make of your last letter – "What do I intend?" Well I think it would be better to see and tell you. Shall I come on Sat. evy?
> Yours,
> W.P.

But she was too canny for that:

> My dear Jane,
> I think you are rather out of temper. You would not let me come on Saturday – and you do not say when I may. I wish you would fix a time.
> Any day but Thursday next week will do for me.
> Yours,
> Wm. Palmer

William Palmer's cavalier way with women was catching up with him. Something needed to be done soon about the pregnancy.

> My dear Jane,
> I can't make you out – of course I am sorry that you are unwell. Perhaps the face ache is caused by that. I shall be over tomorrow.
> Yours,
> Wm. Palmer

The next letter in the sequence is the longest, most detailed and most sensitive of all. It is clear, despite the euphemism, that an abortion is to be arranged and it names who is to do the deed. It is almost sinister in its briskness. This time, the instruction to burn the letter is triple underlined. From the reference to Ascot, it must now have been early summer: the Ascot meeting that year began on 2 June and Palmer's diary shows that he went down to London and then on to the races on Monday 4 June. The diary also notes for Sunday 3 June: "At home. Eliza came." Tharme's baby was due later in the month, so that day it looks like he was juggling his relationships with two pregnant women:

> My dear Jane,   <u>Burn this</u>
>   Ascot tomorrow so I must repeat by letter what I said to you on Sunday because I wish you very much to do it – it won't hurt you worth mentioning and as I said you have had a toothache and Cooke is known as the best dentist in Stafford. Your handkerchief to your mouth – and you can't talk will do it.
>   He won't keep you ten minutes. Say the word and I will write to him and you will only have to ask him to draw the tooth that hurts you. He will know where to look for it!!!
>   So don't be surprised at what he may do.
>   <u>The man is as silent as death</u> and you may depend on him. Send word that I may write to him there's a dear girl.
>   Yours,
>   Wm. Palmer
>   P.S. You see I am <u>not</u> afraid "to write as I speak" because I am sure that you will burn this as you have burnt the others.
>   W.P.

Surely this did not refer to a toothache, otherwise why the secrecy? The Cooke in this letter was probably a man called James Cook who gave his occupation as a druggist in the 1861 census. At the time Jane went to see him he was a man of fifty and he had premises in Foregate Street, Stafford. The operation might have been quick – though 10 minutes may have been meant as a reassurance rather than a prediction – but, as with drawing a tooth in the mid-nineteenth century, it would not have been painless. Cook would probably have used the standard technique of inserting a sharp point, maybe a knitting needle, a wire or a knife, into the uterus to induce the rejection of the foetus and placenta. It was a surreptitious but very common operation. It has been estimated that in the US in the middle of the nineteenth century there may have been as many as one abortion for every six live births and such a figure is unlikely to have been substantially different in the similar society of Britain, though any such statistics must by their nature be speculative.

The operation on Jane prompts the question why Palmer did not use a condom, especially if he had already fathered illegitimate children. Such devices, which were made of sheep gut (they would not be made of vulcanised rubber for some time yet), were easily available and relatively cheap. Contraception might not be mentioned in polite society, but it was discussed in books of the sort to which a doctor such as Palmer would have had access. The Chartist Francis Place had written *The Principle of Population* in 1822; there was Richard Carlile's *Practical Hints on How to Enjoy Life and Pleasure without Harm to Either Sex*; and the American Charles Knowlton's *The Fruits of Philosophy*, first published in Britain in 1841, gave extremely detailed advice on how to use a douche and what to soak it in. From the tone of Palmer's letters, however, it seems likely that his assignations with Jane were too frantic and fervent for that sort of consideration.

The next letter indicates that the deed had been arranged:

My dear Jane,   Burn this
You are a good plucked one. I have written to Cooke – do just
as he tells you – send me word how you get on.
Yours,
W.P.

The following letter jocularly indicates that the operation had been carried out. It contained two halves of different £5 notes – a precaution to prevent them being abstracted in the post, or possibly a means of exerting control over what Jane did next. Currency notes of course were large paper documents either drawn on local banks or, more often following the passage of the Bank Charter Act of 1844, issued by the Bank of England. Notes were still less common than gold coins, but safer in the post. They were presumably sent to reimburse her for the cost of the abortion.

My dear Jane,   Burn this
All's well that ends well. I am glad that you were so little hurt –
in a week or two you will be all right again. I enclose halves of
two £5 notes. Say you have got them and I will send the others.
Yours,
W.P.

The remaining halves were sent with the next letter. Clearly Jane had not got over her operation, so Palmer's breezy tone was presumably unwelcome. He was certainly not bothering to visit her, even to check on her condition.

> My dear Jane,   <u>Burn this</u>
> I am deucedly sorry to hear that you are so unwell – but you have got rid of the cause and now as old Tylecote would say the effects will cease.
>   Remaining halves enclosed – send me word you have them and that you are better.
> Yours,
> W.P.

The next two letters contained more money, probably to mollify Jane, or at least to keep her quiet. Perhaps she had demanded more. They seem to have been written on or about 3 July 1855, just before Palmer left to attend York's summer race meeting.

> My dear Jane,
> I enclose the halves of four £5 notes. Acknowledge receipt and I will forward the others – <u>they can't be traced</u>.
> Yours,
> W.P.

> My dear Jane,
> Enclosed are the remaining halves – drop me a line by return to York to say they are all right.
> Yours,
> Wm. Palmer

There is then a gap of several weeks. It does not seem likely that Palmer visited Jane during this period. The next letter can be more precisely dated. It must have been shortly after Walter's funeral on 20 August.

> My dear Jane,
> Walter's funeral went off very well.

I caught sight of you at the window – when shall I call?

Hope you are alright now?

Yours,

Wm. Palmer

He was obviously still thinking of resuming their affair, though perhaps fortunately there is no mention of resuming the search for insurance cover for Jane. But by now people's tongues were starting to wag, presumably about Walter's death, the strange mortality of the Palmers and William's part in it all, and the rumours had evidently reached Jane. As well as sensing a danger, maybe the possibility of an opportunity was already in her mind:

My dear Jane,

Your letter is hard to understand. What queer things are people saying? Some damned chatterboxes can't mind their own business and are looking after mine, are they? You can't say I have used you ill. Let us speak of a man as we find him is my motto.

Please write and say why you think "I had better not call for a few weeks."

Yours,

Wm. Palmer

Again there must have been a gap of several weeks. Jane evidently delivered a considerable shock in her next communication with Palmer. She had not burned their correspondence as requested and now wanted money in return for his letters. The realisation that the notes had not been destroyed and exactly how incriminating they were – signatures and all – must have appalled Palmer, who was already wrestling with mounting debts running into thousands of pounds and struggling to fend off threatening letters sent by the moneylender Pratt – not only to himself but to his mother, who was blissfully ignorant that she had been signed up for loans on her own account. And on top of that, there was the decision of the Prince of Wales insurance company and its investigator Inspector Field not to pay on Walter's policy, together with the veiled threat that he might be prosecuted if he persisted with the claim. Everything was closing in and now his mistress was demanding money too. She probably asked for £100. Palmer was cornered. The next

letter was written – and dated – on 13 November 1855, which was the day
John Parsons Cook's horse Polestar won the Shrewsbury handicap:

> My dear Jane,   Rugeley, Nov. 13th 1855
> It's <u>damned hard </u>for a fellow to find his friends turning against him
> and I was surprised to learn that you have never burned one of my
> letters – I cannot do what you ask.
>   <u>I should not mind giving £30 for the whole </u>of them though I
> am hard up at present. If you agree you shall have the money in the
> course of a week or ten days.
>   I enclose the only letter of yours I can find.
>   I shall always think with pleasure of our intimacy and can say
> with Moore:
> "We've had some happy hours together
> But joy must change its wing
> And Spring would be but gloomy weather
> If we had nothing else but Spring."
> Oblige me with an early reply and believe me, Dear Jane,
> Yours truly,
> Wm. Palmer

The words "damned hard" were underlined twice. The verse is from
Thomas Moore's poem *A Parting*. The recently deceased Moore (1779–
1852), one of Ireland's national poets (though he is buried near his home
in Wiltshire), is now best remembered for his songs *The Minstrel Boy*, *The
Last Rose of Summer* and *Oft in the Stilly Night*. But it is evident that all
Palmer now wanted was to get out of the relationship as quickly and cheaply
as possible. He attended Shrewsbury races that day, then returned home
feeling sick, before going back to see his horse The Chicken lose two days
later. Had the horse won, he could have gained time with Pratt and easily
paid off Jane. As it was, Polestar's victory and Cook's £3,000 winnings just
made matters more difficult. No wonder he was still feeling queasy himself
on the return journey to Rugeley.

The next letter to Jane, also dated, was written the following Monday,
two days after Eliza Tharme's baby son had died and the day he went to
London, while Cook was ill at the Talbot Arms, to raise money on his

friend's winnings and settle some of his debts with Pratt. He clearly no longer trusted Jane:

> My dear Jane,   Nov. 19th
> I am agreeable to split the difference and will send you £40 in notes tomorrow or the day after and shall expect you – <u>honour bright</u> – to let me have the letters on return of bearer.
> Yours,
> Wm. Palmer

The next letter came two days later. It was written within hours of Cook's writhing death at the Talbot Arms, probably at about the same time he was writing to Pratt promising to pay him £75 the following day. Now Palmer had the money to pay off Jane:

> My dear Jane,   Nov. 21st
> Enclosed you have the halves of eight fivers. Please acknowledge receipt and I will send remainders.
> In great haste.
> Yours,
> Wm. Palmer

The final letter in the sequence shows Palmer honouring the agreement and hurt at the way the relationship has ended:

> My dear Jane,   Nov. 24th 1855
> Remaining halves of notes enclosed.
>   Please keep letters for me until I send for them.
> Yours,
> Wm. Palmer
> P.S. You have no reason to be unfriendly to me, remember. W.P.

The fact that the thirty-four letters still sit in the files at the William Salt Library shows that Jane never did return them. By the time he might have sent for them, William Palmer had other things on his mind: he was too preoccupied and to have them found in his possession would have further incriminated him. He probably thought that on balance they were safer with Jane for now, despite her perfidiousness in keeping them. There were enough rumours about his infidelities flying around the district without the letters blackening his name further. No one knew about them, or his relationship with Jane, either at the time or during his trial, when they would certainly have been used against him. It looks as though Jane was a clear winner in the transaction, financially at least: she received £40, she got to keep the letters, she survived her relationship with one of the most notorious murderers of the nineteenth century, and she presumably kept her good name and anonymity. Perhaps it is just as well, too, that Dr Waddell had turned her down for life insurance earlier in the summer. It is only recently, more than a century after they were written, that the letters have been thought fit to be seen, and this is the first time they have received wide publication.

It is thought that Jane eventually sold the letters privately. Maybe her moment to inflict damage had passed now there was no one to blackmail, or she realised, or was told, that they were unpublishable. Perhaps they did not bring her much more money. In the early years of the twentieth century, they appear to have been in the possession of a Stafford tobacconist named W. S. Wile, who certainly showed them and may even have sold them to George Fletcher, the man who wrote a book about the case as an old man in the 1920s. The existence of the letters has evidently been known for more than a century, and Fletcher probably showed them to G. H. Knott, who wrote up the Palmer volume in the Notable British Trials series. If so, neither of them thought the letters fit to be printed. They only confirmed their view of Palmer as a disgusting and wicked creature, engaged in unspeakable behaviour. "I have had the original letters . . . submitted to a great expert on handwriting and he says they are undoubtedly all in Palmer's writing," Fletcher wrote in his 1925 book:

> They consist of 34 letters written . . . in a most lascivious, degrading style . . . They show unmistakeably the nature of the illicit intercourse existing between them both and Palmer gives the name and address of a doctor in Stafford who, he says, would be "*silent as death*" and who performed an illegal operation successfully on her . . . I need scarcely say the letters are not fit for publication. But they are well written and clear, showing a man of education, though of a most disgusting nature.

In Knott's book, first published in 1912, there is a brief, tasteful reference to the letters, with the "silent as death" quote but little else, and in a further book by Dudley Barker, published by Duckworth in 1935, brief extracts also crop up. Barker had clearly seen the letters and said they were then in the possession of the great-grandnephew of Superintendent Woollaston, who had been responsible for guarding Palmer during his trial – by this time Fletcher had died – but Barker too was discreet in referring to them, saying that they simply revealed a desire to avoid unpleasant consequences, "never one passing thought of sympathy or one suggestion of real help". Clearly, even eighty years later, they were still too direct to be published in detail.

It took nearly 120 years for the letters to be printed in full, in an article by Ann Kettle in the *Transactions of the Stafford Historical and Civic Society* of 1971. They had been assumed to be lost for many years – the author Robert Graves, who wrote a book about Palmer in the 1950s and whose uncle inherited Fletcher's medical practice, certainly thought them to be so – but they have in fact been in the William Salt Library's archives since the 1940s. Kettle describes Palmer as an accomplished seducer, with touches of poetry and some heavy sexual innuendo, and says that the abortion letter is the most unpleasantly suggestive in the whole collection.

So, who was Jane? Several names have been suggested over the years. Fletcher, who had the original access to the letters, thought her name was spelled Jane Bergen, but Knott and Barker named her as Jane Burgess in their later books. Both names were listed in the 1851 census, but there was also a Jane Burgin in that census who seems on the face of it to be the likeliest candidate. She was a 26-year-old milliner living in Stafford with her parents and siblings in 1851. They lived in Station Road, Stafford – perhaps more easily spotted by Palmer on his way to the train? – where her father, Francis, was listed as a clerk to the commissioner of land taxes while her mother, Sarah, was also a milliner. Of course, Burgin and Bergen might simply be a misspelling of the same person. Burgess was a nursemaid to a builder in Baswich, then a village, now a suburb of Stafford, between there and Rugeley. But there was also a Jane Bergen, the daughter of Daniel Scully Bergen, who at that time was the Irish-born chief superintendent of the Staffordshire rural constabulary, living in Burton on Trent nearly twenty miles from Rugeley. Is it possible that Palmer would have been having an affair with a senior policeman's daughter? Who knows? Jane's real identity remains hidden, thanks to Palmer's discretion and her own nerve. Both Jane Burgin and Jane Bergen had disappeared from Staffordshire by the 1861 census, by which time Jane Burgess was working as a house servant to the superintendent of the Coton Hill lunatic asylum.

There is, however, one other intriguing possibility. By the time of the 1861 census, the taxation clerk Francis Burgin and his wife Sarah had moved to Gaol Road, Stafford, just down the road from where William Palmer had been hanged. Living with them then there was a grand-daughter, Janet Burgin, aged five. She would have been born in 1856, just about at the time when Jane's pregnancy might have come to term. Is it possible that Jane Burgin finally double-crossed William Palmer, took his money, and after all avoided the ministrations of Cooke, the man as silent as death, the best dentist in Stafford? If so – and it is pure speculation – she took the secret to her grave.

9

"Dreadful reports current at Rugeley"

O N THE NIGHT AFTER HIS ARREST, SUNDAY 16 DECEMBER 1855, WILLIAM Palmer was taken to Stafford prison, where his own clothes were removed for fear that he might have poison concealed in them and he went straight to bed. His clothing was minutely examined – the seams unpicked, the coat, waistcoat and trousers shaken and beaten to force out any powder that might be inside – but nothing was found. This took two weeks, and in the meantime Palmer refused to wear the clothes that were given to him and went on hunger strike in protest at his treatment. After six days of this, the prison governor Major William Fulford threatened him with force-feeding. As ever, the *Illustrated Times* had the details:

> [Fulford] procured a stomach pump and, ordering a bowl of soup to be made, visited the prisoner . . . Palmer answered that he had no appetite. The governor replied that his looks were those of a healthy man, that his pulse was good and that there was no apparent reason why he should not make the effort . . . if he did not take his food quietly, he should have to place the tube of the stomach pump in his mouth and inject the soup into his stomach. He pointed out to Palmer that his resistance was useless, for in less than five minutes – if he was forced to have recourse to compulsory measures . . . all he had to do was summon his officers, to place a small gag in his mouth and introduce the coil and the soup would be down his throat . . . Palmer

seemed to think better of the idea and ever since he has continued to eat his meals.

Thereafter he put on weight, so that by the time of his trial five months later
he was becoming portly enough for the court reporters to mention it in
their copy. His request for the food to be prepared at his home in Rugeley,
nine miles away, was denied: he was told he could order whatever he liked,
but it had to be prepared in the prison. Inside the walls, the prison had its
own bakehouse, producing slabs of bread three feet long to feed the con-
victs, its millstones grinding the corn powered by a large treadmill on which
thirty-two prisoners at a time would trudge.

Stafford prison, Gus Mayhew reported, had the appearance of a large,
squat brick castle – it still does, though without the crenellated corner tur-
rets that it had in Palmer's day. The sense the reporter felt then of a "red
hot glare about the pile, as if you saw it through red glass" now appears to
have waned. Whether prisoners ever thought that the imposing stone-
fronted gatehouse with the turnkey's lodge was "quite refreshing . . . like
being in the cool shade" must always have been doubtful. Earlier in the century hangings had taken place on a scaffold perched high on top of the gatehouse roof, until in 1817 the structure collapsed during an execution;
thereafter they took place on a portable platform in the roadway directly
outside the main entrance.

Meanwhile, as rumours spread that Palmer had murdered other victims, the graves of Annie and Walter in the churchyard at Rugeley were dug
up so that the bodies could be dissected in post-mortems. Later, Cook's body
was also exhumed for more tests to be made, at Professor Taylor's behest, on
the dead man's spinal cord. It was either then or at the first post-mortem
that the doctors took the opportunity to examine Cook's penis, in the light
of Palmer and Bamford's suggestion that he had had syphilis (Cook himself
seems also to have suspected this, given his own doctor's recollection that
he had been dosing himself with mercury earlier in the year). Two reports
on this interesting appendage were added to the prosecution's file. Charles
Devonshire, the medical student who had conducted the first, botched, post-
mortem, reported that he had seen no chancre (a sore or lesion) or scar on
the organ – "I particularly examined the penis in consequence of it having
been stated by Palmer and Bamford that he had been affected by syphilis" –

and that when he cut out the dead man's throat, he had found no ulceration or sores. But Dr Harland, the pathologist who had forgotten his instruments, looked more closely and said there was indeed a chancre on the penis which had nearly healed and "was not larger than a pea". Neither ventured an opinion on whether the sore was syphilitic or not.

Walter and Annie's coffins were dug up two days before Christmas, both taken from the Palmer family's vault behind St Augustine's church. They were then taken across the road to the nearest pub, which was also called the Talbot, though not the Talbot Arms this time, in deference to the local aristocratic family. The coffins were placed in the pub's meeting room in front of Coroner Ward and a jury of twenty-three locals. The top was prised off Annie's oak coffin first. After fifteen months, the corpse, it was said, was comparatively dry and the smell endurable: any noxious fumes had evaporated through the wood. By contrast, when a hole was bored through the lid of Walter's lead coffin, the room was filled with the stench of putrefaction. He had been hermetically sealed in four months earlier, and the corpse, when it was viewed, was swollen, rotting, blackened and gangrenous. More than half the jury had to rush out to be sick and the whole pub was filled with a terrible smell which took months to dissipate, even after the wallpaper had been stripped and replaced and the floors re-sanded. A few weeks later Gus Mayhew found the pub's landlord, William Williss, "a stout, jolly-looking man" of forty-five, sitting disconsolately in the bar with his equally plump child happily munching an apple between his father's knees. Williss was talking of ruin because the commercial travellers who were his best customers no longer wanted to visit. He was sighing and drinking ale by turns while his wife tried to jolly him along:

> He occasionally thrust his hand into his brown velvet waistcoat and glanced around at the rows of ale mugs and barrels of spirits, as though he was calculating what they would sell for if the worst came to the worst . . . it was difficult to tell whether he or the beer engine was groaning . . . he muttered something about it being perhaps better to die young before it had come to want.

The order to use the pub for the post-mortems had been landed on him without consultation:

I knew they were going to do so because two police officers stayed here all night. About seven in the morning, when we were in bed on a bright frosty morning, one of the policemen, by name of Chesham came to our room and says he: "Here you must get up, they are going to bring these bodies into the house; Mr Bergen says they are to come here." I told him there was an outhouse and coachhouse where they could take 'em. Then Bergen told me they was to come here and that he had a letter from the Secretary of State . . . We have had the coachhouse all cleared out on purpose but Bergen says it's too cold there, the doctors can't manage their work; they must come here because the Secretary of State says so. I told him we could warm up the coachhouse but he wouldn't. They brought the corpses here. We were obliged to put 'em in the commercial room because that was the only place where the passage would let the coffins enter. Only fancy, twenty-three jurymen and I am among the number, the coroner, four police officers and lookers-on in that little room, as is only about five yards by three. When the lid was lifted up the stench was awful. I don't know as ever I smelt anything like it, it was uncommon bad . . . it seemed to soak into everything. It was against the walls and in the paint and in the looking glass even. We were obliged to have the passage took down (and it near killed the man as worked) and the woodwork painted and the ceiling whitewashed . . . it was as if things had been soaked in a liquor and took it up in 'em. Of course the boards where the stuff dropped from the coffin was all done for and had to be taken up and burned. Ah! It was a nasty business. The affair has been as good as £200 or £300 out of my pocket. Commercial gentlemen that used to come here before now and have done some of them for 20 years won't come to the house now.

Taylor at Guy's was sent what samples could be obtained from the sludge that was what remained of Walter's corpse. A month later his report came back that he could find no traces of poison, and although he was confident that Walter had been murdered with prussic acid, he had to concur that he had died as originally stated from apoplexy. The jury nevertheless ignored this and returned a verdict of wilful murder – a verdict which was itself later overturned by the grand jury, which was formally considering the accusations against Palmer in Stafford to decide whether he should be sent for trial. By that stage no more victims were needed for the indictment. The allegations about Mary Thornton, Palmer's mother-in-law, and Leonard Bladen, both of whom had now been dead for several years, were not pursued, and they were allowed to lie in their graves at Rugeley in peace. A murder suspect could only be tried on one count at a time and Cook's death had the strongest evidence. Had Palmer been acquitted of Cook's murder, he would have been tried, sequentially, for Annie's death and then, if he had got off that, probably for Walter's.

Annie Palmer's stomach and intestines were removed at the December inquest and sent to Taylor. When the hearing resumed in mid-January, a series of witnesses, including Eliza Tharme and Sarah Palmer, William's sister who had been with his wife in Liverpool, testified to the illness she had had when she returned to Rugeley, the constant vomiting, debilitation and slow decline. They also spoke of how attentive William had been to her, what good terms he had been on with his wife, and how, when Bamford suggested that her guardian Dr Knight should be called in to give a second opinion on her illness, Palmer had sent for him at once. The handywoman Mrs Bradshaw – the one who had once claimed Palmer was killing his babies – now gave evidence that she had prepared the patient's food herself: "I tasted most of it before it went upstairs for I prepared it." One of the jurymen asked facetiously whether she had also tasted the pills given to Annie, whereupon another juryman chuckled ribaldly: "We can answer for it she never did, as she is here today." Clearly there was going to be little doubt about the verdict, even before Taylor's report was received. When it did arrive, Taylor stated that he had found antimony in all the organs of the body that he had tested, including the stomach, liver and kidneys, all given shortly before death; it had built up in relatively small but regular doses, rather than one big amount, and it, and nothing else, must have been the cause of death. This was not necessarily surprising: antimony, a metallic element, though toxic, was widely available, both in make-up and patent medicines, and was particularly used as tartar emetic to provoke vomiting in a patient with an illness such as dysentery – though in too large a quantity it acted like a form of arsenic. If Annie was not getting better in her last week, there may have been a tendency to increase the dose. However, in the circumstances, Taylor's report offered further incriminating evidence against Palmer. Old Dr Knight, who had testified that he thought his ward had died from English cholera, now changed his mind and agreed that she must have been poisoned, both before and after he and Bamford had examined her in her final days. The jury took just 20 minutes to return a verdict of wilful murder.

As if that was not enough, in late January Palmer was taken from prison down to Westminster to act as a witness in a case the moneylender Henry Padwick was bringing against his mother, Sarah Palmer, to recover an outstanding debt of £1,000 (£2,000 had originally been borrowed, but half had been repaid) which had been incurred two years earlier. He was brought from Stafford by train, accompanied by three plain-clothed officers, held overnight at the Clerkenwell house of correction, and rushed in the morning in a cab to the Queen's Bench court in Westminster Hall, past a mob of onlookers who, the *Manchester Guardian* reported, greeted the sight of him with groans and execrations. The court, it was said, was full to bursting two hours before the hearing and was besieged by crowds still trying to get in. The poisoning cases, as the newspapers were calling them, were already exciting a national audience, enthralled by what the *Manchester Guardian* called the "dreadful reports current in Rugeley". In the hearing a baffled Mrs Palmer denied that the handwriting on the bill of debt was hers – as did relatives, solicitors and bank clerks who knew her signature. Palmer himself was then called to give his evidence, with spectators craning to see what he looked like. He coolly testified to his own signature as the recipient of the money and was then asked who had written Sarah Palmer's name in acceptance of the debt. Anne Palmer, he replied simply. "Who is she?" "She is now dead." "Do you mean your wife?" "Yes." "Did you see her write it?" "Yes." The newspapers reported that "a profound sensation" ran through the court at Palmer's assertion that his wife had been a forger. There was nothing more to be said; Padwick had to withdraw his suit, Sarah Palmer was vindicated, and Palmer was taken back to Stafford prison. No one could disprove his claim that his wife had written his mother's signature. There were those who doubted it was true. The *Morning Chronicle* the next day editorialised sternly:

> There is no other case on record where a prisoner who underlies
> a charge of murdering his wife [has] had the opportunity of
> coming into court and murdering her reputation. It aggravates

Henry Padwick, moneylender to the gentry: not someone
from whom you would want to borrow

rather than detracts from the instinctive loathing with which we
regard such a case, that he blasts his own character as well as hers.

Meanwhile, cash had to be raised for Palmer's defence. Family money must
have helped, but his assets had to be realised too. First to go were the racehorses – the stud he had tried so hard to save and whose expense had ruined
him. Seventeen horses, including a number of unraced bay and brown colts
and fillies, were sold at Tattersall's that January. Prince Albert bought Trick-
stress, through the agency of Major Grove, for 230 guineas; Nettle, the four-
year-old who had run off the course during the 1854 Oaks, went for 430
guineas; and the best of them, The Chicken, the horse on which he had
placed all his hopes at Shrewsbury races two months before, was sold for 800
guineas and subsequently (and appropriately) renamed Vengeance. Doubt,
Palmer's first horse, which must have been getting long in the tooth by then,
fetched 81 guineas, and Lurley, a five-year-old – the horse that had been run-

ning at Ludlow in the race Palmer had been so keen to hear about on the afternoon of Walter's death – was sold for 120 guineas. Despite his case against Mrs Palmer, Padwick bought two of the horses, a bay yearling colt and a brown yearling filly, for 480 guineas, nearly half of what he was claiming the Palmers owed him, but both horses, it was said, turned out to be poor racing specimens. In all the sale realised nearly 4,000 guineas. It was still far short of Palmer's debts, but it was not a negligible sum. William Stephens and John Hatton, the chief constable, were present at the auction, and a sign was stuck up asking anyone who had paid money to Cook at Shrewsbury races, or had witnessed any transactions involving him, to make themselves known.

Now, too, the furniture, books and medical equipment at Palmer's house in Rugeley were auctioned off. It was of good quality, according to the sale catalogue: "a rosewood couch with spring seat, squab [cushion] and pillow in blue damask, six elegant rosewood chairs, a handsome mahogany bookcase with plate glass and sliding shelves" came out of the drawing room, as did the fine-toned semi-grand pianoforte that Annie used to play. From the master bedroom there was "a handsome German bedstead with panelled footboard, carved cornice and fringe and figured damask hangings". It was the bed in which Annie had died and which Palmer had afterwards shunned, for he said he could not bear to sleep in it alone, though perhaps with Eliza and Jane he did not have to. There were pictures of his horses, Elizabethan carved oak chairs and the Palmers' grandfather clock, which sold for 15 shillings. And there was quite a cellar, too, for a man who did not drink much: 222 gallons of ale, 67 dozen bottles of port, 43 gallons of spirits: more bottles of wine than bottles of medicine, it was noted – 800 of the former, 137 of the latter. The sale attracted spectators and bidders from across the Midlands. "The sale was too hurried," Mrs Bennett, Palmer's next-door neighbour, told Mayhew. "If they had brought the things out into the open air they would have fetched much more money; but they didn't give the bidding time. The books were almost given away. Loads and loads of things went off from here to Birmingham. The furniture was very good indeed." Occasionally, Palmer mementos still surface: an inkwell here, letters there, while the four-poster bed sold for £12 in 1944. The *Rugeley Times* reported in 1971 that the grandfather clock was still in the possession of the same Walsall family that had bought it at the auction and that it still kept good time.

The crowd trampled through the large, well-kept garden behind the house too: looking at the flower-beds, inspecting the stable and the pigsty with its manure tank, whose contents had been spread over the well-tended bed of rhubarb and the leeks, admiring the fruit trees trained against the wall, and gazing at the plantation of forty raspberry and gooseberry bushes. Later in the year, a photographer, Mr C. Allen, would set up there, respectfully informing the ladies, gentry and inhabitants of Rugeley in an advertisement that he could produce for them very superior portraits in gilt and other frames for prices from one shilling to a guinea, between ten o'clock in the mornings and six in the evenings. The attraction "in premises lately occupied by W. Palmer" was obviously the notoriety of the setting. "The number of fashionably-dressed persons who journey over to Rugeley from the surrounding districts to obtain a sight of Palmer's house is positively astounding," marvelled Gus Mayhew. "The photographer no doubt calculates upon a large proportion of these being seduced into returning home with such an interesting souvenir as their own portraits, actually taken off in Palmer's back garden." He speculated that the house was now so notorious that it would have to be pulled down, but in fact the building remains, much altered and renovated, with a new frontage now enhanced with three windowed gables in the roofline and two shops downstairs: a Gymophobics tanning centre on one side and a pet shop on the other. At the back the outline of the medieval building that the Palmers once lived in is still just visible in a cluster of pitched roofs, gables and chimney stacks.

By January 1856, the law had caught up with Sam Cheshire, the Rugeley postmaster. The police had first thought that William Webb Ward, the coroner, must have tipped Palmer off about the contents of Taylor's letter, and he had to do some fast footwork to evade suspicion. Hatton told him that there was a traitor somewhere and he was determined to find out who it was: "he would use every exertion to get him discovered . . . The coroner observed that it was a most mysterious affair and he thought the best plan would be for him to send by that evening's post a copy of the letter to the Secretary of State, inquiring whether he had acted right or wrong." When confronted, though, Cheshire immediately admitted that he had scanned the letter which Taylor had sent to Stephens's Rugeley solicitor James Gardner and that it was he who had told Palmer about the contents. The *Staffordshire Advertiser* recorded what Cheshire said had happened:

> I went to Mr Palmer's house about half-past eight in the morning with his letters. I found him in bed. Mr Palmer said to me: "Well, have you seen or heard anything?" I told him that I had, but that it would be wrong of me to tell him. He said: "What have you heard?" and I told him that I had seen a letter and that they had found no poison. He said he knew they would not and that he was as innocent as a baby . . . On opening the London letter bag that morning I [had] found a letter, the envelope of which was open and my attention was particularly drawn to it by observing on the enclosure the words "cause of death". I took the enclosure from the envelope, cast my eye over it and the signature of Dr Taylor struck my attention. I returned the enclosure to the envelope, wetted the gum and secured it . . . I think I mentioned the word "strychnin" to Mr Palmer.

For this, Cheshire, "an extremely respectable looking man", lost his job and went to prison for two years. He would have to leave Rugeley, where he had lived all his life, and was last heard of in 1861 living in Everton, Liverpool, with his wife and three small children and working as a stationer.

The question was how Palmer could get a fair trial. It was a long-standing principle that the accused were tried in the districts where their crimes occurred, but feelings were said to be running so high against him that finding an unprejudiced jury anywhere in the Midlands was looking increasingly impossible. So, in January, Palmer's solicitor, John Smith of Birmingham, applied to the Queen's Bench for the trial to be moved. "Honest John Smith" was known as an assiduous and tenacious lawyer and had made an early appearance in Rugeley to keep his eye on the sale of Palmer's furniture. Probably he had approached the Palmers to be William's lawyer: brother George, who had advised in the early stages before the inquests, would not have been a professionally appropriate choice, and although Jerry Smith had scampered between the hearings to Palmer's house to let him know what was going on, he was strictly a local lawyer and had been too close to what was happening. John Smith had experience of handling important cases and would stick with Palmer to the end.

Smith's application for a writ of certiorari in the case – a ruling from the higher court to the Staffordshire justices – was heard in the Queen's Bench court on 31 January 1856. The lawyer had sworn an affidavit that:

> he was informed and believed that Palmer could not have a fair trial in Staffordshire or elsewhere in the Midland counties inasmuch as the prejudice against him was so great that he could not believe that among an ordinary panel of jurymen 12 men could be found unbiased and unprejudiced. In the neighbourhood of Stafford he was also accused of having murdered several other persons; which rumour was very generally believed to be true.

Smith added that the expense of bringing medical experts to a trial in Stafford would be very great and could not be afforded, so that Palmer would not get a fair trial:

> it would be necessary that the deponent should have a sufficient number of scientific persons to give evidence on his trial, most of whom were resident in London and the expense of such witnesses would be £1,000 or thereabouts if he were tried in Stafford, that he had no funds wherewith to meet such expense and was entirely dependent on his friends and relations and he feared he could not be well or properly defended unless he could be tried where the expense of such witnesses would be much less.

Palmer's counsel at the hearing, William Smith – yet another lawyer named Smith – added that, by means of newspapers, the inhabitants of Staffordshire, Warwickshire and other neighbouring counties were greatly prejudiced against the defendant and eager for his conviction. One of Palmer's defence counsel at his trial, Edward Kenealy – a notoriously perverse character – reckoned later that, contrary to these assertions of local prejudice, he would have got off if the case had been heard in the Midlands, but judging from the local coverage and the behaviour of the crowds who gathered in Rugeley and later at Stafford, he was probably better off being tried in London. His case had been so fully reported nationally that people everywhere already had an opinion about Palmer's guilt.

Lord Campbell, who would also preside at the trial in May, dismissed the lawyers' argument about expense, pointing out that the government would be conducting the prosecution and therefore would defray the cost of the trial. But he agreed that the ends of justice required the case to be removed from the Midlands:

> It appears that a great prejudice prevails and a fair trial cannot be had in Staffordshire . . . I do earnestly hope that from this time to the trial there will be no further discussion on the case. After the trial it will be perfectly legitimate to discuss the conduct of the jury and judge and the question as to the innocence or guilt of the defendant. Till then, it is most desirable that nothing of the sort should take place: if anything of the kind were to be done and that were to be brought to the notice of the Court it might be the subject of punishment, meanwhile the defendant is to be presumed innocent.

This was ironic, in view of the fact that throughout the trial Campbell clearly assumed that Palmer was guilty, and he was ambitious to conduct such a notorious case himself. But if he hoped that his stern words would inhibit press comment, he was woefully mistaken: two days after the hearing, the *Illustrated Times* published its Rugeley supplement, stuffed full of prejudice. Three days after that a bill that was to become known as the Palmer Act was introduced in the House of Lords by the Lord Chancellor, Lord Cranworth, to allow trials to be removed from the areas where crimes had occurred and held at the Central Criminal Court – the Old Bailey – in London instead if there was a risk of prejudice. It was legislation specifically to deal with the situation in which William Palmer found himself and was only the first of a number of changes to law and regulations that his case would ultimately cause. The Trial of Offences bill went through Parliament with scarcely any debate and occupied very little time: less than 10 minutes in the Lords – long enough only for Lord Campbell to thank the Lord Chancellor formally for a great improvement in criminal procedure and to acknowledge that often a fair and impartial trial could not be had in the county where the offence was committed – which rather begged the question why the reform had not been introduced before. He added: "In the

Central Criminal Court, however, such a case could very well be heard, and very little delay arise in bringing on a trial in this way."

There was scarcely more debate in the Commons when the bill reached there in early March: it took less than an hour, after midnight, and there was no division. The chief objections came from Irish MPs, fearful that Irishmen could be tried in London for offences committed in Ireland – they were told that the bill would not apply across the Irish Sea – and from the MPs for Stafford, aggravated that it might be thought that their constituents would not try a case impartially. Arthur Otway, one of the MPs, who was a barrister as well as a Liberal supporter of the government, said it was notorious that the bill had been introduced to meet a particular case, that of Palmer, because it was pretended that he would not obtain a fair trial from a jury in Staffordshire: "He would undertake to say, for the jurymen of Staffordshire in general, that such an accusation was most unjust and unfounded." His colleague John Wise also believed that there was no reason for apprehension that an impartial jury could not be obtained at Stafford. At the third reading a week later there was grumbling that the government might use the law for political convenience, to remove a sensitive case – such as a trial for treason – to London, but the measure was promoted merely as a tidying up of the law, to remove anomalies, and the legislation passed effortlessly with only a formal vote without division.

The Act, CAP XVI, to empower the Court of Queen's Bench to order certain offenders to be tried at the Central Criminal Court, was passed into law on 11 April 1856, five weeks before William Palmer's trial. It is quite short, running to twenty-nine clauses, and lays down such details as who would pay for the expense of a prisoner's maintenance in prison in Newgate: "at the average daily cost of each prisoner according to the whole number of prisoners confined in said gaol, such average to be taken yearly, half-yearly, quarterly or at such other intervals as the visiting justices of said gaol shall from time to time determine" (the answer was that the county treasurer where the offence had been committed would pay the bill). It also laid down that a person convicted in such circumstances would be sentenced to be punished back in the county where the offence had occurred.

With this, the legal obstacles to William Palmer's trial were cleared away. Six months almost to the day since John Parsons Cook had breathed his last, writhing in agony in Room 10 of the Talbot Arms in Rugeley, his

The official text of the indictment

close friend would stand trial for his murder in the most famous and awesome criminal court in the land.

The indictment against him, now formally returned by the grand jury in Stafford in March 1856, was both sonorous and ornately, not to say floridly, inscribed in immaculate copperplate, though without much in the way of punctuation:

> Staffordshire. The Jurors for Our Lady the Queen upon their
> oath present that William Palmer late of the Parish of Rugeley
> in the County of Stafford Surgeon not having the fear of God
> before his eyes but being moved and seduced at the instigation
> of the Devil on the 21st day of November in the year of our Lord
> 1855 with force and arms at the parish afsd in the County
> aforesaid feloniously wilfully & of his malice aforethought did
> kill and murder one John Parsons Cook Against the Peace of
> Our Lady the Queen Her Crown and Dignity.

The invocation of God and the instigation of the Devil was a standard rubric on 19th Century chargesheets.

Palmer had not, and never would, publicly speak in his own defence, at the coroner's inquest, at the court in Stafford, or at the Old Bailey. But now the law would take its course.

10

"History when properly written"

I NITIALLY AT LEAST, THE *STAFFORDSHIRE ADVERTISER*'S REPORTS ABOUT THE death of John Parsons Cook, the most celebrated story in its area in the whole of the nineteenth century, were brief to the point of perfunctoriness. The weekly newspaper gave the case four paragraphs in its first available issue, on 1 December 1855, ten days after Cook's death, rather less than it devoted to a report about the visit to London of the king of Sardinia and a meeting of the Staffordshire schoolmasters' association. Under the heading "Mysterious death of a sporting gentleman at Rugeley", as if reporting an event that had occurred on the other side of England, it wrote: "Some excitement has arisen in this town during last week in consequence of the somewhat sudden death of a sporting gentleman J. P. Cooke [*sic*]." The following week it added more detail: before Cook's death "his symptoms had become more decided", but a post-mortem had been made by Dr Harland. The report did not mention how chaotic it had been. It added lightly, with a touch of local pride: "On Thursday evening an inquest was commenced before a highly intelligent and respectable jury."

Such limited coverage did not last. By the time the inquest on Cook was held a couple of weeks later, national newspapers were taking an interest. On 18 December *The Times* gave a verbatim report of the inquest running to several thousand words over two columns under the headline "Mysterious Death at Rugeley". By Christmas its report was headlined "The Suspected Poisoning Case at Rugeley" and already the newspaper had located its villain, William Palmer. Astounding facts were promised and there was an intimate account of his hunger strike in prison – "he is in tolerably good health and perfectly free from any disease"; also included was the full story of his attempt to bribe the postboy to overturn the wagon taking the jar of stomach and intestines to Stafford railway station, not to mention a rundown of his financial difficulties. *The Times* was far from alone: every regional and national newspaper with pretensions to comprehensiveness was giving each twist of the case extensive coverage, often with the sort of details that no newspaper would publish today – the colour of the fluid in Cook's stomach, the removal of the bone marrow from his spine, all was grist to the mill. Palmer's name was soon as well known to readers of the *Bath Chronicle*, the *Liverpool Daily Post* and the *Dundee, Perth and Cupar Advertiser* as it was in the Black Country.

The story was too good to miss for newspapers that had finally been freed, six months earlier in June 1855, from the shackles of government stamp duty on papers and tax on their advertisements, and so had been able to lower their prices and increase their circulations. The *Manchester Guardian* was typical: previously a bi-weekly paper, published on Tuesdays and Saturdays, it immediately reduced its price from fivepence (a penny of which was tax) and became a daily, selling at twopence. Many others followed similar paths, took the gamble that readers would pay a shilling a week for six days' papers, rather than tenpence a week for two, and found that indeed they would. With literacy on the rise, the readership was broadening. Newspapers might not reach the poor yet, but an artisan could read the paper now and know that he was getting fresher daily news from more sources than ever before. There were good stories about: the end of the Crimean War was coming closer, there was politics, and there were daily trade and commodity prices to report. And there were "human interest" stories. What could be better than a juicy murder at Christmas time to boost sales?

In this, William Palmer was, as so often, unlucky in his timing. His trial would always have been a sensation, but without the recent unshackling of the press it would have been a more limited one. As it was, the story was followed in minute detail; everyone had an opinion and every turn in the evidence was avidly discussed. Even the queen, as her private journal shows, was following the case. It was a sensation which kept on giving fresh angles. This was not a common or garden robbery or coshing in the street. It was the insidious administration of a new poison by a middle-class professional man. There was money involved, a lubricious whiff of illicit sex, and deathbed scenes retold in graphic and affecting prose to enthral a highly literate audience. No wonder the *New York Times* would say, when it caught up with the story a few months later: "this horrid story . . . distances all the fancies of Bulwer's romance."

By the time the inquests into Annie and Walter's deaths were held in Rugeley town hall in mid-January, there were at least thirty journalists present, most of them from the national press. Not to be outdone for its local readers, the *Staffordshire Advertiser* was now devoting columns of verbatim coverage too, and published a special twopenny supplement so they could catch up. All the reporters present were primed to write word-for-word accounts of the proceedings and telegraph them back to their offices in London. Thousands of words were being filed each day: two and three columns' worth of tightly printed, small-type lines, each witness closely scrutinised, each question reported, each answer given. Only occasionally did attention flag. Deep in the *Morning Chronicle*'s account, as the inquests entered their second week, was the following:

> Gentlemen connected with various insurance companies were examined at great length as to attempts which have been made by Palmer to effect insurances on his wife and brother's life. There was nothing however in their evidence beyond that which had already been fully detailed in the statements we have already published.

The ephemera of even the best-kept newspaper archives does not usually permit reporters to be identified at such a distance. *The Times* may have dispatched one of its leading young reporters, John Cameron Macdonald, who was only thirty-three but had already been on the paper for more than a decade and had specialised in what would now be called investigative reporting: exposing the scandal of the treatment of inmates at the Andover workhouse in the mid-1840s, for instance, and writing from Ireland during the potato famine. The paper's editor John Thadeus Delane certainly had it in mind for Macdonald to cover the Rugeley poisonings. *The Times*'s archive contains a memo to that effect. Sent by Delane to his deputy George Dasent in January 1856 and written in the ironic and terse style still common to editors, the scrawled note says: "I congratulate you on another murder. Pray make the printers display it well and set Macdonald to attend the examinations. I shall send him for Stafford when Palmer comes on for trial." Delane, who was largely absorbed in the great events of national politics and international diplomacy (he was a close friend and confidant of Lord Palmerston), was certainly interested in the Rugeley poisonings. Another memo from about the same time urges Dasent to ask one of the paper's leader writers, Alexander Knox, to write about them: "I think you should make . . . Knox [write] on the new complication of the Rugeley affair. You will have seen the coroner is now deep in the mire of denying the receipt of the second letter from Palmer." He writes again, maybe on the following day: "Chenery to write on Col. Tim's case, an enlistment of Italian legion, Knox on Baron Martin, Dallas on Rugeley poisonings." Eneas Sweetland Dallas was another leader writer (aged twenty-seven at this time, so clearly a bright young man); Delane added: "Dallas has two articles, one which I read last night upon the Rugeley poisoning & he will write another on the Eastern Counties report . . . "

That January, Rugeley was crawling with smart young men from the metropolitan papers. Of these two are identifiable: Edward Whitty of the weekly paper called the *Leader* and Augustus Mayhew of the *Illustrated Times*. Both were what newspapers now call colour writers, sent to report the background details, circumstances and human interest of what was rapidly becoming the biggest domestic story of the year. Their approaches were recognisably modern and startlingly vivid, contrasting with the normal image of Victorian newspaper reporting as a turgid recitation of ponderous facts in laborious prose. With only marginal tweaks of style – and not even much updating of the descriptions – Whitty and Mayhew's copy with its mixture of colour, reportage and opinion could slot straight into a newspaper today. It is their accounts of the Palmer story that have shaped the telling of it ever since. They were the men who ferreted out the gossip, the jokes and the rumours, and it was they, probably more than anyone else, who directed the way the Victorian public saw William Palmer long before he ever came to trial. It was their depictions of him as notorious, a wretch, a rogue, a monster and a liar – all terms they used – more than any others that ensured his trial would be prejudiced. Palmer's solicitor John Smith might argue that he could not get a fair trial anywhere in the Midland counties, but actually he probably could not have received a trial in front of unbiased listeners anywhere in Britain.

Whitty and Mayhew wrote anonymously, but it is possible to identify them. Whitty's paper, the *Leader*, was edited by the high-minded George Henry Lewes, best remembered now as George Eliot's long-term partner but then the man who had just published an acclaimed biography of Goethe. That did not stop him sending his rather supercilious special correspondent to Rugeley to write a lengthy, patronising article about the place, which appeared on 16 January 1856, just after the inquests had ended. The report, in self-consciously mocking, purple prose, depicts the town as an idyllic rural place whose Arcadian ambience had been torn apart by the monster in its midst. The account was written up as if in terms of a mythical French visitor descending on the place – it might as easily have been a man from Mars. Rugeley was, he wrote, a harbour of refuge from the vanities and vexations of a frivolous or malicious world, a promised land, a land flowing with milk and honey – maybe the only time that phrase has ever been applied to Staffordshire in January: "here, if anywhere [one] might hope to exhume the simple virtues hitherto buried in the dull dribbling of pastoral rhapsodies." Eventually Whitty got on to Palmer: "his personal appearance if not heroic, was by no means disagreeable ... there is not a chambermaid or waitress within thirty miles who does not speak of him as 'a nice, pleasant sort of gentleman'." But Palmer was from a family that was all-powerful locally, requiring "as cautious handling as a hedgehog". He was almost certainly right about the local influence and wealth of the Palmers. And then there were the inquest hearings themselves: a ponderous coroner and a jury not made up of the highly intelligent and respectable men predicted by the local paper, but instead a group characterised by "open countenances and lips well apart, of average provincial misunderstanding and no doubt as weighty as any twenty-three men in the kingdom". The spectators were "local chaw-bacons who stand for hours 'obstruction's apathy', occasionally snoring on their legs, laughing consumedly when Mr Lawyer makes fun of a witness". Presumably Whitty hoped never to return to Rugeley. He was, it was said, a man whose "bright extemporaneous flippancies" had lightened the office of the *Leader*, as he bantered irreverently with the likes of philosophers such as Lewes and Herbert Spencer. No wonder Whitty found Rugeley provincial and dull. He was also the author of an unsuccessful novel and a parliamentary reporter and – almost inevitably – drank himself to death in 1860 on board a ship taking him to Australia in an attempt to cure him of his alcoholism.

Whitty's reporting chimed perfectly with the *Leader's* contemporary obsession with the insidious crime of poisoning – the ideal means of stirring its middle-class readership. In its issue of 15 December 1855, before Palmer had ever been heard of outside Rugeley, the *Leader* had published an article – "The Poisoner in the House" – in the wake of two other recent poisoning cases that was calculated to make anyone squirm:

> If you feel a deadly sensation within and grow gradually weaker, how do you know that you are not poisoned? If your hands tingle, do you not fancy that it is arsenic? How can you be sure that it is not? Your household perhaps is a "well-regulated family"; your friends and relations all smile kindly upon you; the meal at each period of the day is punctual and looks correct; but how can you possibly tell that there is not arsenic in the curry?

A week later the magazine was at it again: "The very regularity of our lives suggests a means for the malefactor to arrive at his purpose." And that malefactor might easily be a trusted, respectable doctor: "Give a medical man motives for getting rid of his patient and it is clear that he has the man at his mercy. Without a metaphor, your medical man can always poison you if he chooses; and unless he is very clumsy . . . he can poison you without detection." Right on cue, Dr William Palmer was making his first appearance in the public prints. No wonder the papers were interested in him.

Then there was Augustus Septimus Mayhew, the man sent up to Rugeley by the *Illustrated Times* whose reports have already been mentioned. He was another archetypal journalistic figure, now long forgotten. Gus, as he was known by his colleagues, was the younger brother of Henry Mayhew, a radical journalist and the founding editor of the magazine *Punch*, whose book *London Labour and the London Poor*, written in the early 1850s, remains a key text in understanding what working-class life was like in the capital during the period. The older Mayhew pioneered the technique of interviewing and quoted his subjects verbatim in their own words and idioms. They were the sort of people – labourers and costermongers, milkmen and street sellers, dustmen and crossing sweepers, cab drivers and vagrants – whose views journalists had never bothered with before. It was an innovation then, but the "vox pop" has been a newspaper staple ever since. Henry and Gus had also collaborated before on a couple of satirical novels, which verged on the documentary. They have a strikingly recognisable modern flavour: *The Greatest Plague of Life, or The Adventures of a Lady in Search of a Good Servant*, published in 1847, concerns an upwardly mobile coal merchant's family with pretentions to gentility, while *Living for Appearances*, which came out in 1855, the year before Palmer's trial, is a satirical account of a smart young couple living only to be in fashion.

Not much is known of either man's life, but it is quite clear from Gus's report, which filled the fifteen-page special issue of the paper on 2 February 1856, that he had learned from his brother's techniques. It is a formidable piece of work, running to more than 40,000 words and complete with thirty-three line-drawing illustrations. Gus had interviewed many of the local participants and observers and relayed what they said in their own striking phrases, so that even the Midlands accents are distinctly audible. This is his account of being shown the room in the Talbot Arms where Cook had died a few weeks before:

> "That's where he lay," says the maid who officiated as showwoman. "That's just the spot, poor fellow! And he was curled up, just there, poor fellow! He was put in the bed near the door because it's nearer the fire and you see the bell's handy, poor fellow. Dr Jones slept in the other bed and you see it was so convenient because they could lie and look at each other. There was always a fire burning and after he was dead, poor fellow, all three of the doctors stood round it looking very serious and never saying a word. It's a nice comfortable room, that's one consolation and he had of the best, poor fellow!"

The *Illustrated Times* had been launched the previous year, in the wake of the lifting of stamp duty, as a cheaper, sprightlier, smaller-sized and more populist version of the more stately *Illustrated London News*, which it undercut for price (twopence as opposed to sixpence) and in sharpness. It was not quite a tabloid, but it had a tabloid's verve. Its cover page – illuminated with a frieze of naked cherubs prancing tastefully around an acacia border in which lurked the busts of Shakespeare, Bacon, Newton and "Raffael" – promised "numerous first-class engravings of the chief events and all the news of the week" and claimed that it was published not only in London but as far afield as Montreal, New South Wales and Van Diemen's Land. It did not disappoint. It covered the news of the world, but as it said in an editorial in 1856:

> History when properly written gives its due prominence to do-mestic topics, even when painful and repulsive. We have not only fulfilled the bounden duty of a newspaper but have sup-plied the moralist and the philosopher with materials for their study. Those again who learn from the narrative how crimes may be committed will learn too how they may be detected and punished and that science is its own avenger.

The two magazines competed fiercely and not without a certain degree of internecine skulduggery. It was not unknown for the first page proofs of il-lustrations to find their way from the printers to the rival magazine's offices, where they could be reproduced with marginal alterations and used as their own. These weeklies offered something daily newspapers could not: a more discursive style and line drawings of various sizes – full-page portraits and thumbnail sketches, some as accomplished as paintings, others as lively as cartoons. There were pictures of foreign lands and strange, alien people in native costumes, of charging cavalry and exotic sites of the sort that readers would never have seen before. The magazines employed considerable artists: Dickens's illustrator "Phiz", Hablot Browne, George Cruikshank and even the French artist Gustave Doré, who would draw a full page for them for £6. Such ephemeral pictures were not only innovative, but also established an image of the age – and also, in the case of the story of William Palmer, show us what most of the participants looked like at a time when photographs were still new and could not be reproduced in print. The success of the Ruge-ley supplement – over 250,000 copies were sold – surprised even the news-paper staff, and following Palmer's trial it was immediately reissued in an edited, though slightly truncated, version, as a book, which did equally well.

The founder and editor of the *Illustrated Times* was the dapper, neatly bearded Henry Vizetelly, who had started his career in the family's Holborn business as a printer and engraver. Maybe his stories grew in the telling, but

Vizetelly was certainly a charismatic and raffish figure. He was one of three brothers of Anglo-Italian origin, all of whom would become famous: the older brother James was a publisher and the younger brother Frank became a notable war artist. The Vizetellys were like the Mayhews, Lewes and Whitty, George Augustus Sala, Thackeray and Wilkie Collins, Dickens and his friends: all part of a London literary and journalistic circle, setting up newspapers and magazines, writing for each other, laughing, drinking, getting into trouble, having tiffs, tantrums and feuds, avoiding creditors, flitting back and forth to France and Germany, and always moving on. Henry, later in his career, after going to France as a foreign correspondent, would become one of the first English wine writers. The spirit is caught very much in his long-forgotten memoirs *Glances Back through Seventy Years*, published in two volumes in the 1890s, which contain one of the liveliest accounts both of Palmer's trial and of the *Illustrated Times*'s coverage of it:

> The *Illustrated Times* came out with a Rugeley number filled with portraits and views sketched on the spot and a narrative of this and other crimes of a similar nature of which Palmer was supposed to be guilty; together with the private family history of the accused and all the incriminating gossip concerning him that could be picked up in the place . . . Today one cannot but express one's amazement that a quarter of a million copies of this number of the paper were allowed to be sold without the courts being appealed to on behalf of the accused and special correspondent, editor, printer, publisher and proprietor being all promptly packed off to gaol for so outrageous a contempt of court. The paper published column after column of statements made by the landlord, housekeeper, boots and postboy . . . Augustus Mayhew was one of the most jocose and lighthearted of special correspondents and the lugubrious details he was sent to pick up in Rugeley were not by any means in his line.

The paper was understandably a little defensive about flouting the injunction against prejudicial reporting, but at the time it offered its readers a public-interest defence, as well as the added bonus of illustrations which could not be matched by the daily press. Its editorial in the Rugeley supplement was a splendid example of hypocrisy:

We conceive in what we have this day done we have only fulfilled the office that devolves on us as the conductors of an illustrated journal. We cannot agree with that squeamishness which allows long, wordy descriptions of places and individuals to be perfectly admissible and which refuses to tolerate those productions of the pencil, the skilfully indicated lines of which are more suggestive than columns upon columns of the best written descriptions. Does even one of our readers believe that the Times or any other of the morning journals would not readily avail themselves of the means which we possess and make use of, were it only possible to adapt them to the exigencies of a daily newspaper? The labour that we have for weeks been engaged in and the results of which are now before the reader was not entered upon with the idea of pandering to a mere vulgar curiosity. Our object was to lay bare a great social vice which is gnawing away at the very core of society and which every day shows to be rapidly on the increase – namely the fearful amount of gambling in human life for the sake of pecuniary gain. Anyone who scans these columns with attention will approve the spirit in which we have performed our task.

The great labour had involved sending Mayhew and at least one of the *Illustrated Times*'s illustrators, C. H. Bennett, to Rugeley – although several artists were used for its coverage, Bennett's is the only signature visible. His portraits verge on the caricature – Vizetelly thought him a poor draughtsman, but possessed of a "highly original humorous fancy". Perhaps he was the only man able to go to the Midlands in January – it is a pity that Doré was not available instead.

The supplement, however, did not just contain Gus Mayhew's report. His older brother Henry was also enlisted to write an investigative piece about the insurance industry and, presumably because he was so well known, the paper made a point of naming him, unlike his brother. It is an exemplary piece of reporting. Henry – portly, balding, respectable and middle-aged if his sole line-drawn portrait is anything to go by – went round a number of insurance offices in London seeking a life policy and came back with a lengthy report that has a ring of modern familiarity about it. "We of course found some persons more communicative than others, but on the whole the information obtained was of a similar nature wherever we addressed ourselves," he wrote. Of visiting one unidentified office, he added:

> Our appearance seemed to excite a hope that we were about to insure our life . . . we were shown into the boardroom. The splendour of the furniture at once revealed to us that we were in one of the young offices the appearance of which bears the same relation to that of the old offices, which a fashionable Paris bank does to one of our banks in the City. A French banker who makes no display obtains no customers; an English banker who exhibits signs of extravagance causes his customers to withdraw their deposits.

Mayhew wandered round the room taking notes: a massive mahogany table covered in a green cloth like a billiard table (mahogany tables were regarded as a sign of conspicuous extravagance, much as some sorts of executive desk would be 150 years later), luxurious chairs "inviting you to be seated", knick-knacks on the mantelpiece, a card outlining the benefits of the company's policies, a carafe of water and upturned glass, and a stethoscope – all designed to impress.

He visited a dozen or so companies and found not only that the sort of scam Palmer was said to have indulged in was widespread, but that the number of premature deaths was greater among the insured than the uninsured, just as fires in insured houses were more common than those in uninsured properties. The Irish seemed particularly prone to fraudulent claims, he reported, including concealing drinking problems and alcoholism in those being insured. The lives of confirmed alcoholics – such as Walter – were often insured in the knowledge that, if they did not soon die naturally, their deaths could be brought on prematurely: "intentionally done to death by unlimited supplies of drink, the worst cases . . . in connection with Irish policies, the lives of confirmed whiskey drinkers being heavily insured by strangers who took good care to provide these bibulous dependents with a plentiful supply of their favourite liquor." Germans – who preferred to insure with English companies rather than with their own, where checks were more rigorous – enjoyed pretending to be dead and then claiming on the policies they had taken out. Some insurance companies made it a policy never to insure doctors' relatives, particularly their wives, because of their knowledge of and ready access to poisons. The sort of fraud that Palmer had tried, making Walter seem healthier than he really was, was also a common try-on: "clients stop drinking, take a hot bath and have new clothes for their medical examination." It was largely down, he concluded, to unregulated competition between companies and the recklessness of agents in pursuit of commission:

> Tampering with life with a view to become possessed of the insurance money is far more general than the public believe and than some of the companies are disposed to state . . . The overeagerness of insurance offices to do business arises from the great number of companies and the excessive competition between them . . . they are mostly started by adventurers with a view to obtain the lucrative situation of actuary, secretary, solicitor, medical officer, chairman or director.

This reporting was part of a generalised mid-Victorian concern about the meretriciousness and general corruption and moral shadiness of much modern business practice, of which the burgeoning insurance industry was a particularly striking example. These had disastrous effects in the periodic panics and slumps of real life: speculative bubbles and manias and suddenly booming and collapsing companies that arose out of unregulated markets and unsupervised business practices. Such companies were gradually being brought under constraints – the Limited Liability Acts were passed in 1855 and 1856, reducing shareholder investment risks – but the middle classes had been severely bitten by scams, frauds and failed investments over the previous few years and a suspicion of flashy new schemes and sharp-suited, narrow-eyed men doing well out of honest but gullible strivers was strong. In *The Times*'s words in March 1854: "A man assumes the appearance of inexhaustible wealth, buys and buys and buys again, each time with the credit derived from former but still unsettled transactions", but then "father, mother, uncles, aunts, brothers, sisters – all are ruthlessly plundered to save from exposure a 'victim' who never had a farthing that he could rightly call his own".

Mayhew's solution, in an era when governments saw their regulatory role in private commerce as strictly limited, has a familiar ring too: "It is the duty of the Government, as the great protector of society to suppress by every legitimate means in its power the various causes above enumerated as productive of such disastrous results." The following week's *Post and Insurance Monitor*, serving the industry, acknowledged that Mayhew's investigation was true – "*corruptio optimi pessima* – nothing so bad as the abuse of a good thing," it said sagely, adding:

> It appears that some insurance companies are culpably lax in granting policies on the lives of third parties without exacting the proper legal proof of interest . . . in some of the insurances the question seems to have been scarcely raised and even when death ensued in startling proximity to the date of policy payment does not appear to have been resisted . . . The facilities afforded for life insurance are liable to gross abuse and in the hands of unscrupulous parties may be turned to the very worst purposes. Such companies cannot too soon be pilloried throughout the country and their shameless promoters consigned to their true quarters, the prison or the hulks.

William Palmer's insurance scams were far from unique, except perhaps in his being caught because his attempts were just too desperate and too blatant.

Public interest in the case and appetite for every detail of the alleged murders was fully served when Palmer came to trial at the Old Bailey in May 1856. All the newspapers carried column after column of near-verbatim transcripts of the evidence heard in court; in papers usually about eight pages long, depending on the day of the week, at least a page and often more would be devoted to the trial. On the first day *The Times* alone carried approximately 18,000 words over three pages. The newspaper's court correspondent was a middle-aged man called Alfred Clyatt, who also covered public meetings and general elections but was mainly employed sitting at the Old Bailey day after day. He would eventually go freelance and supply court copy more widely, and he reported from the court almost until his death nearly forty years later in 1891. When he died, *The Times* carried no obituary, but Mr Justice Hawkins expressed regret at hearing the news before the commencement of the day's business. We can probably imagine Clyatt handing running copy, written in pen and ink, doubtless in immaculate copperplate, to a succession of boys who would then run across Ludgate Hill and down to the paper's offices in Printing House Square near Blackfriars.

Deep in the trial's transcript, on the fifth day, there was a spat between Professor Taylor and Palmer's barrister Serjeant Shee over Mayhew's efforts in the *Illustrated Times*, with the discomfited medical expert expressing his outrage at being doorstepped by the reporter over the evidence he was to give at the Palmer trial. Taylor had been remarkably free with his opinions, and in a letter to the *Lancet* in February – coincidentally on the same day that the *Illustrated Times* published its Rugeley supplement – he had come close publicly to declaring Palmer's guilt, three months before he would be called to give evidence as a witness at the Old Bailey. His letter had read:

> During a quarter century which I have now specifically devoted to toxicological inquiries I have never met with any cases like these suspected cases of poisoning at Rugeley. The mode in which they will affect the person accused is of minor importance compared with their probable influence on society. I have no hesitation in saying that the future security of life in this country will mainly depend on the judge, the jury and the counsel who may have to dispose of the charges of murder that have arisen out of these investigations.

Privately, Taylor had gone further, writing to the attorney general before the trial in May: "If Palmer escapes no person's life in England will be safe from poisoning where an interest may exist to take it." But his *Lancet* letter was quite clear enough and Shee wanted to know about it and remarks he had also made to Henry Mayhew which the *Illustrated Times* had published. Taylor had told Mayhew that poisoning was on the increase, but that chemists could almost always detect the presence of poison in a body and that where small doses of strychnine had been administered, physiology and pathology would invariably be enough to establish the cause of death. This is not what he argued either at the trial or afterwards, but in the light of his appearance at the inquest and prospective evidence at the trial it was highly prejudicial. Had he ever met the editor of the *Illustrated Times*, one Augustus Mayhew? "I have seen him once or twice," Taylor replied evasively.

Actually, Shee was wrong: Gus was not the editor, and the reporter who had turned up on Taylor's doorstep at St James's Terrace, Regent's

Park, had been Henry Mayhew. But there was another, more compelling reason why Taylor could not really have been taken completely by surprise: the line drawing of him and Dr Rees sedately carrying out tests in their laboratory, which had been published in the supplement (see page 229). It is such an evocative picture that it has been used to depict Victorian scientists ever since. Shee asked: "Did you allow pictures of yourself and Dr Rees to be taken for publication?" Taylor bridled: "Be so good as to call them caricatures. No, I did not." This must have been a discomforting untruth for Taylor and Shee spotted it: "There may be a difference of opinion as to that. I think it is very like. Did you receive Mr Mayhew at your house?" Taylor answered: "He came to me with a letter of introduction from Professor Faraday. I never received him in my laboratory." "Did you know that he called in order that you might afford him information for an article in the *Illustrated Times?*" Taylor huffed:

> I swear solemnly I did not. The publication of that article was the most disgraceful thing I ever knew. I had never seen him before, nor did I know that he was the editor of the *Illustrated Times* ... On my oath, it was the greatest deception that was ever practised on a scientific man. It was disgraceful. He called on me with another gentleman ... I received him as I should Professor Faraday and entered conversation with him about these cases. He represented as I understood that he was connected with an insurance company and wished for information about a number of cases of poisoning which had occurred during many years. After we had conversed about an hour he asked if there was any objection to the publication of these details. Still believing him to be connected with an insurance office I replied that so far as the correction of error was concerned I should have no objection to anything appearing ... he went away without telling me that he was the editor of the *Illustrated Times* or connected with any other paper. I did not know that until he called upon me on Thursday morning and showed me the article in print. I remonstrated verbally with him. He only showed me part of a slip ...

"Why did you not tell your servant to show him the door?" asked Shee. "Until we had had the conversation I did not know anything about the deception. It was not until the Thursday morning that I knew he was connected with a paper. He told me it was an illustrated paper." There is a sense of Taylor's lip curling. He might almost have said "tabloid".

"I objected to its publication," Taylor added. "Peremptorily?" asked Shee. "No. I said, 'I do not like this mode of putting the matter. I cannot however interfere with what you put in your journal.'" "Did you not protest as a gentleman, a man of honour and a medical man that it was wrong and objectionable?" "I told him that I objected to the parts which referred to the Rugeley cases. It was most dishonourable ..." "Did you not know that ... an interview with Dr Taylor on the subject of poison must be taken to apply to those cases?" Taylor was defeated: "I did not think anything about it ... I thought it was a great cheat. I remonstrated with him. I was not angry with him in the sense of quarrelling."

Shee asked about Taylor boasting that he would give Mayhew and a colleague called Cook Evans (was he the "other gentleman" who had visited him?) "strychnia enough before they had done"? The professor bridled: "No. I never used any expression so vulgar and improper. You have been greatly misinstructed." Perhaps, insinuated Shee, that was what he had said about Palmer? "It is utterly false."

Henry Mayhew was understandably affronted by Taylor's remarks that he had been underhand in the interview. He and his editor Vizetelly sought out the attorney general, Alexander Cockburn, who was prosecuting the case, during the next break. Vizetelly wrote in his memoirs:

> It was ... commonly believed that this note of warning [in the *Lancet*] sounded by Professor Taylor induced Lord Campbell to try Palmer's case himself ... Taylor [sought] to escape from the inferences drawn by accusing Mayhew of having violated private confidence ... When the court adjourned for luncheon I accompanied him in search of Cockburn whom we found washing his hands in one of the upstairs lavatories. He listened to the explanation which appeared to perfectly satisfy him and laughingly remarked that the badgering Taylor had met with in the witness box had driven him to make a mountain out of a molehill.

In any case, Mayhew had his very public revenge in that week's paper, pointing out in a letter written from his home in Percy Street, central London, that he had not only identified himself to Taylor when they met and made clear that he was interviewing him for publication, but that he had even sent him the page proof, which had been returned with amendments in Taylor's own handwriting "which I still retain". He added:

> I would in charity conclude that Dr Taylor was so confused by his long and rigid cross-examination this morning that he was not exactly aware of the serious charge conveyed by his words. I have within the last few years received some hundreds of statements from all ranks of people [and] this is the first imputation that has ever been made of my having obtained any information in a dishonest and surreptitious manner.

Public fascination with the case did not end with Palmer's trial. At least two verbatim transcripts were published, one of them by *The Times*, immediately after the trial, illustrated with the same drawings that had been used by the *Illustrated Times* in its earlier supplement. Vizetelly tried to cash in too:

> There was such a tremendous excitement over the Palmer affair and the public showed themselves so eager for information respecting the prisoner's past career that I was induced to get together a so-called life of the sporting doctor including all the trivial gossip retailed about him. As time was an important element in the affair, half-a-dozen hungry young literary ghouls were set to work to rake up any kind of information respecting the early life of the condemned man within the forthcoming eight and forty hours and the result was a strange medley of materials, in which I have not the slightest doubt fiction played a far more important part than fact. These, after being hastily hashed together, were sorted into chapters and within a week a shilling life of the great poisoner of the nineteenth century was in all the booksellers' shops and on all the railway bookstalls. The life was illustrated with no end of "appropriate" woodcuts, gathered from all manner of sources . . . The book went like wild-fire. Night and day for a fortnight printing machines rolled off their thousands upon thousands of copies without the orders

that had come in being overtaken. A small fortune was made
out of the affair.

As it happened, Vizetelly did not himself benefit much from the book,
falling foul of the sort of mishap that creates a characteristic journalistic
tale of misadventure. You can almost imagine him telling it over a good bottle of wine in years to come: "Although I was a half proprietor in it, only a
trifling sum fell to my share owing to an unlucky accident." Vizetelly had
been at a dinner of the Royal Agricultural Society in Chelmsford a few days
before publication and had returned to London on the last train. As he
sauntered down Ludgate Hill on his way home to Fleet Street, his cigar went
out. "Much to my annoyance I discovered I had no fusees about me," he
recalled in his memoirs:

> The streets were deserted, so that there was nobody from whom
> a light could be obtained . . . I noticed that the glass of a gas lamp
> perched high up against the wall was broken. There being a
> slanting ledge . . . I placed my foot on it and, springing up, suc-
> ceeded in lighting a paper spill which I had improvised, but in
> my rapid descent one of my feet unluckily caught the edge of
> the curb and I dislocated my ankle and broke the small bone of
> my leg. Quick as thought, I wrenched the ankle into its place
> again but it was not so easy to unite two pieces of fractured
> bone, so I hopped to a neighbouring post and there awaited the
> protecting peeler's periodic round.

The policeman put Vizetelly in a cab and accompanied him back to the *Illustrated Times* office further up Fleet Street, where a surgeon was called to
set his leg and pack him off to bed for a month:

> While I was fretting under this involuntary confinement . . . my
> partner in "Palmer's Life" paid me a sympathetic visit and
> bought me out of the speculation for a mere song, without of
> course saying a word to me of the phenomenal success our joint
> venture had already met with. Owing to this circumstance I
> have always reckoned that my cigar going out as it did cost me

about £1,500 . . . After such a result any sensible man would have given up smoking, but I am sorry to say I lacked the resolution to do so.

A few years later, Vizetelly would sell his share in the *Illustrated Times* and go to work for its hated rival the *Illustrated London News*, becoming its Paris correspondent, covering the Franco-Prussian War and staying throughout the subsequent siege of the French capital. He put his wine drinking to good use with pioneering books about sherry and champagne. Vizetelly also published a book entitled *Four Months among the Gold Finders in California* about the 1840s gold rush, without actually going to the trouble of visiting America. Later still, spotting a gap in the market, he became the publisher of English translations of the novels of Zola, which led to him being prosecuted and heavily fined for bringing such obscene literature into the country. He was incorrigible.

11

"As calmly as the
question of the
moon's rotation"

WILLIAM PALMER HAD NO SHORTAGE OF LEGAL ADVICE BEFORE HIS TRIAL.
His brother George was a solicitor, but his representation was coordinated by the energetic and assiduous young solicitor John
Smith from Birmingham. The court-room drawing of Smith shows a
plump, smiling, youngish man with crinkly hair – Vizetelly in his memoirs
describes him with just a touch of metropolitan condescension as "a provincial buck with hair in ringlets and gilt buttons to his waistcoat" – but he
was certainly not foppish or in any way indolent in his approach to the case.
He had already built up a large practice in Birmingham and had a reputation for taking immense and tenacious trouble on his clients' behalf.
Fletcher, writing in 1925, says churlishly: "he had defended many prisoners
for all sorts of offences and restored to society some who had better have
been under lock and key." The National Archives contain numerous polite
letters from him requesting access to documents and permission to visit his
client in prison. His assiduousness clearly annoyed Taylor, who would be
the chief witness for the Crown. Indeed, Smith's cross-examination of Taylor at the inquests still rankled with the pathologist several months later, as
on 26 March 1856 he wrote privately to H. R. Reynolds, the Treasury solicitor coordinating the prosecution, describing the solicitor as "an impudent
fellow" who had cross-examined him for three hours – which was a gross
exaggeration. He was equally peeved to be asked by Smith to supply a copy
of his witness statement to show his evidence for poisoning. This was an
earlier letter to Reynolds on 5 March:

Mr John Smith's request that I would furnish him <u>now</u> with the substance of the evidence which I propose to give hereafter at the trial is not only unreasonable but unprecedented. I have been more than 20 years engaged in medico-legal practice and this is the first time that a request for information with a view to dress up a cross-examination has been made to me ... in a case of alleged murder, Mr Smith might as reasonably ask for a copy of the intended address of the Attorney General in order that his counsel for the defence may be fully prepared to meet the case set up for prosecution. If Mr Smith has a just case to defend he has no reason to fear my opinions or chemical accuracy, if he has an unjust one he must bear the consequences.

Smith was not cowed in the least. He just kept asking. Taylor repeatedly declined to show the defence his evidence and was criticised for his secretiveness by the *Lancet*. It was not alone in thinking that such defensiveness was counterproductive and unhelpful to scientific progress and the development of consensus, creating professional rivalry and undermining the quest for truth. Eventually, under pressure from Sir Alexander Cockburn, leading the prosecution, he seems to have made the disclosure. In a book written after the trial, he stated: "Although contrary to usual practice, but in accordance with the wish of the Attorney General, who was desirous of giving every possible advantage to those who were defending William Palmer, Dr Rees and I furnished the prisoner's solicitor the subjoined statement regarding the processes pursued by us for the detection of strychnine and antimony in the body of Cook." He clearly did so reluctantly however, adding:

[Palmer's] counsel, legal and chemical ... had full opportunity of anticipating the statements of the witnesses for the prosecution and framing their questions for cross-examination accordingly. There can, I conceive, be no objection to this course when scientific questions are likely to be dealt with *bona fide* and with a view to public justice ... I need hardly observe however to those who are acquainted with the special pleading which may be brought to bear on scientific questions to the confusion of the Court and jury that such a practice must be in the end detrimental to the course of justice.

It is easily possible to detect a certain chippiness on the part of Taylor, a sea captain's son from Kent, originally apprenticed to a doctor in Maidstone, who rose by his own diligence to be appointed a professor at Guy's Hospital at the age of twenty-five. By 1856 his expertise in toxicology was widely acknowledged and he had been giving evidence in criminal trials for more than twenty years. There was an aura of infallibility about him – one that he seems to have been happy to cultivate.

Taylor was not the only pioneering forensic toxicologist, specialising in medical jurisprudence, working in Britain in the 1850s. All four of the most eminent – Taylor, Robert Christison of Edinburgh, William Herapath of Bristol and Henry Letheby of London – appeared at Palmer's trial, the last two for the defence. The scientists were crucial to the case and central to the trial: of fifty-four witnesses called by the prosecution, seventeen were medical men, as were sixteen of the twenty-three produced by the defence. But Taylor was probably the best known by reputation. He had an acute understanding of how expert evidence ought to be given in court. He was, his *Dictionary of National Biography* entry states, "a man of commanding stature, calm and earnest in his manner", and he was regarded as discreet and astute. Taylor maintained to his students at Guy's Hospital that chemical analysis could provide only a degree of probability in criminal cases and was never incontrovertible and that standards of legal and toxicological proof were different. It was a dictum that failed to inform his conduct in the Palmer case, where his opinion of what he believed must have happened far exceeded any proof of poisoning that he could offer. Nevertheless, the indignation powering Taylor's rapid, black ink scrawl above a flamboyant and wayward signature in his correspondence about the case is palpable. He had long since made up his mind that Palmer was a mass-murderer and his regular letters to the Treasury solicitors show that he enthusiastically threw himself into the prosecution case, suggesting witnesses who would be supportive and deriding evidence to the contrary. If his letter published in the *Lancet* in February had nearly given the game away, there was no disguising his view in another private letter to the prosecution lawyers, written from his home at 15 St James's Terrace, Regent's Park, on 9 May, the week before the trial. In it he advised them to call Alexander Tweedie, a physician at the Fever Hospital, if they needed evidence on prescribing tartar emetic to patients, as they would do if Annie Palmer's death was referred to at the trial:

he has witnessed its effects in medicinal doses. I did not gather from him when I saw him this evening that he had <u>ever gone so far as to poison a patient</u> with small doses at intervals, but I think his experience will enable him to say that a person may as surely be killed by this treatment as by giving a large dose at once.

In the same letter, he is anxious that the prosecution should secure Christison's services in case the defence do so instead. Robert Christison, a tall, sonorous and commanding presence in court and in the lecture theatre, was the author of a standard work on poisons and professor of materia medica at Edinburgh University; he was almost as highly regarded as Taylor was in court and had better qualifications than he did, so there was always a possibility that the other side might recruit him. Taylor added: "There is some difference about Dr Christison's fees which may prevent him coming. If John Smith could secure Dr Christison's services for £500 he would pay it at once." A fortnight later, Christison appeared powerfully for the prosecution, though he certainly did not get such a huge fee: Taylor, always insistent on being paid appropriately for his work, was probably exaggerating.

Taylor's views on the case certainly had one effect: they ensured that the trial would be heard by the Lord Chief Justice himself. John, Lord Campbell was aged seventy-seven – the oldest Lord Chief Justice to hold the office – when the trial took place. He had been planning to retire, but stayed on when he realised the prominence of the case, even though he was no longer at the height of his powers. No one had ever doubted the old man's ambition. The son of an obscure Church of Scotland minister, he had been to St Andrews rather than Oxbridge and unsuccessfully tried to eliminate his Scottish accent after he came to London. In more than fifty years at the bar, he had exhibited diligence rather than flair. His *Times* obituary said of him that "his industry atoned for his want of genius" before going on to damn him with what sounds very much like faint praise: "his kindness of heart and liberality of sentiment reconciled men to the absence of refinement ... [there was] little that was attractive in his manner and nothing that was graceful ... abundance of anecdote supplied the place of wit." A large, severe-looking man with heavy side-whiskers, Campbell was a workaholic who slept for only a couple of hours a night. Such reputation as he ever had rests largely on the lengthy group biographies he wrote of his fellow chief justices and lord chancellors in the gaps between serving the government and sitting in court – though perhaps he ought also to be remembered for reforms to the libel laws, helping to make truth and publication in the public interest defences against defamation.

The American author Harriet Beecher Stowe, who met Campbell on a tour of England, was rather impressed, describing him as a "man of most dignified and imposing appearance. Tall with a large frame, a fine forehead, and strongly marked features." The young barrister James Fitzjames Stephen, meanwhile, who sat through the Palmer trial, was "overpowered with admiration at his appearance. He was thick set as a navvy and hard as nails, still full of vigour at the age of 76."[2] Less impressed, an early biographer wrote that his "selfishness, desperate eagerness to push to the front and perpetual air of calculation . . . leave an unpleasant taste behind", while Walter Bagehot noted that: "He has a steady, comprehensive, abstract, distinct consistency, which elaborates a formula and adheres to a formula; and it is this which has raised him from a plain – a very plain – Scotch lawyer to be Chief Justice of England." His judicial eminence was also due to his conservative Whiggishness as a loyal and unrebellious party member: Daniel O'Connell, the Irish nationalist, described him as "a tool of the base and bloody Whigs". Twenty years earlier he had been MP for first Stafford and then Dudley, so presumably he knew the Rugeley area at least a little – and he was determined to convict Palmer. During the trial he addressed him with an icy politeness and ordered that he should be "accommodated with a chair" – allowed to sit down. "Ah," muttered one of the ushers on hearing this, "He means to hang him." Vizetelly wrote in his memoirs: "No more damaging summing up ever proceeded from a judge's lips. He was minutely careful over the evidence, persisting in taking every word of it down and while so engaged constantly pulled up the witnesses with his impatient 'Stop now! Stop, stop!'"

Two other judges sat with Campbell for the trial, although he does not seem to have consulted them much. One was Baron Alderson, the man who had presided over the Running Rein Derby-fixing trial a decade earlier, the other the unimaginatively named Justice Cresswell Cresswell. Sir Edward Alderson, who had been a brilliant scholar at Cambridge many years before, was a firm conservative and one of those judges who thinks that his position on the bench gives licence for the sort of jokes that people feel obliged to

---

[2] Stephen underestimated Campbell's age by a year.

laugh at. His *Dictionary of National Biography* entry notes that "he was later remembered, with varying degrees of enthusiasm, as a clever, analytical, and forthright judge . . . quick to take a view of a case, and exceedingly hard to talk out of it. He was popular with the bar and juries, if not always with his colleagues, not least because of his relentless jocularity, on the bench and off." Alderson had few such opportunities in the Palmer case, but he may have given the defence some grounds for hope in being previously critical of the wide application of the death penalty – though he thought its use ought to be restricted rather than banned. A few months after the trial, he died of a stroke brought on by shock on learning of the death of his son, whereupon his obituarist in *The Times* noted that he had:

> a careful, learned and conscientious mind, naturally inclined to take a rather hard and dry view of the question at issue. His intercourse with members of the Bar was uniformly courteous and friendly and his good humour and perhaps over-frequent jocoseness made him generally popular.

The third judge, Cresswell Cresswell, had had a dim academic record at Cambridge followed by a long, largely undistinguished career, presiding as a judge mainly over property cases. Described by the *Dictionary of National Biography* as tall, slim, pale and arrogant in bearing, a martinet who could treat counsel with contempt, he would come into his own two years after the Palmer case when he became the first judge appointed to the new divorce court and surprised everyone, given his past manner, by treating plaintiffs humanely and with sensitivity. A court-room drawing of him during the Palmer trial nevertheless shows a grim-faced, unsympathetic figure. His career, said *The Times* when he died in 1863, was "simply that of a hard-working lawyer, in his later years one of those who seem to love work for its own sake. He was what is called a strong judge, that is to say not only a learned one but a man who would have his own way. He was a . . . conscientious and successful public servant and his life has been useful. How few there are who die of whom so much as this can be said?" He never married.

Leading the prosecution team at the trial was Sir Alexander Cockburn, the attorney general and a man generally regarded as the most brilliant advocate of his day. A small man with a large head, bright, questing eyes, a

The three judges at Palmer's trial: Cresswell, a severe Lord Campbell and Alderson.

melodious voice and a ferrety manner, Cockburn was at the height of his powers, taking a leading role in defence or prosecution in many of the big cases of the period. He had successfully and adroitly defended McNaughton, the deranged man who shot Prime Minister Sir Robert Peel's secretary in 1843, and represented one of the cheats in the 1844 Derby scandal. He had a feline wit and was making £16,000 a year at the bar – nearly £1 million in modern terms – as his fees books at the Middle Temple library show. There was an incongruously racy side to him as well: the library also contains a two-volume romantic novel which he is thought to have penned in his twenties, when he was just beginning to make his way as a barrister. It peters out shortly after the French heroine exclaims: "'I was a timid and trembling girl, but the example of Auguste has taught me courage' . . . Her last wish was fulfilled – our happiness was perfect and uninterrupted – this is the true history of my youth – my tale is done!" Perhaps it was at this point that his legal career began to pick up, for he certainly took his literary one no further. Actually, his personal life was quite as vivid as his heroine's: Cockburn never married, but fathered two illegitimate children, for whom he provided. He knew what it was to be short of money too: on one occasion he escaped bailiffs coming to arrest him by jumping out of the robing-room window at Exeter Castle. It was this private lifestyle that would lead Queen Victoria to deny him a peerage in 1864 on the grounds of his "notoriously bad moral character". This does not seem to have worried Cockburn unduly: he was a lawyer to be feared and the Palmer case would show him at his forensic best. It would also be his swansong as an advocate, as within months he would be appointed Chief Justice of the Common Pleas and later, despite the queen, he would himself become Lord Chief Justice.

By Cockburn's side in the Palmer case was "the somewhat dissipated looking" Edwin James QC, a barrister whose financial problems would soon become as extreme as William Palmer's. Once an actor, his annual income of £6,000 was nowhere near enough to meet his debts, which within a few years would exceed £100,000. In 1861 he was caught borrowing money from the plaintiff in a case in which he was representing the defendant and disbarred, but he then fled to America and started practising as a lawyer there. The third member of the team was Serjeant Huddlestone, a barrister who switched sides during the course of the Palmer case: he had been one of those who represented Palmer in the High Court pre-trial prejudice hearing and Sarah Palmer in the litigation brought by the moneylender Padwick; he had also represented Samuel Cheshire when he was charged with opening the mail. But now he was on the Crown's team, which was completed by two older Treasury prosecutors, Sir William Bodkin and William Welsby.

Palmer's defence was not helped by the defection of Huddlestone, and Smith had some difficulty finding a barrister who would represent him. The first choice, Sir Fitzroy Kelly, was one of the most successful and incisive members of the bar – perhaps the only man who could have rivalled Cockburn – but he was also the most expensive and his demand for 1,000 guineas was beyond the defence's means. The second choice, Serjeant Wilkins, who had studied medicine and so might have been ideal and formidable, represented Sarah Palmer during the Padwick case, but three weeks before the Old Bailey trial he disappeared from the scene. The official reason was that he was unwell, the unofficial one that he had had to flee to France to avoid his creditors. The choice to replace him eventually fell on Serjeant William Shee, a large, blustering Irish barrister with a thick shock of white hair, who was not helped by coming to the case late, nor, probably, by his accent and Catholic background. Shee was not only an Irish MP but also the cousin of Nicholas Wiseman, who was

The Prosecuting barristers at Palmer's trial in May 1856. Sir Alexander Cockburn, the attorney general, a devastating prosecutor, is bottom left, Edwin James, whose financial problems would soon force him to flee to the US is bottom right, Serjeant Huddlestone is top left.

the first Cardinal Archbishop of Westminster since the Reformation but had scarcely endeared himself to the public by calling for the reconversion of England as soon as he took up his post a few years earlier. As the member for Kilkenny, the barrister had struggled largely unsuccessfully to improve the rights of Irish tenants and for the disestablishment of the Irish Anglican Church, to give parity of status to the Catholic hierarchy – something that would eventually be achieved but not until long after he himself had been rejected by the electors. Both were extremely sensitive political issues on each side of the Irish Sea. Among his colleagues at the bar Shee was well liked, a genial if diffident figure. He was a shambling character and, with a difficult case to defend and not much by the way of forensic skills, no match for Cockburn. Henry Vizetelly, watching from the public gallery, was not impressed and forty years later was still scathing about Shee's performance in his memoirs:

> snuffy, slovenly-looking Serjeant Shee . . . the befogged advocate blundered from the very outset over the names of people and places and commonly misstated dates. Once, when referring to

Dr Taylor and tetanus, he transposed the words and spoke of Dr Tetanus and Taylor; and . . . in a lengthy argument, intended to demonstrate that Palmer had no motive for taking Cook's life, he misplaced the names of culprit and victim throughout and only discovered his blunder while deducing his conclusions at the close . . . his bombastic declamations, accompanied by heavy thumps on his desk and his general forced melodramatic action betokened rather the vulgar ranter than the calm sagacious advocate. Every now and then he paused to wipe his perspiring forehead with the result that he invariably lost the thread of his argument and rarely succeeded in recovering it. His efforts too to be pathetic in his allusions to the trembling anxiety of Palmer's aged mother, to his sister sinking under the most dreadful suspense and to the brave and gallant brother striving against all obstacles to save his unhappy relative from an awful doom, fell completely flat on listeners in the last stage of weariness.

Shee himself confessed to his son George that he had never made a speech with less preparation, and if so, it was probably because he had been recruited to the defence team so late. It evidently showed as he attempted to make up with bluster what he lacked in incisiveness. At the conclusion of the case the *Illustrated Times* would compare and contrast Cockburn's Scottish style – "lucid, logical and strong" – with Shee's representation of the Irish: "bold, plausible and glowing". Shee seems somehow older than Cockburn, yet he was actually two years younger. His legal career was nowhere near as stellar, though he would eventually become a judge.

Shee's second was William Grove QC, a Welshman and primarily a scientist, who was presumably brought in to apply scientific forensics to the medical evidence, but whose expertise and interest lay chiefly in the development of electric batteries: first the nitric acid battery and then a gas battery which was the forerunner of the modern fuel cell. Naturally, these did not make him any money, which was why he had to devote his time to legal practice. There were those – Vizetelly among them – who believed that, had Shee allowed Grove more scope, his more forensic manner might just have raised more doubts about Palmer's guilt than his leader's bombast.

The third member of the defence team was another unbalanced char-

Palmer's defence team. The hapless Serjeant Shee is bottom left, the unbalanced Edward Kenealy is top right.

acter, the Irish barrister Edward Kenealy, whose chequered career had already included a spell in prison for harshly chastising his illegitimate son. It would go on through a string of high-profile cases until his wild accusations and vehement bluster eventually got him disbarred following the long-running Tichborne Claimant case in the 1870s. In that he represented a drunken Australian butcher who had come to England claiming to be the lost heir to an aristocratic fortune. Kenealy's passion and emotional instability – which may have been the result of undiagnosed incipient diabetes – threw him then against none other than Cockburn himself, who was the judge in the Tichborne case, but the men had originally been friends and Cockburn was godfather to Kenealy's son. In the defence of Palmer, there are perhaps early intimations of Kenealy's private furies. A lengthy pamphlet published after the verdict, purportedly written by the Rev. Thomas Palmer, attacks the judges' conduct of the case in a very similar style to the barrister's blustering manner. If it was intended to overturn the outcome, comparing Chief Justice Campbell to Judge Jeffreys of the Bloody Assizes and describing the trial as "the late mockery at the Old Bailey" may not have been the best way to do it – and Thomas Palmer himself later disowned it.

If Kenealy was indeed the pamphlet's anonymous author – as Campbell clearly suspected – it was a remarkable piece of advocacy, for the barrister himself later made clear in his memoirs that he had always fully believed Palmer was guilty and found him distasteful. The pen portrait of his client is very vivid and the closest any of those professionally involved in the trial came to a description of the man in the dock. Kenealy said his suspicions were first aroused by the fact that Palmer would not look him in the eye when they spoke:

> [He] quickly dropped his lids as though he feared lest I might read there something he wished to conceal. Palmer was one of those who could not meet my gaze: he invariably drooped and seemed uncomfortable. Otherwise he displayed the greatest composure on every occasion. His manners were courteous, bland and sympathetic. Yet there was something in their very smoothness which reminded me of some creeping reptile, not repulsive, on the contrary attractive, but suggestive of the gliding, stealthy movements of a snake. He entered the room with a gentle tread, making no sound, like a man walking on thick carpet. Gliding forward, he laid in one's grasp a soft, small hand which seemed to slip from the touch so soon as taken. His voice was low, unctuous, almost tender. One can picture this gentle, quiet man inviting his victim in the most soothing tones to drink the fatal draught . . .

What Kenealy did not believe, however, was that Palmer received a fair trial.

These, then, were the lawyers who would dispute the case: men from very different backgrounds, socially and educationally. Most were neither public school nor Oxbridge men, as it happened; some were clinging uncertainly to respectability, others teetering on the edge of financial disaster; some were eminent in their profession and bound for the judiciary and high office, others heading for disgrace, humiliation and disbarment; some were forensic in their skills, others overwrought and unbalanced in their passion; some were jocular or witty, others dull. And all were about to wrangle for a man's life: whether or not he dangled in a few weeks' time at the end of a rope depended entirely on their skill, wit and acuity. Certainly no lawyers before that time can ever have been watched more intently or by a wider international audience. The stakes, as Palmer might have said, could not have been higher, either for them or for their client.

As far as the prosecution was concerned, the chief weakness in their case was that it was entirely circumstantial in the absence of any traces of poison in Cook's body. No one had actually seen Palmer administer poison to Cook, the death had been certified by two doctors, and the line of proof linking Palmer directly to Cook's money was potentially problematical. Nor was it only the absence of strychnine that was awkward, but the fact that it was still an unfamiliar poison, discovered only in the previous thirty years, and its effects on humans had only been seen in a very few instances, following accidents. No one had ever been convicted of using it to kill before; the symptoms it produced were similar to the relatively common tetanus (and it killed by suffocation in much the same way); and the best tests for it were still debated: did it stay in the organs like a metallic poison such as arsenic, or – as the product of a vegetable, the nux vomica – was it easily absorbed and lost to the body? Medical men were using strychnine in minute doses as a treatment for paralysis, though the dangers were only too apparent. Nevertheless, the case against Palmer was still formidable, given the evidence of his financial difficulties, the closeness of his relationship with Cook, his presence throughout his illness and his behaviour following his death. All this and the previous suspicious deaths had been helpfully spelled out in the press before the trial. There was also a string of witnesses hostile to Palmer and, in Alfred Swaine Taylor, a most impressive professional pathologist to bear down on the scientific evidence for Cook's symptoms and cause of death.

The defence had these obstacles to overcome, but they were not necessarily insurmountable if they could pay for and produce pathologists as eminent as Taylor to argue that Cook's death could have been caused by something else – his general debility, for instance, or an undiagnosed natural disease with similar symptoms such as tetanus; if they could create a credible alibi and prove that Palmer had not bought poison; or if they could show that his financial problems were not as grave as alleged or could have been overcome. There were also gaps in the evidence of some of the prosecution witnesses. By such means, they would perhaps be able to show unprejudiced minds that murder could not be proved.

The defence was, however labouring not only under the difficulty of a late-recruited team, but also under procedural problems inherent to the defence in all contemporary criminal trials. Remarkable as it seems now, professional legal defence in trials was still a comparatively recent innovation, dating back only to the Prisoners' Counsel Act of 1836, and in these circumstances tactics and strategies were still being developed in the face of frequently hostile judges who saw little need for prosecution evidence to be challenged. Palmer's family could afford to pay for senior barristers and so his trial was much more protracted and detailed than it would have been had he been from an impoverished or working-class background. Much was weighted against defence teams, including the need to pay the expenses of all witnesses they called. And there were deeper questions too. The nature of evidence itself – how it should be presented and what part it should play in the proof of guilt or innocence – was still contested. If a killing could be established, did the burden of proof shift from a presumption of innocence to a presumption of guilt unless the defence could prove otherwise? What evidence was admissible? And, of particular relevance in Palmer's trial, was a scientific deduction the same as a legal proof: Taylor thought not, except seemingly in the poisoner's case.

In a trial such as Palmer's, in the 1850s, the accused was not allowed to give evidence on oath and so most – like Palmer – did not speak. This only changed following the Criminal Evidence Act of 1898. Though barristers were, and are, aware that defendants can condemn themselves by what they say in the witness box as easily as they can prove their innocence, it meant that the accused could be sent to the gallows without ever speaking a word in their own defence. An educated, articulate man such as Palmer might have been better able to defend himself than most, but like many after him he might well have proved shifty and unreliable in the face of the circumstantial evidence against him. His charm, if he could summon any, would not have availed him under terrier-like cross-examination by Sir Alexander Cockburn.

More crucial were the limitations imposed on the defence. After the closure of the prosecution case, Serjeant Shee was given the opportunity to outline the case on Palmer's behalf and to present witness evidence. But the prosecution was given the last word in a closing speech, so Cockburn had the opportunity to make two presentations to the jury, at the beginning and end of the case, Shee only one. Then, following the prosecution's closing speech, the case was summed up by the presiding judge, in this case Lord Chief Justice Campbell, who spoke for a day and a half, largely against Palmer, before sending the jury out. This imbalance – of one speech for the defence, two for the prosecution – was only corrected a decade later with the passage of the Criminal Procedure Act (the so-called Denman's Act) of 1865, which allowed the defence counsel to rebut evidence and summarise their client's case. In Palmer's trial, however, the defence case occupied less than three days of a twelve-day trial and the jurors went out having listened to the case for the prosecution for most of the last three days. From their verdict, moreover, there was no appeal – the Criminal Appeals Act was another half-century away.

Now, in early May 1856, defence and prosecution teams were in place for what was already being regarded as the trial of the century. As *The Times* said later:

> Strangers who came to London that year found everybody talk-
> ing of the Rugeley murders. The crimes excited a terrible interest
> at every fireside in the land and the principles of circumstantial
> evidence by which the verdict was decided were discussed in so-
> ciety of every rank of intellectual qualification for the task.

Was Palmer one of the new, calculating *scientific* murderers, using his medical skills perversely and wickedly to kill his nearest and dearest for personal gain? Or was he the hapless victim of circumstance and tragic misfortune? Everyone had a view. And the next fortnight would tell.

12

"Extraordinary disclosures of a most frightful character"

THE TRIAL OF WILLIAM PALMER AT THE OLD BAILEY IN LONDON FINALLY got underway on Wednesday 14 May 1856, nearly five months after his arrest: an unusually long time to wait in those days. The Central Criminal Court in the 1850s was a large Georgian room, designed by George Dance the Younger eighty years earlier, with high windows and a deep well in the centre where the lawyers sat in rows at right angles to both the dock and the judges. High above them to one side was the dock for the prisoner and higher still on the other was the judges' bench, with a row of desks for them and, further along, for the High Sheriff of the City, the aldermen and various other notables – of whom there would be many, crowding to see the trial.

Dance's building, connected to Newgate prison, was a grim and daunting place and was replaced early in the twentieth century when the prison was finally removed and the court rebuilt. The "new" court has much the same layout as the old: its judges still have desks and large armchairs and still sit under the sword of justice and the royal coat of arms, gazing across the void where the barristers sit, facing them now, to the wretched prisoner in the distance. It has seen many famous trials and notorious murderers: Crippen and his mistress Ethel Le Neve stood here in 1910; Seddon, the Edwardian poisoner, made a masonic sign to the judge at his trial hoping unsuccessfully to stave off his punishment; Ruth Ellis, the last woman to be hanged, and the Kray twins, who would have been had their crimes occurred a few years earlier. They and many others have stood in the dock, as William Palmer did before them. The current court has a lower ceiling than the old one, so it feels somewhat more intimate. These days laptops are on the desks, rather than pens and inkwells, and microphones amplify what is said – an advantage over Palmer's day when lawyers and journalists struggled to decipher what the Lord Chief Justice muttered through his Scottish burr. Nothing quite brings back the atmosphere like the scribbled notes of the barristers and solicitors, gathered up with the witness statements and lawyers' letters at the end of the proceedings and still in the bundles in the National Archives – inconsequential, hasty messages in faded sepia ink: "To the Under-Sheriff and Officers: It is really peremptorily necessary that the medical <u>witnesses</u> should <u>be in court Immediately</u>. John Greenwood for Treasury." Anyone who bemoans the decline in penmanship in modern life has not tried to decipher the scribbles on some of these documents.

Newgate prison and the Central Criminal Court were enough to induce dread in anyone. The walls were thick and high, the stench of unwashed bodies and inadequate sanitation must have been nauseous, and the reek of fear and panic strong. Many of those incarcerated would step outside again only to be hanged on the scaffold wheeled out into the Old Bailey thoroughfare just beyond the door for the occasion. In England and Wales in the 1850s there was on average one public execution a month, and between a quarter and a third of the annual tally took place outside Newgate prison. The young Charles Dickens caught the atmosphere in a piece called *Criminal Courts*, which he had written as a young reporter twenty years earlier, in 1834, for the *Morning Chronicle* and which was subsequently printed in his first book, *Sketches by Boz*:

> How dreadful its rough heavy walls and low massive doors . . . the latter looking as if they were made for the express purpose of letting people in and never letting them out again . . . we never pass the building without something of a shudder.
>
> Curiosity has occasionally led us into both courts at the Old Bailey. Nothing is so likely to strike the person who enters them for the first time as the calm indifference with which the proceedings are conducted; every trial seems a mere matter of business. There is a great deal of form, but no compassion; considerable interest but no sympathy. Take the Old Court for example. There sit the Judges with

whose great dignity everybody is acquainted . . . then there is the Lord
Mayor, looking as cool as a Lord Mayor can look with an immense
bouquet before him and habited in all the splendour of his office.
Then there are the Sheriffs, who are almost as dignified as the Lord
Mayor himself, and the Barristers, who are quite dignified enough in
their own opinion, and the spectators, who having paid for their
admission, look upon the whole scene as if it were got up especially
for their amusement. Look upon the whole group in the body of the
Court – some wholly engrossed in the morning papers, others care-
lessly conversing in low whispers and others again quietly dozing
away an hour – and you can scarcely believe that the result of the trial
is a matter of life or death to one wretched being present.

In this sense only, Palmer was lucky: many prisoners arraigned for murder
had only the briefest of trials. They were getting longer now that they could be
represented by counsel, but a trial could still be over in minutes or hours even
for capital crimes. For lesser crimes it was estimated that the average trial time
was under ten minutes, sometimes as little as three. Business was dispatched
with little opportunity for consideration or reflection, with jurors scarcely bothering to leave the box to decide their verdict. In lasting twelve days, Palmer's
trial was both exceptional and exhaustive, much more like a modern trial,
though with longer sitting hours (running into the early evening), shorter
breaks – less than half an hour for lunch – and hearings on two successive Saturdays while the trial lasted. It would be a very protracted and tense experience.
Henry Vizetelly, naturally, said he was present throughout the trial
and recorded more vividly than anyone else what it was like:

During the twelve days the Palmer trial lasted I was present on
every one of them at the Central Criminal Court and took notes
of the principal incidents. Admission was only to be obtained
by tickets issued by the sheriffs and, on the first day, when many
thought to secure entrance to the court by means of liberal tips
to the doorkeepers, the crush was tremendous. Of course these
Old Bailey janitors indulged in the stereotype inquiry as to "the
good of pushing," with the usual unsatisfactory result. Once inside the court, on glancing round, I saw a few early aldermen in

their great gold chains already installed on the bench and, looking as if they had been deprived of half their accustomed sleep,
chatting languidly with the portly, rose-gilled ordinary [chap-
lain] of Newgate (recognisable by his clerical band and gown),
though it was fully a week before he was likely to be called upon
to intone "Amen!" to the sentence pronounced by the lord chief
justice after donning the ominous black cap.

The Times reported:

Notwithstanding the interval which has elapsed since this extraordinary case was first brought under the notice of the public,
the intense interest and excitement which it then occasioned
seemed in no degree to have abated. Indeed, if the applications
for admission to the court which were made so soon as the trial
was appointed and the eager endeavours of large crowds to gain
an entrance may be regarded as a criterion of the public anxiety
upon the progress and issue of the trial, the interest would seem
to have augmented rather than diminished. At a very early hour
every entrance to the court was besieged by persons of respectable
appearance, who were favoured with cards giving them a right
of entrance. Without such cards no admittance could on any pre-
tence be obtained and even the fortunate holders of them found
that they had many difficulties to overcome and many stern janitors to encounter before an entrance to the much-coveted
precincts could be obtained . . . although there may be individual
cases of complaint as there always will be when delicate and
important functions have to be performed with firmness it is but
justice to testify to the general completeness and propriety of the
regulations which the Sheriffs had laid down.

Of course, not everyone had to endure such pushing and shoving to get into
the court. Vizetelly, like all the other court journalists, took careful note of
the celebrities present. At times the first paragraphs of their reports each
day read almost like gossip columns about who was spotted in attendance.
On the first day notables included the Tory party leader and former prime

minister the Earl of Derby, the former Whig minister Earl Grey, Lord Lucan, the disastrous cavalry commander now back from the Crimean War, and Prince Edward of Saxe-Weimar. Vizetelly wrote:

> Earl Grey limped into the court and at once hid himself behind an open sheet of *The Times* newspaper and Lord Derby, attracted I suppose by the sporting elements in the case, soon afterwards joined him. Both these peers were pretty regular attendants throughout the trial and occasionally other magnates, such as the Dukes of Cambridge and Wellington – not the great Arthur, but his son – the Earl of Albemarle and General Peel kept them company. One of the under-sheriffs, a dapper little man in lace frills and ruffles, strutted about with his sword at his side, nervously awaiting the arrival of the judges . . . Suddenly everyone rose to his feet as the judges sailed in like three staid dowagers, each adorned with a handsome bouquet, as though the affair were some fete. Lord Campbell at once installed himself in the centre seat, while Creswell dropped into the seat on his right hand and Alderson into that on his left.

This was at 10 a.m. Vizetelly continued:

> The moment the three judges had taken their places, the usher shouted "Silence!" and the case of William Palmer being called on, the governor of Newgate was seen to pop up from the stairs communicating between the cells and the dock, followed by a fair-complexioned, sandy-haired, good-natured looking individual of medium height and stoutish build, clad in a glossy black surtout, light grey trousers and carefully fitting gloves and with nothing particularly striking about him, save a somewhat thickish neck. This gentlemanly personage was the Rugeley apothecary, accused of plundering his intimate friend.

The *Manchester Guardian*, less politely, described him on the day as having grown exceedingly stout since his committal to prison. Perhaps he could have done with a longer hunger strike.

He pleaded, said *The Times*, "in a clear, low, but perfectly audible and distinct tone, 'Not Guilty' . . . His manner was remarkably calm and collected throughout the whole of the day. He was altogether devoid of bravado, but was respectful and attentive and was calculated to create a favourable impression." The paper that day would devote three solid pages of unrelieved type to the trial of the man described in the court calendar as William Palmer, thirty-one, "surgeon of superior degree of instruction".[3] The *Manchester Guardian*'s coverage was only slightly briefer. The public interest in their reports was phenomenal: George Fletcher says in his book about Palmer that as a nine-year-old boy living in Birmingham in 1856 he would be sent by his father every day to New Street Station to buy a copy of *The Times* when the papers arrived from London and would often have to pay three or four shillings – the cover price was fourpence – to secure a copy.

Some of the papers even reported the names and at least some of the addresses and professions of what *The Times* described as a most respectable jury. It was also socially and professionally a most diverse one: William Mavor, the foreman, was a veterinary surgeon of Grosvenor Square; Thomas Knight, baker, Leytonstone; William Newman, a bootmaker from Pimlico; George Oakeshott, a confectioner from West Ham; Charles Bate, a brewer of Surrey; William Ecclestone, a grocer from West Ham; John Over, a grocer of Pimlico; William Nash, Bond Street; George Miller, Duke Street; William Fletcher; Samuel Mullin; and Richard Dumbrell. These were men who deemed themselves unprejudiced by the pre-trial publicity, though one potential juror named Mason declared himself so decided that he did not feel competent to act and was summarily dismissed by Campbell. The jury would be kept together incommunicado for the next week and a half. Every evening they were taken under escort to the London Coffee House, where they had their meals, slept and washed together in a large dormitory, with a valet in attendance to look after them. It was, quite possibly, the nearest some of them came in their entire lives to mixing intimately with members of other classes, occupations and locations. In the mornings, before the day's hearings, they

---

[3] A letter from W. Foster White of St Bartholomew's Hospital to the prosecution a fortnight before had declined to confirm this, pointing out that it was the Royal College, not the hospital, that awarded qualifications: "There is no record at this hospital concerning William Palmer's qualifications who, I should say, was <u>simply a student</u> here." It sounds as if the hospital was trying to distance itself as far and fast as possible from its alumnus.

were allowed to walk – under supervision – in the gardens of the Middle Temple, and in the short lunch breaks at court they could walk, again under surveillance, in the prison yard. On the Sundays during the trial, they were escorted to church and then were given an excursion to Epping Forest. Such brief breathers were necessary, after being shut up in stuffy rooms all day: "they walked alone of a morning, weather permitting," the *Illustrated Times* reported afterwards, "tasting a little of the outer world and (what was much more important considering the asphyxiation of their lot) a little sweet, good air and calm." They served on the jury, without payment or recompense for their lost earnings. For some this would be a real hardship.

Now the trial was underway and Cockburn was on his feet to outline the case against Palmer. He proceeded, said *The Times*, amid breathless silence in the court. The attorney general spoke, without referring to notes, for four hours, while Palmer stood all the time, listening intently and occasionally writing comments to his solicitor Smith. This was the first time that Palmer and his defence team heard in precise detail the case against him. Slowly, methodically and forensically, Cockburn outlined the case, starting with a warning:

> The peculiar circumstances of this case have given it a profound and painful interest throughout the whole country. There is scarcely a man perhaps who has not come to some conclusion on the issue which you are now to decide . . . I feel it incumbent on me to warn you not to allow any preconceived opinion to operate on your judgement this day.

Then he came to the nub:

> The case which, on the part of the prosecution, I have to urge against Palmer is this – that, being in desperate circumstances, with ruin, disgrace and punishment staring him in the face, which could only be averted by means of money, he took advantage of his intimacy with Cook, when Cook had become the winner of a considerable sum, to destroy him, in order to obtain possession of his money.

Cockburn outlined Palmer's dealings with "a person named Padwick", "a gentleman named Pratt, a solicitor" and "Mr Wright, a solicitor of Birmingham".

Then he went through the attempt to get George Bates's life insured and on to Cook's health: "a young man . . . slightly disposed to a pulmonary complaint . . . in all other respects hale and hearty" except for one or two slight eruptions in his throat, for which he had been taking mercury "having mistaken the character of the complaint". Perhaps the jury understood the delicacy of this description. Next, Cockburn outlined the events at Shrewsbury races and the fact that once Cook arrived in Rugeley, he had constantly received "things" from Palmer, including antimony: "it was not that however of which this man died. The charge is that having been prepared by antimony, he was killed by strychnine, a subtle and fatal poison . . . a half or a quarter of a grain will destroy life – you may imagine therefore how minute is the dose." Then, carefully, the attorney general described the symptoms "known to medical men under the term of tetanus" – which was not correct as strychnine does not cause tetanus but suffocating spasms. Cockburn anticipated the defence case: "an attempt will be made to confound those different classes of disease and it will be necessary therefore for the jury to watch with great minuteness the medical evidence upon this point." With tetanus the paroxysms continued without intermission, but with strychnine the convulsions might subside for a time. Most importantly, tetanus took hours and days to develop while strychnine could kill in minutes: "the paroxysms commence with all their power at the very first and terminate after a few short minutes of fearful agony and struggles in the dissolution of the victim." Palmer would know this as a medical man, he added, and he had a book of medical notes in his handwriting to prove it.

Cockburn moved on to Palmer's Monday visit to London. Why had he chosen Herring as the intermediary to settle up at Tattersall's, not Cook's normal contact Ishmael Fisher? Then: "beyond all controversy, Palmer did not hesitate to apply Cook's money to the payment of his own debts." That evening Palmer had returned to Rugeley and bought three grains of strychnine at Salt's. Meanwhile, Dr Bamford had himself also prescribed pills. "There is no doubt that Cook took pills on Monday night. Whether he took the pills prepared for him by Dr Bamford . . . or whether Palmer substituted some of his own concoction consisting in same measure in strychnine, I must leave for the jury to determine." That night Cook suffered convulsions before becoming calm. On the next day, Tuesday, Palmer had gone to the chemist Hawkins – a druggist with whom he did not normally deal – and had asked his assistant Charles Roberts for two drachms of prussic acid.

While he was there, Newton, the assistant to Mr Salt, from whom Palmer had obtained the strychnine the night before, came in. Palmer had hustled him outside, talking to him on a matter of "the smallest possible importance", until Newton was distracted by another passer-by and Palmer had gone back into the shop and asked for six grains of strychnine in addition to the prussic acid. After he had gone, Newton went in and asked "out of passing curiosity" what Palmer had bought, and Roberts told him. This was damning stuff – a direct link between Palmer and the poison on the day of Cook's death – and Cockburn underlined it heavily. But he also had to explain why Newton had not mentioned that there had been two separate purchases of strychnine before and he neatly glossed over it:

> it was only as recently as yesterday that, with many expressions of contrition for not having been more explicit, he communicated to the Crown the fact that Palmer had also bought strychnine on Monday night. It is for you gentlemen to decide the amount of credit to be attached to this evidence, but you will bear in mind that whatever you may think of Mr Newton's testimony, that of Mr Roberts on whom there is no taint or shadow of suspicion is decisive with respect to the purchases which the prisoner made.

Cockburn now went through the rest of the day: how William Jones had been summoned from Lutterworth by a letter from Palmer stating that Cook was suffering from a severe bilious attack – "utterly untrue" – and how Jones had examined Cook's tongue and remarked: "That is not the tongue of a bilious fever." So on to the evening and Bamford's prescription of more pills which Palmer might have substituted: "half or three-quarters of an hour elapsed from the time he left Dr Bamford's surgery until he brought the pills to Cook." Cook had been forced to take the pills against his will, but had then settled down "easy and cheerful . . . no symptoms of the approach of disease, much less of death". Then the screams, the fetching of Palmer "and now ensued a terrible scene . . . then suffocation commenced . . . the tide of life was ebbing fast . . . gradually, all was over – he was dead." Scarcely was the breath out of Cook's body than Palmer began to think what was to be done. He was seen searching the pockets of Cook's coat and hunting under the pillows and bolsters: "what is very remarkable is that from that day to this nothing has been seen or heard either of the betting book or of any of the papers connected with Cook's money affairs." Palmer had subsequently attempted to get Cheshire, the postmaster, to attest to a paper supposedly bearing Cook's signature and acknowledging liability to £4,000 of Palmer's debts:

> Forty-eight hours after the death of the man whose name it bore, Palmer did not hesitate to ask Cheshire to be an attesting witness. Cheshire though, unfortunately for himself too much a slave of Palmer, peremptorily refused to comply; whereupon Palmer carelessly observed: "It is of no consequence; I dare say the signature will not be disputed, but it occurred to me that it would look more regular if it were attested."

Cockburn went through the arrival of Cook's stepfather Stephens and the dispute over the dead man's debts and the missing betting book; and then over Palmer's request to Bamford to certify the cause of death:

> The doctor expressed his surprise and observed: "Why, he was your patient." But Palmer importuned him and Bamford taking his pen filled up the certificate and entered the cause of death as apoplexy. Dr Bamford is upward of eighty and I hope that it is to some infirmity connected with his great age that this most unjustifiable act is to be attributed. He shall be produced in court and he will tell you that apoplexy has never been known to produce tetanus.

There was also the story of Palmer asking Newton how much strychnine was needed to kill a dog. Now, on to the post-mortem: Palmer had said Cook was full of disease and all kinds of complaints, but that was not so – the organs were healthy. Cockburn glossed over the chaos of the spilled stomach but outlined Palmer's attempt to remove the jar containing the organs and said he had insisted that it should not be sent away for analysis:

> if he had been an ignorant person not familiar with the course likely to be pursued by medical men under such circumstances, there might be some excuse for this; but it is for you to ask yourselves whether Palmer, himself a medical man . . . might not have relied

with confidence on the honour and integrity of the profession to which he belonged. You must say whether his anxiety to prevent the removal of the jars was not a sign of a guilty conscience.

The attorney general outlined the conversation with the postboy who was to take the organs to the London train: "They have no business to take them; one does not know what they may put in them. Can't you manage to upset the fly and break them? I will give you £10 and make it alright for you." Now came the inquest and Palmer's letters to the coroner, including the one telling him that Taylor had failed to find poison: "Why should he have done this if there had not been a feeling of uneasiness upon his mind?" Palmer was now flush with cash, whereas none of the £800 Cook had had when he left Shrewsbury had been found. Cockburn laboured the point with heavy irony:

> It may be that Cook who, whatever his faults, was a kind hearted creature, compassionating Palmer's condition and influenced by his representations, assisted him with money. That I do not know. I do not wish to strain the point too far, but one cannot imagine that Cook, who had no money but what he took with him to Shrewsbury, should have given Palmer everything and left himself destitute.

This was a man overwhelmed with pecuniary difficulties, Cockburn said, obliged to resort to the desperate expedient of forging acceptances, hoping to meet them by the proceeds of insurances, disappointed in that by the insurance company, under pressure from the gentleman moneylender, ruin staring him in the face: "You gentlemen must say whether he had not sufficient inducement to commit the crime." But there was more: he had tried to lay claim to more of Cook's money and to the horse Polestar. And then there was the fact that Cook had been mixed up in the attempt to insure Bates. And then there was the evidence of the paroxysms of Monday and the mortal agony of Tuesday: "I shall show that things were administered . . . by the hand of Palmer, by a degree of evidence almost amounting to certainty."

Now Cockburn tackled the prosecution's chief difficulty, that no poison had been found: "although the presence of strychnine may be detected by certain tests and although the indications of its presence lead irresistibly to the conclusion that it has been administered, the converse . . . does not hold. Sometimes it is found, at other times it is not. It depends upon circumstances." In Cook's case, it would have been a minute amount and would have been absorbed into his system, depending on how it had been administered. As a vegetable-based poison, the tests were "infinitely more delicate and difficult" than for a mineral poison. The attorney general was all too aware of the scientific controversy over whether it could be detected in such tiny amounts. He had a neat riposte:

> It would indeed be a fatal thing to sanction the notion that strychnine administered for the purpose of taking away life cannot afterwards be detected! Lamentable enough is the uncertainty of detection! Happily Providence, which has placed this fatal agent at the disposition of man has marked its effects with characteristic symptoms distinguishable from those of all other agents by the eye of science.

So what of the poison that *was* found in the body: antimony? Cook's symptoms earlier in the week were exactly what one would expect from that. Now Cockburn, maybe with an eye to a trial over Annie Palmer's death if this trial failed, speculated: "It may be that the original intention was to destroy him by means of antimony – it may be that the only object was to bring about an appearance of disease so as to account for death." All he had to prove now was that Cook was killed by strychnine, administered by the prisoner's hand – and he would do so, even if it must occupy a considerable portion of the jury's time. He ended with an elegant tribute to Serjeant Shee – "one of the most eloquent and able men who ever adorned the bar" – and the standard admonition: "If in the end all should fail in satisfying you of his guilt, in God's name let not the innocent suffer! If on the other hand the facts that will be presented to you should lead you to the conclusion that he is guilty, the best interests of society demand his conviction."

Cockburn's lengthy statement had created a formidably lucid case against Palmer. It was at this point that Campbell allowed Palmer a chair to sit down. The court was still not finished for the day. It was past two o'clock in the afternoon; there was a short break and then the court would hear the first five witnesses: those who had been present at Shrewsbury. Ishmael Fisher, the London

wine merchant, spoke about Cook telling the other guests at the Raven that the
brandy he had just drunk was burning his throat. It was at this point that Campbell made his first intervention. Edwin James, taking over after Cockburn's
exertions, had just asked Fisher: "Did he state what he was suffering from?"
Shee objected to the leading question but was overruled by the judge. Fisher
replied that Cook had thought "that damned Palmer had dosed him". In cross-
examination, Shee managed to get Fisher to say that he had not noticed anything peculiar when he smelled the brandy, but then Cockburn took over and
had a second go. Fisher told him that Cook had not had any great respect for
Palmer and that he himself had not tasted the brandy that night.

The last and most important witness of the first day was Elizabeth
Mills, the chambermaid at the Talbot Arms, now dressed in her best poke
bonnet. She was guided slowly through her evidence about what she had
seen during Cook's illness at the hotel by Edwin James, including the broth
that had been sent over for the patient, which she had tasted and which had
made her sick. She had watched Cook's convulsions:

> There was a sort of jumping or jerking about his head and neck
> and his body. Sometimes he would throw back his head upon
> the pillow and then raise it up again. He had much difficulty in
> breathing. The balls of his eyes projected very much. He
> screamed again three or four times . . . he was moving and
> knocking about all the time. Twice he called aloud: "murder!"

She had fetched Palmer from his house across the road on the night of the
death and seen the doctor afterwards going through the dead man's pockets.
She said she could remember letters on the mantelpiece and the betting
book going missing. Again, Campbell intervened at one point to overrule
Shee's objection to a leading question, saying: "It seems to me that the
examination is being conducted with perfect fairness." Her examination in
chief took the rest of the day and the court at last adjourned at 6.20 p.m.
after eight solid hours of the prosecution's case.

The following morning, Mills returned to the witness box for cross-
examination by Shee and a slightly different picture emerged of her evidence. She had left the inn a month after Cook's death and got work at
Dolly's Hotel in London instead, where she had been visited "not more than

**Elizabeth Mills, the chambermaid at the
Talbot Arms telling her story in court**

six or seven times" by William Stephens. "He only came to see whether I liked the place or whether I liked London." She admitted they had talked about his stepson's death, but insisted that he had "never given me a farthing of money or promised to get me a place". The last time had been just the previous week when Stephens had been accompanied by Hatton, the Staffordshire police chief, and James Gardner, the Rugeley attorney:

> Mr Cook's death may have been mentioned. Other things were talked of which I do not wish to mention . . . I cannot remember what they were. I do not know whether we talked about the trial. They did not ask me what I could prove. My deposition was not read over to me and Mr Stephens did not talk to me about the symptoms.

It sounds very much as though that is precisely what had happened. Elizabeth Mills had read about other strychnine cases in the papers. She had not mentioned being made sick by the broth before because it had not occurred to her: "I did not at the time think it was the broth that caused the sickness."

She had not previously mentioned that Palmer had given Cook pills, nor that Cook had beaten the bedclothes, nor that he had called out "Murder!"; nor had she spoken before about the food he had been given, or about him snapping at the spoon. None of this had come up because she had not been asked: "I should have answered all those questions if they had been put to me . . . I merely answered the questions and I was not told to describe all I saw. I don't know what brought the sickness to my mind afterwards, but I think that someone else in the house brought the fact to my memory." With that, Mills was allowed to go. She had stuck doggedly to her story and, thanks to the incompetence of Coroner Ward and his failure to ask her questions, neither side could prove whether her story had been developed since the inquest.

Now came William Henry Jones, Cook's friend, the Lutterworth surgeon who had stayed in the same room with him. He told the court Cook's spirits had been very good that evening, laughing and joking about what he would do with himself that winter and objecting only to taking Bamford's pills because they had made him ill the previous evening. Jones had been present when he died: the only medical man there in the final moments, though the room had been so dark that he had not been able to see Cook's face properly. "When I was rubbing his neck his head and neck were unnaturally bent back by the spasmodic action of the muscles. After death his body was so twisted or bowed that if I had placed it upon the back it would have rested upon the head and feet." Jones said he was sure that Cook had died from tetanus. He had seen one case before, resulting from a wound, so he knew what it looked like. But he realised that Cook had not died from epilepsy, or apoplexy.

Then it was the turn of Dr Henry Savage, Cook's London doctor, who said that the ulcers on his tongue earlier in the year had been caused by two bad teeth: "There were no indications of a syphilitic character about the sores . . . there was in my judgement no venereal taint about him at the time . . . he was timid on the subject of his throat and was apt to take the advice of anyone. No, I don't think that he would take quack medicines. I don't think he was so foolish as that."

The last witness of the day was Charles Newton, the 22-year-old chemist's assistant who said he had given Palmer three strychnine grains on the Monday night: "the whole transaction did not take more than two or three minutes." He had never mentioned this publicly before the trial started. Now he told of meeting Palmer outside Hawkins's the next day and of their subsequent conversation in Palmer's kitchen about how much would be needed to kill a dog: "He asked me what would be the appearance of the stomach after death? I told him that there would be no inflammation and that I did not think it could be found. Upon that he snapped his finger and thumb in a quiet way and exclaimed as if communing with himself, 'That's all right.'" That caused a gasp in the court. Then there was the day of the post-mortem, when Newton was one of the assistants: "He said: 'It will be a dirty job; I will go and have some brandy,' I went with him . . . he gave me two wine glasses of neat brandy and he took the same quantity himself. He said: 'You'll find this fellow suffering from a diseased throat – he has had syphilis and has taken a great deal of mercury.'"

Cross-examined by Grove, Newton grew hazy about when he had mentioned the strychnine transactions to anyone else. Maybe a few days later: "I think I may undertake to say that it was not a fortnight afterwards." He had not mentioned Palmer's visit to Salt's shop at all because he knew that there was evidence about the sale at Hawkins's shop: "I did not mention the circumstance of my having given the strychnine to Palmer because Mr Salt and Palmer were not friends and I thought it would displease Mr Salt if he knew I had let Palmer have anything." Shee intervened: "Have you not given another reason . . . that you were afraid you could be indicted for perjury?" Newton replied no, but he was aware that a young gentleman at Wolverhampton had been threatened with a charge of perjury because he had said he had sold William Palmer prussic acid, but had not entered it in the book, so could not prove it. Maybe that really was the reason, or maybe it was because it would have implicated Newton himself in the murder. That further point was not raised, for it would have undermined the defence's case that there was no strychnine and no murder. But nor did the defence ever seek to find out whether Palmer could have reached Salt's shop before it closed at nine o'clock on the Monday evening when he came back from London: the train had got in to Stafford at 8.45 p.m., so he could not have done so if what Newton said about the time of their meeting was true. Some said the postboy from the Junction Hotel, who had driven him home from Stafford that night, had disappeared, or had been spirited away. But he alone could have independently proved whether Newton's story was true and he was not produced in court. Nor was Newton's part in the whole affair ever untangled: why would Palmer need to ask a chemist's assistant about the poisonous properties of strychnine? But then, why would Newton only belatedly

Palmer's trial at the Old Bailey: prisoner in the dock, left, barristers in the middle, jury in front of the windows, judges under the canopy to the right

tell the prosecution about their meetings just before the court case? His evidence was what linked Palmer directly to strychnine in the hours before Cook's death. Why did he do it – and why did the defence not press him harder to explain?

Friday 16 May saw seventeen witnesses hustling through the court, all accounting for the events in Rugeley and London in the week before Cook's death. Palmer, *The Times* noted, appeared rather more anxious than previously, though apparently he was still calm and collected. He was paying the greatest attention to the evidence, it said. He was the quietest person in the court, beadily watching a contest whose outcome would determine whether he lived or died within a month. As he listened, he scribbled anxious notes and passed them down to his barristers.

The first witness of the day was Charles Roberts, the apprentice druggist at Hawkins's shop, who said that on the Tuesday morning he had sold Palmer six grains of strychnine, two drachms (a quarter of a fluid ounce – one drachm was a teaspoonful) of Batley's Sedative (an opium solution), and the same amount of prussic acid – which was a surprise because he had not bought anything from Hawkins for two years, getting all his drugs from Thirlby. Roberts had not bothered to note down the purchases: "When articles are paid for across the counter I am not in the habit of making entries of them in the books." His evidence was as crucial as Newton's – and more reliable – in placing Palmer in proximity to poison, but he was scarcely questioned by the defence.

Next came William Stephens, Cook's stepfather, who took the court through his involvement with Palmer in the days after the death. He built up a steady pattern of the accused's shiftiness, but seemingly without the remorseless vengefulness he had displayed in his private correspondence and with no indication that his first thought on hearing the news was that Cook had been poisoned. His stepson had not been a robust man, he said – his complexion had been pale – but the last time he had seen him, at Euston station a fortnight before his death, Cook was looking better than he had seen him for a very long time. When Stephens saw him in his coffin at the Talbot Arms a fortnight later, his fists had been "clinched", but apart from that he had not looked dead at all. On the Saturday afterwards, when he and Palmer had found themselves on the same train together from London back to Rugeley, Stephens recalled saying to him during the refreshment stop at Wolverton: "Mr Palmer, this is a very melancholy thing, the death of my poor son happening so suddenly. I think for the sake of his brother and sister, who are somewhat delicate, it might be desirable for his medical friends to know what his complaints were." This is the only reference to Cook's sister and half-brother in the whole story: if they took any active part in the case, it has not been passed down and not even their names are known. Palmer had replied: "That can be done very well." When they got to Rugeley that evening, Stephens tested him by asking if he knew of a local solicitor to look after his interest. "I know them all intimately and I can introduce you to one," Palmer had said. Stephens then told the court the story of how he had purposely altered his tone and said: "Mr Palmer, if I should call in a solicitor to give me advice, I suppose you will have no objection to answer any questions he may put to you?" He said: "I looked steadily at him but although the moon was shining I could not see his features distinctly. He said with a spasmodic convulsion of the throat which was perfectly apparent, 'Oh no, certainly not.'" Later during the weekend, Palmer had sidled up to him in the hotel and handed him a piece of paper. Funnily enough, it had Jerry Smith's name on it. "Pray, who is Mr Smith?" said Stephens, carrying on writing at a desk. He had to ask the question several times before Palmer replied: "He is a solicitor in the town." Stephens said: "I ask you because as the betting-book is lost, I should wish to know who had been with the young man." Then he changed the subject: "Did you attend my son in a medical capacity?" "Oh dear, no," said Palmer.

Then John Harland, the man who had supervised the post-mortem and had turned up without his instruments, defended himself by saying: "I had only been requested to be present at the examination." Palmer had met him in the street outside the Talbot Arms. "I said: 'What is this case? I hear there is a suspicion of poisoning.' He said: 'Oh no, I think not. He had an epileptic fit on Monday and Tuesday last and you will find old disease in the heart and in the head.'" Harland then went through the findings: all the organs normal without a sign of the cause of death. And he described the shove that had caused the two students to drop the stomach. Lord Campbell intervened: "Might not Palmer have been impelled by someone outside him?" "There was no one who could have impelled him," Harland replied. "I saw Mr Newton and Mr Devonshire pushed together and Palmer was over them. He was smiling at the time." Then he had heard Palmer, looking on, say: "They won't hang us yet." He had said it several times in a loud whisper. Harland said he had not had a lens at the post-mortem: "I made an examination which was satisfactory to me without one." He sounded exasperated by the intervention of the London medical men:

> I do not know who suggested that there should be an examination
> of the spinal cord two months after death . . . There were no indi-
> cations of wounds or sores as could by possibility produce tetanus
> . . . There was nothing whatever in the brain to indicate the pres-
> ence of any disease of any sort; but if there had been I never heard
> or read of any disease of the brain ever producing tetanus.

Young Charles Devonshire, the other medical student at the first post-mortem, came next and described the same findings from the first, botched examination, then the second a few days later at which more organs were removed. He had found no indications of syphilis. The second judge, Alderson, then intervened: "When you have all the medical men in London here, you had better not examine an undergraduate of the University of London upon such points, I should think." So Devonshire, the man who had actually carried out the post-mortem on Cook, was stood down.

Then it was the turn of James Myatt, the postboy at the Talbot Arms, a sallow, lank-haired youth in a muffler, to tell the court of Palmer's attempt to bribe him to upset the fly: "If you could, there's a £10 note for you." The court gasped. "I told him I could not. I then said: 'I must go, the horses are ready for us to start.' I said if I didn't go somebody else would. He told me not to be in a hurry for if anybody else went he would pay me." Answering Shee, he said he did not think Palmer had been drunk: "He said it was a humbugging concern altogether – or something of that. He said Stephens was a troublesome fellow and very inquisitive."

The postmaster Sam Cheshire came next, brought from Newgate prison. Palmer had persuaded him on the day before Cook's death to write out a cheque for £350, payable to Palmer, which he said he would take to the sick man to sign. It was to be drawn on Cook's betting account at Tattersall's, but Palmer said he could not write it out because Weatherby, the treasurer of the Jockey Club who supervised the account, knew his handwriting. The cheque was refused and had now disappeared.

Cheshire said that after Cook had died, Palmer had called him in to witness a document, apparently signed by Cook, claiming some £1,500, but he had refused as he had not seen it being drawn up and he feared that he might be witnessing a lie. "I thought the Post Office authorities would not approve of my mixing myself up in a matter which might occasion my absence from my duties to give evidence," he said. Palmer had told him it did not matter as the signature would not be disputed. But a fortnight later he had told Palmer that Taylor's letter to James Gardner, the Rugeley solicitor advising Stephens, had said he had found no strychnine: "for reading which I am now under sentence of punishment."

Next came Ellis Crisp, the police inspector in charge of Rugeley's two constables. He showed a book he had picked up at the auction of Palmer's furniture which allegedly contained the words, in Palmer's handwriting: "Strychnia kills by causing tetanic fixing of the respiratory muscles." Vizetelly remembered that all the opera glasses in the public gallery swivelled onto Palmer, but Lord Campbell just said: "That may be merely a passage extracted from an article in some encyclopaedia." Cockburn replied: "No doubt it may. I put it in for what it is worth." Point satisfactorily made. If it is the notebook now in the National Archives at Kew, the phrase does not appear in it.

George Herring, the betting agent, was called to say that he had been at Shrewsbury with the others and had watched Cook count the banknotes he

Samuel Cheshire, the Rugeley Postmaster, whose reputation was ruined by his involvement with his friend Palmer

had won after Polestar's race: "He unfolded them in twos and threes. There was a considerable number of notes." Then, the following Monday, Palmer had summoned him to a meeting in London and asked him to settle Cook's account at Tattersall's and pay £450 to Pratt and £350 to Padwick; he should send the cheques to them first, before collecting the money: "I refused to comply as I had not yet received [it]," Herring said. Palmer said to him that it would be all right for Cook would not deceive him: "he wished me particularly to pay Mr Pratt." Herring offered to visit the moneylenders and pay them after he had received the money at Tattersall's, but when he went there later in the day, he received only £99, not the £200 he had been led to expect. Unfortunately, by that time he had sent Pratt his cheque, and now – although he held signed bills of exchange from Palmer and Cook – he was still out of pocket and planning to take proceedings against Palmer, adding to the list of creditors. Such an experience probably taught Herring a lesson, never to be so trusting again.

The court sat through the following day even though it was a Saturday. Among the notables present was George Dallas, the former US vice-president, newly appointed as the American ambassador to the Court of St James (and the man after whom Dallas, Texas is named). First up was the trusting George Bates, the respectable farmer and odd-job man, whose life Palmer had wanted to insure. For looking after some of his horses – four brood mares, four yearlings and a three-year-old – in the stables round the back of Palmer's house in Rugeley, Bates said he had received no fixed salary, just the occasional one or two sovereigns from which he had to pay his weekly rent of six shillings and sixpence. It was a good job he was a bachelor. Edwin James was asking the questions; when he started asking about the attempted insurance, he was stopped by the judges, but not before he had raised the issue in the jury's minds.

After Bates came the first of the medical witnesses who would take up most of the following week. Thomas Blizard Curling, a surgeon at the London Hospital, had been called to give evidence on tetanus and carefully explained the two sorts. Idiopathic tetanus he described as self-generated, caused by something internal – possibly arising from a cut or sore but then exacerbated by exposure to damp, cold "or from the irritation of worms in the alimentary canal" – but he admitted he had never seen a case. Then there was traumatic tetanus, which arose from an infected cut; he reckoned he had seen a hundred cases of this kind in twenty-two years at the hospital. This caused a stiffness in the neck and jaw muscles and increasingly regular and worsening paroxysms, which led to the body bending backwards:

> the disease if fatal may end in two ways. The patient may die somewhat suddenly from suffocation, owing to the closure of the . . . windpipe; or he may be worn out by the spasms. The disease is generally fatal. The locking of the jaw is an almost constant symptom. It is an early symptom. Another . . . is a peculiar expression of the countenance . . . I never knew or read of traumatic tetanus being produced by a sore throat or chancre. I know of no instance in which a syphilitic sore has led to tetanus. The disease when once commenced is continuous.

Cockburn asked: "Did you ever know of a case in which a man was attacked one day, had 24 hours' respite and was then attacked the next day?" Curling answered: "Never." He then dismissed the accounts of Cook's suffering given by both Jones and Mills, adding: "The sudden onset of the spasms and their rapid subsidence are consistent with neither of the two forms."

Shee tried to shake the evidence by suggesting tetanus could be caused

George Bates "possessed of a good property and a capital cellar" but in reality a farm labourer, done up in his Sunday best for the trial

by a fishbone sticking in the gullet, vibrations from a musket shot, the stroke of a whip under the eye, "the biting of a finger by a favourite sparrow", the blow of a stick, or the extraction of a tooth. Curling agreed these could have that effect. He was followed by Dr Robert Todd, a physician, this time, at King's College Hospital and lecturer on tetanus and diseases of the nervous system. Todd was asked about strychnine and said it was usually given in large doses to animals to kill them quickly – he thought a grain would certainly kill an adult human: "death would probably ensue in a quarter of an hour or so." No one mentioned that strychnine was available over the counter at a penny a grain from any of Rugeley's three chemists. Todd added:

> The difference between tetanus produced by strychnine and other tetanus is very marked. In the former case the duration of the symptoms is very short and instead of being continuous . . . they will subside if the dose has not been strong enough to produce death and will be renewed in fresh paroxysms, whereas in other descriptions of tetanus the symptoms commence in a mild form and become stronger and more violent. I think it is remarkable that the deceased was able to swallow and there was no fixing of the jaw, which would have been the case with tetanus proper . . . From the evidence I have heard I think that the symptoms which presented themselves in the case of Mr Cook arose from tetanus produced by strychnine.

Todd was followed by the imposing figure of Sir Benjamin Brodie, the senior surgeon, doctor to the royal family and pioneer rheumatologist at St George's Hospital, now in his seventies and immensely distinguished. His account of tetanus endorsed that of his predecessors in the witness box. The *Times* reporter was impressed: Brodie, he wrote, gave his evidence with great clearness, slowly, audibly and distinctly, "matters in which other medical witnesses would do well to emulate," he added with feeling. Brodie had seen plenty of cases: "I never knew the symptoms of ordinary tetanus to last for a few minutes, then subside and then come on again after 24 hours." Shee tried to shake him on the descriptions given by Elizabeth Mills and Dr Jones, who had diagnosed tetanus in Cook: "Which would you rely upon – the medical man or the chambermaid?" Judge Alderson intervened: "That is hardly a question to put to a medical witness although it may be a very proper observation for you to make."

Then a succession of witnesses – a lady's maid, a surgeon and a chemist's assistant – was called to describe the terrible story of a Mrs Sarjantson Smyth of Romsey, who had been given medicine containing strychnine because of a mistake by the chemist (he had meant to prescribe salacite, willow bark). She too had died in agony in just over an hour. This was the case that William Stephens had read about in the newspapers and which had sprung immediately to his mind for some reason when Jones arrived at his door in Kensington to tell him his stepson had died. Charles Blocksome, the chemist's assistant, said simply: "My master made a mistake in preparing a prescription. He destroyed himself afterwards." By then it was past five o'clock and the Lord Chief Justice called it a day, asking for the jury to be taken out on Sunday, "though not to any place of public resort". The first witness on Monday would be the prosecution's key: Alfred Swaine Taylor.

The *Manchester Guardian* reported after this day's evidence: "Palmer still entertains a confident expectation of being acquitted and at the consultation with his professional advisers on Friday evening, very sanguine opinions were expressed as to the success of the defence." This sounds like a form of lawyerly spin, perhaps by the solicitor John Smith, and is not the sort of comment that would be published today. Most other observers thought that the noose was tightening around Palmer's neck with every day that passed.

13

"The most memorable proceedings for the last 50 years"

THE COURT WAS AS CROWDED AS EVER ON MONDAY 19 MAY. THE PAPERS noted reverentially that the Earl of Denbigh and Lord Lyttelton were granted seats on the bench next to the judges. Alfred Swaine Taylor took to the witness box immediately and self-confidently. Yes, he said, he was the author of a well-known treatise on poisons and medical jurisprudence and had made strychnia the subject of his attention. He had tested it in various strengths upon rabbits, but had never seen its action on humans. He added: "I have never had under my own observation the effects of strychnia on the human body; but I have written a book about the subject." Taylor was in his element describing how the poison could be tested for, using a colouring test on the dried residue and watching it turn blue, then purple; but there was also another fact helpful to the prosecution case – that the tests for the poison's presence were not invariably correct. "Vegetable poisons are more difficult of detection by chemical process than mineral poisons; the tests are far more fallacious," he said. He had tried four tests on animals he had poisoned and only found definite evidence of strychnia in one of them. He was sure the reason was that it had been absorbed into the blood and was no longer present in the stomach. Small amounts, such as half a grain, could kill an animal but were just too small to be detected. Nevertheless, in the current case he had no doubts. Cockburn asked: "As a professor of medical science, do you know any cause in the range of human disease except strychnine to which the symptoms in Cook's case can be re-ferred?" "I do not."

Now it was Shee's turn. He quoted the letter Taylor had written to James Gardner, Stephens's solicitor in Rugeley, in early December following his tests. This was the letter whose contents Sam Cheshire had described to Palmer. It stated:

> We do not find any strychnine, prussic acid or any trace of opium . . . it is now impossible to say whether any strychnine had or had not been given just before death, but it is quite pos-sible for tartar emetic to destroy life if given in repeated doses; and so far as we can at present form an opinion, in the absence of any natural cause of death, the deceased may have died from the effects of antimony in this or some other form.

He had not mentioned strychnine as the cause of death until he heard sus-picions of it later. Was it his opinion that antimony was the cause of death at the time? asked Shee. We could infer nothing else, said Taylor. "May not the injudicious use of quack medicine containing antimony, the injudicious use of James's powders, account for the antimony?" "Yes, the injudicious use of antimonial medicine would account for it." "Or even their judicious use?" "It might." "You gave it as your opinion that he died from antimony?" "You pervert my meaning entirely. I said that antimony in the form of tartar emetic might occasion vomiting and . . . in large doses it would cause death, preceded by convulsions . . . There was no natural cause to account for death and finding antimony existing throughout the body we thought it might have been caused by antimony. An analysis cannot be made effectually with-out information." This was getting tetchy. Shee asked whether he needed a long statement of symptoms first before conducting an analysis; "a short statement will do," snapped Taylor.

Shee turned to the animal tests. "Do you not think a rabbit is a very unfair animal to select?" "No." "Would not a dog be much better?" "Dogs are very dangerous to handle," Taylor replied, as the court tittered. Shee: "I will take from your answer that you are afraid of dogs." Taylor: "Rabbits are much more manageable." This was important for the defence too: Taylor admitted that he had only observed the effects of strychnine on a small

Swaine Taylor and Rees carry out their analysis. It was this illustration in the *Illustrated Times* which caused consternation in court (see page 181).

mammal, not on a human. Shee: "As respects the effect of strychnine on the human body you have no knowledge of your own at all?" Taylor: "I have not seen a case; I have some knowledge." Shee: "By knowledge of your own, I mean personal observation: but you have written a book upon the subject?" Taylor: "Yes." He added that he did not feel justified in sacrificing a hundred rabbits when the facts were ascertainable from other sources. This was an important but novel principle for the period: that an expert did not need to have personally observed symptoms or seen their effects in order to reach a conclusion based on others' findings.

Shee would return to this point, emphasising that the defence's witnesses, on behalf of Palmer, had observed strychnine's effect on humans, not from reading about the experiments of others or writing books. Taylor said that he had been told about Palmer's purchases of strychnine and prussic acid, but that had not influenced his report. Shee said: "You knew of course that his life depended in a great degree on your opinion?" "I simply gave an opinion as to the poison, not as to the prisoner's guilt," he replied disingenuously.

Maybe he had forgotten his February letter in the *Lancet*. Shee pounced: "Did you write a letter?" "Yes, to contradict several misstatements on my evidence which had been made." "What about the reference in it to the life of one man being of minor importance?" "The lives of 16 million people are of greater importance than that of one man." Shee turned to Cook's symptoms. Had there been a case of patients beating on the bedclothes? There had only been about fifteen cases and in none had the patient been in bed, Taylor replied; Cook's were exactly the sort of symptoms he would expect. Re-examined by Cockburn, Taylor pointed out that Cook's heart had been empty of blood, which he attributed to the victim's final paroxysms: "I think the emptiness of the heart is owing to spasmodic affection." In this diagnosis Taylor was quite wrong.

Professor Robert Christison of Edinburgh University – the man Taylor had feared might give evidence for the defence – followed, and his evidence was powerful, even though he had not examined Cook's body:

> I have heard the evidence of what took place at the Talbot Arms and the result of my experience induces me to come to the conclusion that the symptoms exhibited by the deceased were only attributable to strychnia . . . there is no natural disease of any description that I am acquainted with to which I could refer these symptoms . . . When death is the consequence of the administration of strychnia, if the quantity is small, I should not expect to find any trace in the body after death . . . Vegetable poisons are more difficult of detection than mineral ones.

He too could not be shaken.

When the court adjourned at six o'clock that evening, it had been a satisfactory day for the prosecution. The court had heard from the two most eminent experts on poison and both had concurred about strychnine's effects on the body and absorption after death. They had not been shaken by rival theories and they had given the reasons why the poison might not be detected in the organs after death and why it had not been found in Cook's body because of the way the post-mortem had been conducted. The prosecution case was nearly complete. The newspaper reporters still marvelled at Palmer's composure when they glanced at him in the dock: "The prisoner presented his usual calm and collected demeanour," said the *Manchester Guardian* as if it half-expected him to burst into hysterics in the manner of a penny-dreadful villain. "His appearance has undergone no perceptible change. He appeared to pay marked attention to Dr Taylor's evidence and . . . communicated frequently with his solicitor." As he sat impassively, it is little wonder that Palmer's reputation as a cool criminal mastermind grew.

The sixth day began with yet another medical witness, John Jackson, to bolster still further the contention that Cook had not suffered from tetanus. "I have never seen a case in which the disease ended in death in 20 minutes," he told the court.

Then came the elderly Dr Bamford, who had recovered from a bout of dysentery which prevented him appearing earlier, to give evidence about his treatment of Cook. He confirmed that he had given Palmer pills for Cook on the evening of his death – he had wrapped them in paper and sealed the box, but he had not seen the patient after that until he was called as Cook was dying. By the time he arrived he was dead:

> the body was stretched out, resting on the heels and the back of
> the head, as straight as possible and stiff . . . I filled up the cer-
> tificate and gave it as my opinion that he died from apoplexy.
> When Palmer asked me to fill up the certificate I told him that
> as Cook was his patient it was his place . . . He said he had much
> rather I did it and I did so.

Bamford was not asked why he had made the diagnosis he did. After the postmortem he said Palmer had remarked: "We ought not to have let that jar go."

Afterwards it was the moneylender Thomas Pratt's turn. He was more composed than he had been at the inquest and recited the ins and outs of their financial transactions. He read out the letters that had passed between them; the impression given could only have been of Palmer's breathtaking financial trouble. He was followed by Rugeley tradesmen, who confirmed that Palmer had paid off his debts to them following the race meeting at Shrewsbury. John Wallbank, a local butcher, said that the day before the race meeting Palmer had asked him to lend him £25. "I said 'Doctor, I'm very short of money but I'll try if I can get it.' He said: 'Do, that's a good fellow; I'll give it to you again on Saturday morning.'" And he had.

Finally for the day came Herbert Wright, the solicitor brother of the Birmingham moneylender Edwin Wright. He said that in the previous November, when Cook died, Palmer owed them £10,400, more than half of it secured on bills of exchange carrying the forged signature of Sarah Palmer. The bills were overdue for payment and the Wrights had taken out a notice to sell Palmer's property, including his horses. Would he have given Palmer more time to pay? asked Shee. Probably not, he replied. Would the loans have been renewed at 60 per cent interest? asked Cockburn. Probably, yes. Palmer had told them that the money would be paid off in November after the Cambridgeshire race meeting at Newmarket. The court adjourned for the day three hours early.

The seventh day was when the defence would start its case and the court was more crowded than ever: every seat was filled an hour before the start and there were queues waiting outside. Now, at last, after a week of evidence building up into a formidable prosecution case, it was Serjeant Shee's one chance to outline the defence. He spoke for eight hours, throughout most of the day, and made an immediate plea for sympathy. He had only ever once before defended a person on a capital charge:

> a trial of this kind is sufficient to disturb the calmest temper and try the clearest judgement . . . how much more trying is it to stand for six long days under the shade, as it were, of the scaffold, conscious that the least error in judgement may consign my client to an ignominious death and public indignation.

Shee's plea for sympathy was passionate but overdone and fawning. And then he broke the bounds of professional propriety by saying he himself believed Palmer to be innocent: "I say it in all sincerity, having read these papers, I commenced his defence with an entire conviction of his innocence. I believe that truer words were never pronounced than the words he uttered when he said 'not guilty'." It was not Shee's job, of course, to pronounce on Palmer's guilt or innocence, as Cockburn and the judge would tell him in no uncertain terms, and his assertion must have been counterproductive at least. Shee added that he would grapple with every difficulty, meet the prosecution case foot to foot at every stage.

There were three heads on which to challenge the case: whether Palmer had a motive for killing Cook; whether Cook's symptoms were consistent only with strychnine poison and not with natural causes; and whether the circumstantial evidence was so strong as to make any other explanation inexplicable. First, he emphasised the lack of strychnine in Cook's body: "Whatever we may think of Dr Alfred Taylor, of his judgement and discretion, we have no reason to doubt he is a skilful analytical chemist . . . no reason to suppose that he . . . did not do all that the science of chemical analysis could enable man to do to detect the poison of strychnia." Then, he pointed out that Taylor had thought antimony had caused Cook's death until he attended the inquest, heard the evidence of Mills and Jones, and changed his mind. His tests had been partial and wrong. "When we recollect that his knowledge consists – good, humane man! – in having poisoned five rabbits 25 years ago and five since this question of the guilt or innocence of Palmer arose, his opinion I think, unsupported by the opinions of others, cannot have much weight with you." Shee's problem was an abundance of verbiage, a torrent of words, a cascade of labyrinthine, blustering sentences striving for effect and a bathos – in this case about the rabbits – which did not address the seriousness of the case. He lacked Cockburn's deadly precision.

Now he insisted, extraordinarily, that it was not in Palmer's interests that Cook should die; on the contrary, "his death was the very worst calamity that could befall him and . . . it must be immediately followed by his own ruin." Shee got bogged down in the complicated financial dealings of Palmer, speaking through the course of the morning almost as if rationalising to himself, until he finally emerged from the thicket of figures to announce that, if only the insurance company had paid up on Walter's policy, all Palmer's problems would have been over. He came close to implying that the problem had all been got up by the insurers in their correspondence about the policy:

> Gentlemen, that £13,000 is sure to be paid unless that man is convicted of murder and that has a great deal to do with the clamour and alarm which has been excited. So sure as that man is saved and saved I believe he will be, that £13,000 is paid; there is no defence . . . they took an enormous premium.

Cockburn intervened felinely: "Do you mean to prove that?" Shee, stopped in full flow, retorted: "I do not know whether I can show that . . . I say that as sure as he is saved that £13,000 is good for him and will pay all his creditors.

This correspondence saves the prisoner if there is common sense in man." Since Palmer owed in excess of £20,000, it would not have done, of course.

Shee then turned to the state of Cook's health, his vice-strewn life, his sore throat and mercury treatment: ailments "which did not come by an ordinary and chaste mode of life, you may depend upon it . . . he seems to have been about as loose a young man as one is in the habit of meeting without being lost to all sense of honour and propriety, which I do not mean to suggest that he was." Then he was back to Taylor, who had changed his mind at the inquest, deciding the diagnosis of antimony was incorrect:

> he had the incredible imprudence, an imprudence which has led to all this dreadful excitement, an imprudence which has rendered it necessary that this inquiry should take place in this form and in this place, if at all – to state on his oath that the pills administered to Cook contained strychnia and that Cook was poisoned by it. That opinion as delivered was irrevocable. By it Taylor's reputation was staked against Palmer's life . . . it flew upon the wings of the Press into every house in the United Kingdom.

It was an opinion based not on evidence, but on the testimony, "ill informed of the humblest class", of Elizabeth Mills.

There was a short break and then Shee proceeded with his thesis that Cook had died not from poisoning or even tetanus but from general convulsions. He had been overwhelmed by the excitement of winning at Shrewsbury and saving his honour and finances. "He had champagne and we all of us know that when there is champagne there are other things besides . . . I do not mean to say he was drunk," said Shee, having implied precisely that. Cook had stood about in the cold and rain next day and been taken ill – a weakened body, an irritated and excited mind, then sickness. That would account for his state of fright at the Talbot Arms: it must have been a state of very high nervous excitement, arising from a disordered stomach and an agitated and anxious mind, weakened by the medicine he was taking. So the sentences rolled on through the afternoon, winding back on themselves occasionally and meandering through copious subclauses. Despite Shee's charm, his confiding manner and his regular rapping on the table in front of him to emphasise his points, it must have been a challenge to stay alert. Now he was attacking the other medical witnesses: his experts would be of the highest eminence, not mere surgeons in hospitals, but general practitioners, experienced with patients, men enjoying the entire confidence of numerous families – these were the men who knew about convulsions.

On next to Palmer and the local prejudice against him: "in a town like Rugeley there were a great many serious people who could not approve his habits of life, to whom his running about to races would not much recommend him and whom he has reason to know would not very much regret any injury which might happen to him." The same could be said of the insurance company: "there were some persons who did not want to pay him £13,000 . . . who had been doing all they could to undermine his character . . . imputing to him the most wicked conduct respecting a near relation, which none of his own relations ever joined in." His behaviour at the post-mortem, removing the jar to a safe place, was perfectly consistent with innocence, and as for Stephens's vengeful conduct, that was such as would make some men want to kick him, it was so very provoking, supposing Palmer was innocent. Next, he moved on to Newton, who had never mentioned giving Palmer three grains of strychnine on the Monday night until the eve of the trial, or the story about Palmer asking how much was needed to poison dogs: "A man who so conducts himself is utterly unworthy of credit . . . if a man knowing that he is to be sworn . . . the first time he takes the oath omits a considerable portion of what he knows and at a further interval comes forward and tells more, enough in his opinion to drive the guilt home . . . he ought not to be believed." In any case, it was an improbable story:

> That a person should go and buy more the next day at the shop of a rival tradesman with whom he was on bad terms – is to the last degree improbable. Common sense revolts at it . . . Is it credible that a skilful medical man who has studied at the London hospitals would have gone to that dolt Newton to ask him as to what would be the effects of strychnia on a dog's stomach? Is it credible that he should go to that stupid sort of fellow, who gave his evidence in that dogged, mulish, sullen manner?

What was Palmer to do when his friend and racing partner fell ill, but be attentive to him? They were not flush with money when they returned to Rugeley, so it stood to reason that he would buy him cheaper food from down the road than the Talbot Arms served. Palmer was the one who had called in Bamford and sent for Jones. If there was one person that a poisoner would not want to have around, it was a medical man, intimately acquainted with the patient and much attached to him:

> Jones was of all men living the most likely to be the recipient of Cook's confidence, bound by every consideration of honour, friendship and affection to protect him, to vindicate his cause and to avenge his death. Yet this was the man for whom Palmer sent . . . He brings a medical man into the room and makes him lie within a few inches of the sick man's bed that he may be startled by his terrific shrieks and gaze upon those agonising convulsions which indicate the fatal potency of poison! Can you believe it?

As for the missing betting book: many people had been through the room – the maids, jockeys and trainer, the barber, the undertaker's men. It was unfair to blame Palmer for taking it without any assignable reason when the room had not been searched until sometime after Cook's death. Similarly, there was nothing underhand about Palmer searching Cook's pockets, nor his writing about poison in his student notebook.

Shee ended his long peroration with a purple-passage paean to Palmer. There was his love of his wife: "he loved her for herself and for her person . . . with a pure and generous affection", just as he loved his seven-year-old son "who waits with trembling anxiety for a sentence which will restore him to his father's arms or drive that father to an ignominious death upon the scaffold". Then there was his aged mother, a dear sister, a gallant and devoted brother . . . "Expand your minds!" Shee cried. "You have to stem the torrent of prejudice; you have to vindicate the honour and character of your country . . . if you have a doubt, depend upon it the time will come when the innocence of this man will be made apparent and when you will deeply regret any want of due and calm consideration of the case." Palmer sat watching the effect of this torrent on the jury and, said the *Manchester Guardian*, showed signs of emotion at the references to his wife.

Shee sat down and wiped his brow. There were, the court reporters noted, "some slight indications of an attempt to applaud . . . but they were instantly repressed." Vizetelly in the public gallery was less impressed. If, as Vizetelly remembered, Shee occasionally lost his way and confused who he was speaking about, it must have seemed unendurable. It was three hours longer than Cockburn's opening had been, but much of the speech was assertion rather than evidence, and it was submerged in a verbosity which must have seemed wearyingly over-emotional and egregiously partisan. As the court dispersed for the evening and the jury were escorted back to their dormitory at the London Coffee House, it was by no means clear that Shee had swung the case with his one shot at persuasion.

Two-and-a-half days of testimony mainly by medical experts followed for the defence. They disagreed with the diagnosis that Cook had been poisoned, but there was a lack of consensus about what had actually killed him. None of them had had the opportunity of examining his body or organs themselves. They did not have Taylor or Christison's prestige and some were plainly professional rivals. The first to be examined was Thomas Nunneley, the professor of surgery at the Leeds School of Medicine, who said he had listened to the medical evidence, compared it with the different witness depositions, and believed himself that the cause of Cook's death was convulsions. Lord Campbell jumped in: that was not satisfactory – witnesses could not be asked to comment on the statements of others. Nunneley started to say that Cook's previous state of health had influenced his judgement about cause of death, but he was interrupted again by the judge, who told him Cook's previous state of health was irrelevant. Twice within the first five minutes Campbell had intervened aggressively to say that Nunneley's statements were unsatisfactory, which he had not done with the prosecution witnesses. Shee desperately changed the subject, asking about the patient's syphilitic sores, and now it was Cockburn's turn to object, saying that that had not been proved in evidence. The judges started bickering among themselves: Alderson suggested phrasing the question as supposing a person had such sores, Cresswell preferred letting Nunneley describe what he assumed to be Cook's state of health (which is what he had originally been trying to do), and Campbell insisted that the medical men's opinions were not to be substituted for the jury's – though that is precisely what had occurred when Taylor was questioned.

Back on course, but with Nunneley largely nullified as an expert, the witness claimed that Cook would not have been well for a long time, that his condition must have been delicate and liable to nervous irritation, and that excitement or depression would have made his symptoms worse. A man in such a condition would be prone to fits and convulsions, but might be able – as Cook had been – to remain conscious. Campbell intervened once more: had he met anyone like that? No, Nunneley replied, not during a fit. He insisted that nothing could be told by examining the spinal cord so long after death. He too had experimented on animals – mice, rats, frogs and toads, as well as cats, dogs and rabbits – and they had all lost their rigidity after death. Cook's symptoms seemed to him nothing like theirs – "he had more power of voluntary motion" – and furthermore he had never seen a rabbit vomit after taking strychnine, unlike Cook. Then it was Cockburn's turn, and he asked which of Cook's symptoms would have produced excitement and which depression. Flustered, Nunneley replied that there was a good deal of mental depression in Rugeley – he meant Cook, but said the town. He added: "I believe it to be quite probable that convulsions might come on and destroy a person and leave no trace behind." Cockburn was tying him in knots. Had there been anything to show any excitement in Rugeley? Nunneley replied: "You will not allow me to furnish an answer. There was no excitement at Rugeley but morphia when there is sickness will sometimes disagree with a patient when there is an irritable state of the brain." Cockburn tried again: "The stomach was irritated I will allow but where is the evidence that there was any excitement at Rugeley?" Nunneley was defeated: "There was none." "Do you believe he had convulsions?" "To a certain extent, but less in intensity . . ." "Be so good as to tell me, what are the convulsions that will produce convulsions of a tetanic form?" "Any irritation will do it . . . I have known them in children. I have never had such a case in an adult . . . the general statement of all writers is that such cases do occur . . ." So what was the difference between convulsions and tetanic paroxysms? They were very similar, Nunneley admitted, but maybe not at the very moment of death. He had to admit that Cook's symptoms were exactly like the case of the woman who had died of strychnine poisoning in Leeds. He was asked: did he not know that she had asked at the last moment to be turned over, that she had asked for her neck muscles to be rubbed, had difficulty in breathing, wanted her legs straightened? That was just like Cook. Then, Cockburn added the crucial question: "Can you point out any one point . . . in which the symptoms in [Cook's] case differ from strychnine tetanus?" Nunneley thought there might be something about the power of swallowing, but he had to admit that lockjaw was the final symptom of poisoning. The question hung in the air.

Next it was the turn of William Herapath, the professor of chemistry and toxicology at Bristol Medical School, and one of Taylor's chief rivals. They did not like each other. Herapath described his own experiments with strychnine on animals and dismissed suggestions that traces might not be found in the body after death, even when it had decomposed. It ought to have been detectable in Cook's stomach, even after the journey in the jar: "Dr Taylor ought to have found it," he said with what sounds like professional relish. Unfortunately, though, Herapath had let his tongue run away with him. Before being contracted to the defence, he had been overheard saying at a meeting that Cook's symptoms had sounded like strychnine poisoning and that he would have been able to find it in his organs even if Taylor could not. His remarks were overheard by Bristol's magistrates' clerk, a Mr Simmons, who had written anonymously to the Treasury solicitor to tell him what Herapath had said. Simmons was traced through the postmark on his letter and interviewed, and the professor was then subpoenaed to appear. Even worse, his words had got out more generally and been reported by the *Illustrated Times*. So, asked the attorney general, had he said it? "I may have. I had a strong opinion from reading various newspaper reports," said Herapath. "People have talked a great deal to me about the matter and I can't recollect every word I have said." After that admission, the defence had to fall back on Herapath's assertion that he could have found the poison if any of it had been present. He insisted that he was certain he could find traces as small as a 50,000th part of a grain, if not mixed with organic matter. This was incredible and Judge Campbell said as much. The second expert had been shot down.

The next witness was Henry Letheby, a distinguished scientist in his own right and also medical officer of health for the City of London. He too had seen cases of poisoning in animals – he had tested strychnine on fifty of them – and in two humans, one of whom had died. He believed he too could have distinguished traces in Cook's body, even many days after death. His evidence was much more cautious than Herapath's or Nunneley's – he spoke only of the experiments he had done and what he had seen – and it was treated with respect. But when it came to the vital question from Cockburn – "What do you ascribe Mr Cook's death to?" – he admitted: "it is irreconcilable with everything I am acquainted with." Campbell intervened again to ask whether it was reconcilable with any known disease and Letheby said no. All he would say, questioned by Shee, was that he thought the symptoms were irreconcilable with strychnine too.

The defence medical witnesses scarcely strengthened Palmer's case. None of them had proved that Cook had died from something else and they could not really agree how he had died: not having seen his body or investigated his organs, they were guessing. Both the most eminent specialist witnesses, Nunneley and Herapath, had floundered. Shee told the judge he hoped to finish the defence case the following day, but that case was clearly wobbling.

Every morning *The Times* started its report in the same way: the size of the crowd in court – the room was always full to bursting; which notables were attending – on the ninth day they included the Duke of Wellington (son of the victor of Waterloo, who had died four years earlier), General Peel, the younger brother of the former prime minister (and the owner of the horse that ended up the winner of the disputed 1844 Derby), and a slew of peers and MPs; and what time proceedings started. Each day, also, the reporters cast their eyes towards the enigmatic figure in the dock. Palmer was always neatly dressed in black, he stood or sat impassively, periodically scribbling notes for the defence team. He was wholly silent and, as the papers repeatedly said, no alteration took place in his demeanour from day to day, whatever the evidence. But Charles Dickens, who was watching him carefully from the public gallery, was not impressed by the idea that Palmer was impassive. In his essay for *Household Words* on "The Demeanour of Murderers" he wrote:

> he was – not quite composed. Distinctly *not* quite composed,
> but on the contrary very restless. At one time he was incessantly
> pulling off his glove; at another time, his hand was constantly

passing over his face; and the thing he most instanced in proof of his composure, the perpetual writing and scattering of little notes, which, as the verdict drew nearer and nearer, thickened from a sprinkling to a heavy shower, is in itself a proof of miserable restlessness.

Again a succession of medical witnesses trooped through the witness box. They tumbled over each other, offering differing analyses and diagnoses for a person they had never seen, in life or death. Richard Partridge, professor of anatomy at King's College, said Cook's spinal cord should have been examined earlier and, from the evidence he had heard, could form no judgement of the cause of death: "I am only acquainted by reading and hearsay with the symptoms that accompany death from tetanus resulting from the administration of strychnia." The attorney general: "Have you ever seen such a death as this was with the symptoms mentioned proceeding from natural causes?" No.

It was hard to know what the witnesses were adding to the defence case. Dr William McDonnell of the Edinburgh College of Surgeons got into a terrible tangle as he testified that idiopathic tetanus could be caused by mental excitement "arising from causes yet quite undiscovered by science". He had brought his own patient with him, a woman cured of idiopathic tetanus the previous autumn. He too had tested animals with strychnine and watched the results. By now the court must have been astonished at how many animals had been slaughtered in the cause of scientific experimentation. McDonnell was asked whether a fatal dose of strychnine would make a human patient want to have his neck rubbed: it would throw him into convulsions, he said, which rather made the prosecution's point. He thought Cook might have suffered from epilepsy: "I have not exactly arrived at any distinct theory, not quite as distinct as strychnia or tetanus. I have seen one case of death from epilepsy. The patient was not conscious when he died." Cross-examining him, Cockburn was getting testy – the point was that Cook had been conscious: "Being so universally proficient in the science of your profession, do you know of a single recorded case of consciousness at the time of death?" "I do not." Cockburn was soon tying the doctor in knots. He asked him about the excitement at the races that he thought might have triggered the convulsions: "Do you mean to swear that you think the excitement of the three minutes on the course on the Tuesday accounts for the vomiting?" "I do not mean to say anything of the kind." "Do you find any excitement or depression from that time till the time he died?" "There is nothing reported that I can recollect just now." McDonnell claimed that Cook's possible syphilis might have caused his excitement. Cockburn: "Sexual excitement is a cause of epilepsy with tetanic complications. Is that what you say?" "Yes, it might be." "Do you mean to say that you attribute this to some excitement at some anterior period long before?" "I am not called upon to say that." "Do you mean to stand there as a serious man of science and tell me that?" "Yes, the results of sexual excitement – chancre and syphilitic sore throat . . ." "Did you ever hear or know of such a thing as a chancre producing epilepsy?" "Not epilepsy, but tetanus. You are forgetting that." "If I understand it rightly, it stands thus: the sexual excitement produces the epilepsy and the chancre produces tetanic complications?" "You are quite mistaken. I say the results of a sexual excitement." By the time the confused McDonnell stood down he must have wished he had stayed in Edinburgh.

John Bainbridge, the medical officer of a workhouse, came next to say that he had seen cases of epilepsy leading to convulsions and death. Another surgeon then testified that a woman patient of his had had convulsions brought on by the excitement of an argument with her husband, though the blow he had also given her might have had something to do with it. Dr Benjamin Wall Richardson, a London doctor, had also seen a considerable number of deaths from convulsions without them being caused by tetanus. He had had a ten-year-old girl die in agony in 1850: perfectly well at supper, felt ill, got into bed and asked her sister to rub her. Richardson had been treating her for scarlet fever; he had given her some brandy and water, conversed with her, and then nipped out to get some chloroform, and by the time he got back she was dead. He suggested it could have been angina. Shee picked up the point: "Are the symptoms described in the evidence more like the symptoms of angina pectoris or strychnia poison?" "I should certainly say angina."

These supposedly expert witnesses were exhibiting their fallibility and lack of certainty. The limits of their skill had been exposed, their claims to omniscience diminished. *Lloyd's Weekly London Newspaper* pointed out that the adversarial system had pitted the expert witnesses against each other "like rats or prize fighters", undermining the evidence they had given. It suggested that "the purity and brightness of the ore of science" had been tarnished by the dross of human vanity under cross-examination.

The trial's tenth day was another Saturday and it marked the end of the defence case. It would be another long day and one in which Cockburn would fully demonstrate why he was regarded as the cleverest advocate in the country, with the demolition of one last witness and a closing speech which was sometimes claimed to be unrivalled in the nineteenth-century courts.

First, though, Henry Matthews, the police inspector at Euston, gave evidence that the express to Stafford left London at 5 p.m. and should have arrived at 8.42, but actually got in three minutes late on the Monday night the previous November when Palmer returned on it. So Palmer would have had even less time to get to Rugeley nine miles away by nine o'clock. George Myatt, the Rugeley saddler, who had returned home with Palmer and Cook after the Shrewsbury meeting, and John Sargeant, another racing crony, were both called to tell the court that Cook had been in weak health. Sargeant said that his throat had been in a complete state of ulcer: "I told him I was surprised that he could eat and drink with his mouth and throat in such a state. He said it had been like it for months and he did not take notice of it . . . I have heard Cook apply to Palmer to supply him with a lotion called blackwash. This is a mercurial lotion of calomel and limewater."

Then finally for the defence it was Jerry Smith's turn. Jerry's intended role was to testify that he had met Palmer on the Monday evening when he arrived back in Rugeley and so he could not possibly have obtained strychnine from Newton at the same time. Palmer had made it pretty clear what he wanted him to say in two letters which apparently survived. They were seen and copied by George Fletcher and published in his Palmer biography in the 1920s; he said he was shown them by the governor of Stafford prison, though they must have been written at Newgate. The letters are almost the only documents in Palmer's handwriting that survived from the period of the trial and the evidence that Smith saw them is in what he said during his initial examination by Shee. The first reveals Palmer's incandescent anger at Newton:

Dear Jere,

No man in the world ever committed a grosser case of Perjury than that vile wretch Newton – he positively swore last Friday 16th May [actually the previous day] that he let me have 3 grs of Strychnine the Monday night before Cook's death and that I went to Mr Salt's surgery for it and got it from him at 9 o'clock.

It is a base lie for I left London on that very night at 5 o'-clock by Express and arrived at Stafford at 10 minutes to 9, brought a Fly from the Junction and arrived at Rugeley at Masters' door [i.e. the Talbot Arms] about 10 o'clock.

Now as there is a God in Heaven (I am sure you can't have forgotten it) you know that you were waiting for my coming and when I got out of the Fly you told me that my mother wanted to see me particularly and after bidding Cook good night we walked together down to the YARD [the Palmer family home] and got a good brushing from the old Lady . . . and if you recollect she was very cross. We then walked back to my house and you said, "Well, let me have a glass of spirit." I went to the cupboard and there was none – you said "Never mind" and bid me goodnight. This must have been after 11 o'clock – now I should like to know how I could get to Mr Salt's shop at 9 o'clock on that night. You can also prove this truth, that Cook dined with me (and you) at my house on the Friday before his death and that we had a quantity of wine. Cook then went with you and had a glass of Brandy and water – and that he was then the worse for liquor. You can further prove that Cook handed me some money on this day, for he told you so in my presence when he gave you the £10. He told you at the same time I had won over £1,000 on his mare at Shrewsbury and lastly you can prove that he and I betted for each other, that we had 'Pyrrhine' jointly and that we had had bill transactions together. These are solemn truths and I am fully persuaded that they cannot have escaped your memory.

Therefore let it be your bounden duty to come forward and place yourself in the witness box and on your oath speak these great truths. Then rest assured you will lie down on a downey pillow and go to sleep happy.

Bear in mind I only want the truth. I ask for no more.
Yours faithfully,
Wm. Palmer

Newton no doubt calculated upon my coming by the luggage train but this had been discontinued more than a month – thus my reason for going to Stafford.

Palmer then followed that letter – so redolent of panic, desperation and with heavy emphasis on what Smith must say – with a second, fleshing out the story with added details:

Dear Jere,
Do, for God's sake tell the truth – if you will only consider I am sure you will recollect meeting me at Masters' steps the night Monday the 19th of Nov. I returned from London and you told me my mother wanted to see me. I replied: "Have you seen Cook? And how is he?" You said, "No." I then said, "We will go upstairs and see him." We did so. When upstairs Cook said: 'Dr., you are late. Mr Bamford has sent me two pills which I have taken,' and he said to you, 'Damn you Jere, how is it you have never been to see me.' You replied that you had been busy all the day settling Mr. Ingram's affairs and we then wished him good night and went to my mother's.
Yours ever faithfully,
Wm. Palmer

Jerry Smith started confidently enough in the witness box, recounting the meals they had had together at Rugeley that last week: the beefsteak and champagne and three bottles of port the three of them had shared on the Friday night and the boiled leg of mutton and broth that he himself had ordered to be sent over from the Albion when Cook was ill on the Saturday. Then he spoke of the financial dealings they had had together over the years: how he had asked Cook for the £50 he owed him on that last Friday and how he had only been able to pay him £5 but had promised the rest on the Monday after settling at Tattersall's. He more or less faithfully repeated what he had been told to say in the letters, though he less helpfully misremembered slightly and said that it was Palmer who had prescribed the pills Cook said he had taken. This evidence, though, would be entirely subverted in the cross-examination that was to come. Now it was Cockburn's turn. Had Palmer applied to him to arrange insurance on Walter's life? Smith haplessly tried evasion. He could not remember, perhaps if he could see the application? "Will you swear you were not applied to?" "I will not swear either that I was not applied to, or that I was. If you will let me see the document I shall recognise my writing at once . . ." "Don't recollect! Why £13,000 was a large sum for a man like Walter Palmer wasn't it, who hadn't a shilling in the world?" Cockburn was dragging Walter into the case. Oh, he had money, Smith replied, remembering now, from his mother and from William Palmer.

Ah yes, Sarah. "Where, in the course of 1854 and '55 were you living? In Rugeley?" Partly with William, sometimes at his mother's, said Smith. When he did that, where did he sleep? In a room, Smith said evasively. He probably realised where this was leading. He was shaking and perspiring heavily by now. "Did you sleep in his mother's room – on your oath, were you not intimate with her – you know well enough what I mean?" "I had no other intimacy, Mr Attorney, than a proper intimacy." How often did he sleep there? Two or three times a week. "Are you a single or a married man?" Single. How long had that been going on? Several years. "How far were your lodgings from Mrs Palmer's house?" "I should say nearly a quarter of a mile." Was it too far to go home? "Why, we used to play a game of cards and have a glass of gin and water and smoke a pipe perhaps and then they said: 'It is late – you had better stop all night,' and I did. There was no particular reason why I did not go home that I know of." How often did he sleep there when the mother was at home, but the sons weren't? Sometimes two or three nights a week, for some months at a time, and then perhaps he would not go near the house for a month. This didn't have much to do with the case – probably Cockburn (who, of course, was unmarried, yet had two illegitimate children of his own) had been told the gossip by James Gardner, the prosecution's local solicitor in Rugeley – but there was no attempt from the bench to stop him. Unmentioned was the fact that Sarah Palmer was in her sixties, nearly twenty years older than Smith.

Back to the application on Walter's life. Smith was still shifty. "I ask you sir, as an attorney and a man of business, whether you cannot tell me whether you were applied to by William Palmer to attest a proposal for

£13,000 on the life of Walter Palmer?" "I say that I do not recollect it. If I could see any document on the subject I dare say I should remember it." Did he remember getting £5 for attesting the application? Perhaps; he could not positively remember. Now Cockburn produced the document. Here it was: was that his signature? Perhaps. Was it or not? It was very like. Was there any doubt? He had some doubts. "I will have an answer from you on your oath one way or another. Isn't that your handwriting?" "I think it is a very clever imitation of it." Smith thought he had probably been given the document by William, so Cockburn asked again whether the signatures were those of Pratt, Walter and himself. Smith started to reply: "I'll tell you, Mr Attorney . . ." This was a mistake on Jerry's part. Cockburn exploded: "Don't 'Mr Attorney' me sir! Answer my question!" He thought it was not his signature, but he would not swear that it wasn't. The fencing continued: hadn't Smith gone up to Liverpool to try and persuade Walter's widow to give up her claim on the policy? He had, without success. Smith seemed to know quite a lot about the policy. Cockburn tried yet again: had he been asked to witness the application for Walter's life insurance? "I might have been . . . I don't like to speak from memory with reference to such matters." "No, but not speaking from memory but having your memory refreshed by a perusal of that document, have you any doubt that you were applied to?" "I have no doubt that I might have been applied to . . . I see the document but I don't know. I might have signed it in blank." "Will you swear you were not present . . . Now be careful Mr Smith, for depend upon it, you shall hear of this again if you are not." "I will not swear that I was. I think I was not. I am not quite positive."

Smith's credibility had been shot to pieces in a few minutes. He had been revealed to be shifty, unreliable and probably a liar. The most Shee could do was limit the damage by asking him whether there had ever been improper intimacy between him and Sarah Palmer. "They might have said so, but they had no reason for saying so," he replied stubbornly. That closed the defence.

Immediately, Cockburn was on his feet once more to deliver his final address to the jury. He spoke without notes, this time for five hours as, he said, the instrument of public justice, in "a spirit of fairness, moderation and of truth". He proceeded to damn Palmer and his defence with forensic and deadly skill. The two questions were: did Cook die a natural death or was he poisoned, and if the latter, was Palmer the author of his death? The case was that Palmer had weakened Cook by antimony and then finished him off with strychnine. A great deal of time in the case had been devoted to strychnine, much less to antimony, or to the question whether Palmer had administered it, but the attorney general swept onwards. The symptoms showed tetanic convulsions and they had been caused by the poison: whereas tetanus killed slowly, strychnine killed very fast. Cockburn, who was said to have studied the effect of the poison for weeks before the trial, was precisely clear and authoritative about strychnine and its effects now – and coruscatingly scathing about Nunneley's attempts to claim Cook's death was down to something else. No one had ever treated Cook for a cold, there was not the slightest evidence he had had one. "It is a scandal upon a distinguished and a learned profession that men should put forward such speculations as these, perverting the facts and drawing from them sophistical and unwarranted conclusions with the view to deceiving the jury . . . They are unworthy of your notice and discreditable to be put forward by a witness [to] sensible men as you are." Most of the other defence witnesses escaped no more lightly, including Richardson, the angina pectoris man: "The gentleman . . . would not have escaped quite so easily if I had had the books under my hand and . . . [had been] able to expose, as I would have done, the ignorance or the presumption of the assertion which he dared to make."

Slowly, remorselessly, Cockburn went through the symptoms comparing what had been said on both sides:

> I get rid at once of all those vain, futile attempts to distinguish this case . . . and I come back to the symptoms which attended this unhappy man's demise. Can you doubt that when I have excluded all those cases of tetanic convulsions, epilepsy and angina and then lastly exclude traumatic and idiopathic tetanus, what remains? I think you cannot hesitate to come to the conclusion that this was death by strychnia. Medical witnesses of the highest authority agree.

Cockburn pointed out that, despite Shee's assertions that he would contest every point in the case, the defence had not questioned the fact that Palmer had bought strychnine just before Cook's death at all. What motive had

Newton had for "locking the secret" of his giving three grains to Palmer to his breast and not telling anyone until the trial? "What possible conceivable motive can this young man have except a sense of truth?" Newton had only said Palmer had called at "about nine", so maybe he had made a mistake, even of an hour, and then not come to think of it again for weeks.

Then there was Jerry Smith:

> I implore you for the sake of justice not to allow the man who stands at the bar to be prejudiced by that most discreditable and unworthy witness who has been called today on his behalf . . . not to one word which that man has uttered will you attach the slightest value. Such a spectacle I never saw in my recollection in a court of justice. He calls himself a member of the legal profession. I blush for it to number such a man upon its roll . . . There was not one that heard him today that was not satisfied that that man came here to tell a false tale . . . not convinced that he has been mixed up in many a villainy . . . and he comes now to save, if he can, the life of his companion and friend – the son of the woman with whom he has had that intimacy which he sought today in vain to disguise.

Cockburn was comparing Smith's integrity with Newton's. Why would Newton lie about the encounter at Hawkins's shop on the Tuesday? Why would Palmer need to accumulate nine grains of strychnine, enough to kill half a dozen people, in under twenty-four hours? Why go to Hawkins for the first time in three years when he usually used Thirlby? Wasn't that remarkable? It was because Thirlby would know he had no legitimate use for the poison. If it was legitimately for a patient, where was the patient? Shee, he pointed out, had not even mentioned the second purchase. If it was to destroy stray dogs worrying his horses, why had the grooms not come forward to testify to that? Why had no one been recruited to help him lay the poison? If he had tried to buy the poison in London, he would have had to give his name, which was why he had not done so – or perhaps he was rushing to catch his train . . . Why had he called in Bamford to treat Cook? "I speak of that gentleman in terms of perfect respect but I think I do him no injustice if I say that the vigour of his intellect and his power of observation are liable to be impaired by the advancing hand of time ... I do not think he was a person likely to make very shrewd observations upon any symptoms." As for Jones: he had suspected nothing and, if Stephens had not exhibited sagacity and firmness and Palmer had bought a stout oak coffin, nobody would have been aught the wiser. Of course, had Jones not been present in the room, no one would have known of Cook's death until the morning, no one would have known how he died, and his death would have been put down to apoplexy or epilepsy. Why had he had the same symptoms two nights running? Cockburn speculated that the first dose had not been big enough, or had failed for some reason.

Now he came to the antimony which had been found in Cook's system. Cook had got over his sickness at Shrewsbury by the end of the week, but then started vomiting about the time the broth was brought over to him from Palmer's kitchen. Antimony caused retching, it was in Cook's blood, so it must have been administered forty-eight hours before death: who could have administered it but the prisoner? It must have been given to produce the appearance of a natural sickness – but also to prevent Cook going to Tattersall's on the Monday to collect his winnings: "that the sickness was produced and the antimony was afterwards found are incapable of dispute. Put them together and you have cause and effect." If antimony was given, it was probable strychnine was too. The pills were suspicious: why would Palmer go with Bamford to watch him make up the pills when he could have done it himself? And why take them home and wait an hour or so before delivering them to Cook? He would have had plenty of time to make up his own concoction. Why draw attention to the old man's handwriting? Was it part of a scheme, so that he could remind Jones that it was Bamford's pills that had been administered? It would have prevented suspicion: "Any one of these circumstances in itself would not be such ... as [to be] conclusive of the prisoner's guilt ... but following one upon the other, taken as a whole, [they] lead but to one conclusion." Also, what had happened to the strychnine? "It remains a mystery, but this I know, I can look upon it in no aspect in which it does not reflect light upon the guilt ... if you can solve the difficulty for Heaven's sake do, but I can suggest to you no solution."

If poisoning by strychnine was proved and only Palmer could have done it, the question of motive was secondary, but Palmer was in severe financial difficulties and being pressed for repayment by Pratt. Then Polestar won and Cook's own financial difficulties were removed:

> If this accusation is well founded, the mare winning and his being entitled to a large sum of money was the most fatal thing that could have befallen him. Alas! How great is the shortsightedness of mortal man! When we have the highest cause of joy and exultation, often while the sunshine of our prosperity warms and gladdens our heart for a moment, there is lurking beneath our feet a fatal abyss . . . This poor man might have been living now had it not been that upon that fatal day his mare won.

Palmer was in desperate straits with nowhere to turn for money and the usurious moneylender pressing him: "if he once becomes doubtful of the security and uncertain of payment you may as well ask pity of a rabid tiger or . . . pity of stones as hope to find the bowels of compassion in him." Pratt must have seen his reputation sinking as he followed Nunneley under Cockburn's lash. Cockburn was deadly here, remorselessly building a picture of Palmer's debts and how he was trying to siphon off Cook's money in juggling his transactions with Pratt. His debts might have been got rid of by the bankruptcy court, but forgery was a criminal matter, incurring transportation or lengthy penal servitude. Palmer had presented a cheque of Cook's but was it also forged? It had disappeared. If the cheque was an honest one, why had he needed to ask Cheshire to write it out for him? "Does not that transaction bear fraud upon the face of it? What has become of it? Why is it not produced?" Why had Palmer had to borrow £25 to get to the races, but by the end of the week had enough to pay his local debts and make contributions to the moneylender? Palmer had also tried to persuade Cheshire to witness Cook's signature on a document apparently acknowledging a debt of £4,000 and had written to Pratt trying to claim Polestar:

> for all these purposes, from beginning to end, it was necessary that Cook should be put on one side. If Cheshire had had the weakness and wickedness to comply he would have had him in his power and the next thing would have been that he would

have brought him trembling and reluctant into the witness box
of some court to swear that he had seen the dead man put his
signature to that piece of paper.

This was another document that could not be produced: "Who can doubt
that it is either destroyed or purposely withheld?" Then there was Cook's
betting book: where had that gone? It had gone missing immediately after
Cook's death, before other people came into the room: "Does anyone doubt
in his own mind where that betting book had got to?"

Every new section of Cockburn's speech started with words such as
"it does not stop there", "but there is more", "it does not rest here", piling
each new circumstance on the previous one throughout the long spring Saturday afternoon. Now he was onto the post-mortem – the removal of the
jar, the suggested overturning of the carriage, the suborning of Cheshire,
the attempted bribery of the friendly Staffordshire coroner:

> Look at his restless anxiety; it may possibly, it is true, be com-
> patible with innocence; but I think on the other hand it must
> be admitted that it bears strongly the aspect of guilt . . . it is one
> of a series of things, small perhaps each individually in them-
> selves, but taken as a whole . . . leading irresistibly to the con-
> clusion of the guilt of this man.

Finally, Cockburn rebuked Shee for proclaiming his belief in his client's innocence: "It would have been better if my learned friend had abstained from
so strange a declaration . . . The best reproof which I can administer to my
learned friend is to abstain from imitating so dangerous an example." His
bias had led him into error: "Who would not shrink from the conclusion
that he was to advocate the cause of one . . . guilty of the foulest of all imag-
inable crimes?" Then, finally, the peroration:

> Pay no regard to the voice of the country whether it be for con-
> demnation or acquittal; pay no regard to anything but the in-
> ternal voice of your own consciences and the sense of that duty
> to God and man which you are to discharge . . . For the protec-
> tion of the good and the suppression of the wicked I ask for that

verdict by which alone, it seems to me, the safety of society can
be secured and the imperious demands of public justice can
alone be satisfied.

Palmer listened with deep attention and maybe a sinking heart to Cockburn's address. The *Manchester Guardian* detected an air of considerable
anxiety, although still "his usual perfect self-possession".

It was now half past six on Saturday evening. There was only the Lord
Chief Justice's charge to the jury to come, but he would not start it now.
Campbell would labour over his speech all day on Sunday instead. He had
been taking laborious notes throughout the trial and re-reading and revising
them every evening when he got home, but now the 77-year-old had a clear
day to marshal his thoughts. "My labour and anxiety were fearful," he wrote
in his memoirs, "but I have been rewarded by public approbation. The court
sat eight hours a day and when I got home, renouncing all other engage-
ments, I employed myself till midnight in revising my notes and considering
the evidence. Luckily I had a Sunday to prepare for my summing up and to
this I devoted fourteen continuous hours."

That weekend, after watching Jerry Smith's evisceration by Cockburn,
Palmer's solicitor John Smith was writing to the newspapers. The *Morning
Chronicle* published his letter: "As it has been generally supposed that I have
given evidence at the trial of Mr William Palmer, I beg to say that I have not
done so and that the gentleman who has been a witness is not in any way
connected with me. I have simply acted as the solicitor for the defence of the
accused." Clearly, he saw the way the wind was blowing. And he certainly
did not wish to be mistaken for his wretched Rugeley namesake. Palmer
himself told his brother the following week that Smith's evidence had been
very bad.

The jurors themselves had the attorney general's masterful final
speech reverberating in their heads unchallenged for the rest of the weekend. They were still confined at the London Coffee House. One juror whose
wife had gone into labour was told by Campbell that he could not go and
see her "on ascertaining that the lady's life was not in danger". On the Sunday they all went to the service in the chapel at Newgate and were then taken
out to Epping Forest once again for exercise and fresh air. Their incarcera-
tion at least was coming to an end, but there were still two days to go.

14

"It was the riding that did it"

LORD CHIEF JUSTICE CAMPBELL'S SUMMING-UP FILLED ALL OF THE TRIAL'S eleventh day, Monday 26 May 1856, and all the following morning, into the afternoon: more than thirteen hours in all, by far the longest speech of the trial. On the Monday alone, the court sat from 10 a.m. until 7 p.m., which must have been very trying for all concerned in the stuffy, overcrowded, high-windowed room. Among those listening to him was William Gladstone and the court remained densely packed all day. The Lord Chief Justice's prose was ponderous and convoluted, even for a member of the Victorian judiciary, and he tended to read in a low mumbled Scottish burr, which probably did not help. "After reading in court ten hours[4] I had only got through the proofs for the prosecution," he recalled in his memoirs. "I had no doubt of his guilt and I was conscious that by God's assistance, I had done my duty."[4] Indeed, he made his absence of doubt abundantly clear – even when he was seemingly trying to be balanced, Campbell insinuated Palmer's culpability from the start. He began by saying that the jury must not be improperly influenced by evidence of the prisoner's discreditable transactions, especially as they would normally have been excluded:

> It appears that he had forged a great many bills of exchange and that he had entered into transactions not of a reputable nature. These transactions however would have been excluded from your consideration altogether had it not been necessary to bring them forward to assist you in arriving at your verdict . . . the law

---

[4] He exaggerated. It was only nine.

of England presumes every man to be innocent until his guilt is established, it allows his guilt to be established only by evidence directly connected with the charge brought against him.

Campbell seemed temporarily to have forgotten the insinuations about the attempt to insure Walter's life.

Campbell smugly said how pleased he was that the case had been laid out so fully, prosecuted by the government "so that justice may be effectively administered". The prisoner, too, had ample means to conduct his defence, by one of the most distinguished advocates at the English bar. But Shee had committed the mistake of asserting that he believed Palmer was innocent and that had to be squashed:

> Gentlemen I most strongly recommend to you to attend to everything that fell so eloquently, so ably and so impressively from that advocate, with the exception of his own private opin- ion . . . it would have been better if his advocate had abstained from some of the observations he made . . . it may lead to the most disastrous consequences . . . it may lead the jury to believe that a prisoner is not guilty because his advocate expresses his perfect conviction of his innocence.

It was for the jury to decide on Palmer's guilt or innocence, but if they de- cided he was guilty, it would be their duty to say so, for if he were to escape with impunity "there would be no safety for mankind and society would fall to pieces". Circumstantial evidence was all that could reasonably be expected and a verdict of guilty might satisfactorily be pronounced; motive was of little importance – atrocious crimes of this sort might be committed from very slight motives, to gain a small pecuniary advantage. If they decided the symptoms were of strychnine poisoning, they had to decide that it was the prisoner who had administered it: they needed to look at the moral evidence of whether the prisoner had the opportunity to do it and availed himself of the chance to do so.

Campbell proceeded to read through his notes, reciting verbatim large swathes of the evidence, or ordering the clerk to do so – the third time at least that the jury must have heard the case against Palmer. He paused every so often to place his own interpretation on the evidence and the witnesses giving it. When he got to Elizabeth Mills, the maid servant who had moved to London and met William Stephens several times, he added: "It has been suggested that [she] may have been bribed to give evidence prejudicial to the prisoner, but in justice both to Mr Stephens and Elizabeth Mills I am bound to declare that not one fact has been adduced to warrant us in believing that there is the slightest foundation for such a statement." It was all gratuitous assertion, said Campbell, far from supported by the evidence and distinctly denied. As for the fact that Mills had only much later remembered that she had been made sick by the broth and had not originally told the coroner about it, well, the jury would have to determine if there was any material discrepancy. Then he got to the chemist's assistant Charles Newton, "a witness of the greatest importance", and the judge had no doubt about his probity, despite his not remembering the strychnine transaction until the eve of the trial:

> although there is an omission which is always to be borne in mind,
> there is no contradiction of anything that he has said here. Well
> what is the probability of his inventing this wicked and abom-
> inable lie? I see no motive that Mr Newton could have for invent-
> ing a lie to take away the life of another person. If you believe him,
> certainly the evidence is very strong against the prisoner at the bar.

There was still the evidence of the other chemist Roberts that Palmer had bought strychnine on the Tuesday morning:

> Disbelieving Newton you have no evidence of strychnia being
> obtained on the Monday evening; but disbelieving Newton and
> believing Roberts you have evidence of six grains of strychnia
> being obtained by the prisoner on the Tuesday morning and of
> that you have no explanation . . . I should shrink from my duty,
> I should be unworthy to sit here if I did not call your attention
> to the inference that if he purchased strychnia, he purchased it
> for the purpose of administering it to Cook.

Palmer was listening to all this intently, scribbling notes for his solicitor John Smith. One said: "I wish there was 2½ grams of strychnine in old

Campbell's acidulated draught solely because I think he acts unfairly."
Smith kept that one to himself. There were other notes passed down to the
barristers too, on slips of paper not unlike those used for the Jane letters
and in the same urgent handwriting. One, to Kenealy, said: "Did not Campbell sum up sufficiently plain for the jury to say that I am guilty? All I can
say if they do they are great liars. Wm. P." Another said: "If I had a book I
would send it at Campbell's head for I think he behaves ill."

At length Campbell got on to the medical experts. There was Sir Benjamin Brodie, a gentleman of high reputation and unblemished honour,
one of the most distinguished medical men of the present time, so well acquainted with all diseases: "If you agree with him the inference is that Cook
died from some other cause than disease." Shee jumped in to interrupt the
judge's encomium to ask for his cross-examination of Brodie to be read out,
where the witness had agreed that Cook's final symptoms might have been
very similar to epilepsy. "I dare say it is very applicable," said Campbell,
sounding grumpy, then: "The jury have heard you read it. It is for them to
say whether it is important in their view or not." Then there was Taylor and
Rees, their experiments with strychnine on animals and their failure to find
evidence of the poison in Cook's body. "You must bear in mind," said
Campbell, "that we have their own evidence to show that there have been
cases of death by strychnine in which the united skill of these individuals
has failed to detect the presence of strychnine after death." The judge mildly
criticised Taylor's prejudicial letter to the *Lancet*, saying it would have been
better if he had not written it, but suggesting it did not materially detract
from his evidence: "He could have had no enmity and no interest whatever
to misrepresent the facts." By now evening was drawing on and the judge
drew to a close after concluding the prosecution evidence. God willing, he
said, the investigation would certainly close the following day.

After the adjournment, George Palmer was allowed down into the Newgate cells to see his brother, and the following day's *Morning Chronicle* reported
what it supposed William had said to him. The quotations sound very much
as if they were drawn straight from a Victorian romantic novel's notions of
manly steadfastness. "Don't take on, George!" William had apparently cried.
"There is a God above us that will stand between me and harm. I am innocent
of the crime imputed to me. Let that be a consolation to you and, upon my
word, I have never deceived you yet and, however guilty I may be in other

Palmer scribbles his notes to his defence team from the dock at the Old Bailey. The lawyers are sitting on the left.

things, to destroy life has never entered my head." The *Illustrated Times* produced similar but different sentiments, seemingly drawn from the same literary sources. It had William clapping his brother on the shoulder and saying:

> May you sleep as soundly as I do! I have had a good tea with half a pound of steak. May you have as good a night's rest as I shall. Tell my mother and my boy that Newton and Mills are false and that I fear the grave as little as my bed. Tell Willy that his father has had many troubles but the least of all has been the accusation of murder against him. Good night, God bless you. May your mind be as easy as mine is now. Don't feel low.

The religiosity and the resignation may well strike true, but by this stage probably not even Palmer could feel too optimistic about the following day's outcome. Most of the lawyers who had been in court had long since come to the conclusion by now that his guilt was a foregone conclusion.

On the following morning – the twelfth and last day of the trial – Campbell resumed his summing-up, speaking now for a further four hours. "On no previous morning," *The Times* reported, "was there a greater crowd either within the court or waiting on the outside for admission." As the day wore on, the streets outside became blocked with spectators. Campbell started once more where he had left off, with elements of the prosecution, reminding the jury of Palmer's financial desperation and the medical witnesses – "most skilful and honourable men" – who were convinced that Cook had been poisoned by strychnine. He emphasised: "There is no point of law according to which poison must be found in the body of the deceased" – it was just that Taylor and Rees had not discovered any in the parts they tested. Then Campbell added some new thoughts of his own: that the strychnine might have been administered to Cook even earlier than the prosecution had alleged and it had just taken longer to work. Shee lumbered to his feet: "I think that is not so upon the evidence, my lord." Campbell ploughed on: "There are instances in which it has been detected, there have been instances referred to in the course of this trial in which there has been as long an interval." "I believe that is a mistake," said Shee, but Campbell ignored him and continued: "We have to look to the evidence as it implicates the prisoner . . . You must consider the evidence to show that he must have tampered with the health of the deceased." Once again he was back to Palmer's procuring the strychnine, the loss of the betting book, the attempt to tamper with the coroner: "If not answered they certainly present a serious case."

Now, at last, Campbell proceeded to outline the defence argument, but with distinctly less enthusiasm. The Lord Chief Justice, wrote Kenealy, Palmer's junior counsel, was determined to convict: he had shown "an unfairness which gradually increased until his conduct can be justly described by no other word than infamous". Kenealy was unbalanced himself, especially by the time he came to write his memoirs, but he added: "everything in Palmer's favour was met by frowns and dagger look from Campbell, while he made a point of writing down fully everything against, noting scarcely anything to the prisoner's advantage . . . From the very first day he assumed an expression of intense hatred towards the guilty wretch." He noted that Cockburn had told him shortly after the start of the trial that he could "see Palmer's death in Jack Campbell's face".

Campbell said the defence's medical witnesses included a number who were of high honour, solid integrity and proven scientific knowledge, but also others "whose object was to procure an acquittal of the prisoner

. . . a witness should not be turned into an advocate". One by one, the defence witnesses were damned with faint praise. They were respectable men, but it was for the jury to decide how much weight to give to what they said:

> You will have to determine whether Cook's symptoms were or were not consistent with death by strychnia. If they were not, your conclusion will be in favour of the prisoner; if they were . . . I do not say on that fact alone you should find a verdict against him, but, this I say, it will be your duty to consider the fact in connection with other evidence that has been brought before you in order to come to a clear conclusion.

There was a brief adjournment, during which *The Times* noted "as an instance of the tenacity with which the human mind will cling to hope under the most desperate circumstances" that Palmer had tossed a further note to his barristers. Maybe he was briefly more optimistic this morning in spite of everything: "I think they will find a verdict of Not Guilty." If so, Campbell's remarks when he resumed further undermined his chances. The other defence witnesses were compared with the contrasting prosecution case. And then there was Jerry Smith: "Can you believe a man who so disgraces himself in the witness box? It is for you to say what faith you can place in a witness who, by his own admission, indulged in fraudulent proceedings. Of his credit, you are the judges." Campbell rubbed the point home by repeating it twice. By now he was going round in circles, back to the prosecution case, back to the shortcomings of the defence.

As Campbell ground remorselessly on, Palmer could be seen burying his head in his hands. On raising his face, said the *Manchester Guardian*, "the suppressed emotion with which he had been struggling was painfully visible". Presumably that meant he was crying. He must have realised now, more than ever, that he was damned.

Campbell's voice, too, was trembling with emotion by now. His mumbling almost inaudible, the Lord Chief Justice was just preparing to send the jury out with the words, "You will remember the oath which you have taken and you will act upon it . . . and may God direct you!", when Shee was once more on his feet, shouting at him: "It is my duty not to be deterred by any suggestion of displeasure." He, too, invoked God:

it is my duty to a much higher tribunal than even your lordships' to submit . . . the proper question: the question whether
Cook's symptoms are consistent with death by strychnia is a
wrong question, unless followed by "and inconsistent with
death by other and natural causes" and that the question should
be whether the medical evidence establishes beyond all reasonable doubt the death of Cook by strychnia.

Alderson chipped in: "It is done already. You have done it in your speech."
But Campbell, clearly irked to be contradicted like this, also responded,
turning to the jury: "Gentlemen, I did not submit that the question alone
on which your verdict was to turn was whether the symptoms . . . were those
of strychnia, but I said that it was a most material question . . . If you believe
that, it is your duty to God and man to find the prisoner guilty."

In the dock, as Campbell finished speaking, Palmer wrote one more
note which was passed down to Shee. It said: "I thank you for your exertions
on my behalf as I am satisfied that you have done all that mortal could do.
Whatever may be the result, I am satisfied with you and your exertions."

Now at last, at a quarter past two in the afternoon, the jury retired to
consider their verdict. It took them just under an hour and twenty minutes
before they returned. One of the jurors wrote anonymously to *The Times* a
few days later to state what happened, in answer to accusations that they
had not considered the case earnestly enough:

> When we reached our room, there was silence for ten or fifteen min-
> utes. A short discussion on the facts took place, the foreman Mr
> Mavor, intimating that he did not wish any juryman to express aloud
> his personal opinion what the verdict should be for fear of unduly
> influencing a colleague. Each man took pen and paper and wrote
> his decision separately and folded up the paper . . . It is quite untrue
> that we were absent a long time for the sake of appearances – our
> situation was too dreadful and too solemn to admit of humbug.

By 3.35 p.m. the jury were back in court. The verdict was unanimous. They
all thought Palmer was guilty. The prisoner, it was said, "exhibited some
slight pallor and the least possible shade of anxiety", but now recovered his

self-possession and demeanour of comparative indifference. Campbell may have breathed a sigh of relief. It was customary for the most junior judge at a trial such as this to pronounce the death sentence, but Campbell was determined to do it himself and the black cloth square was duly placed on top of his wig. Palmer, he said, had had a long and impartial trial:

> in that verdict my two learned brothers who have so anxiously watched this trial and myself entirely concur and consider the verdict altogether satisfactory . . . whether it is the first and only offence of this sort which you have committed is certainly known only to God and your own conscience . . . your life is forfeited. You must prepare to die; and I trust that, as you can expect no mercy in this world, you will, by repentance of your crimes, seek to obtain mercy from Almighty God. Now I hope that this terrible example will deter others from committing such atrocious crimes and that it will be seen that, whatever art, or caution, or experience may accomplish, such an offence will be detected and punished. However destructive poisons may be, it is so ordained by Providence that there are means for the safety of His creatures for detecting and punishing those who administer them. I again implore you to repent and prepare for the awful change which awaits you. I will not seek to harrow up your feelings by any enumeration of the circumstances of this foul murder. I will content myself now with passing upon you the sentence of the law.

Then, with the invocation that he would be taken back to the gaol of the county of Stafford and the ancient incantation that he would be taken thence to a place of execution, be there hanged by the neck until he be dead and that his body would afterwards be buried within the precincts of the prison, Campbell dismissed Palmer with a loud Amen.

The prisoner, said *The Times* almost admiringly, "maintained his firmness and perfect calmness . . . and when the sentence was being passed, he looked an interested, although utterly unmoved spectator. We think we may truly say that during the whole of this protracted trial his nerve and calmness have never for a moment forsaken him." Asked before the sentencing whether he had anything to say, he had remained silent and he said nothing now. His only words in open court had been "Not guilty" during the first day's hearing. There could be no appeal, unless the home secretary Sir George Grey granted clemency, which he was never likely to do. And so William Palmer now had less than three weeks to live and the prospect of a humiliating public execution before him: dangling throttled at the end of a rope with thousands of people jeering him.

As he was taken down the steps to the cells, Palmer passed one last note to John Smith: "It was the riding that did it." Did he mean it was horse-racing that had brought about his downfall, or the deadly way Sir Alexander Cockburn had prosecuted his case, or the judge's summing-up? Like so many other things Palmer said and wrote, the phrase was ambiguous.

Up in the court, Campbell turned to the jury to offer them his warm thanks:

> Your conduct throughout this protracted trial which you have attended, no doubt, at much serious inconvenience to your-selves, has been such as to merit our utmost commendation. I only hope and I doubt not that you will be rewarded for your patient attention and for the services which you have made by the approbation of your own consciences and the approving voice of your country.

Downstairs in the cells, Palmer protested his innocence to the under-sheriff, saying he had not received a fair trial. The man pointed out that all three judges had agreed with the verdict, but Palmer answered: "Well sir, but that don't satisfy me." He was not allowed to see his relatives, but was told to take off his own clothes and put on prison uniform instead: a dark-grey rough woollen jacket, trousers and waistcoat, a blue checked cotton shirt and heavy boots. Then he was handcuffed and shackled, with a chain at-tached to both ankles and to a warder. It was a great humiliation.

There was a considerable crowd outside, blocking all the streets around. "The prevailing opinion it will not now be improper to say, was decidedly averse to the prisoner," said the *Manchester Guardian* primly. Newgate's governor Weatherhead had arranged for a Black Maria wagon to be drawn up to distract their attention. Meanwhile a hansom cab was

The jury consider their verdict.

brought to the governor's private entrance, and Palmer and the warders were hustled into it to be taken to Euston station, where six months earlier he had bumped into his nemesis William Stephens on the platform. They boarded the 8 p.m. train for the journey back to the Midlands. At the station another large crowd was waiting and surged forward when they saw the warders and their shuffling prisoner. With their shouts of "Murderer!" and "Poisoner!" echoing in his ears, Palmer was hustled down the platform and pushed into a carriage with the blinds drawn. He had asked if he might be taken in a Great Western Railway train as he was so well known on the normal North Western service, but this was rejected out of hand. He had few choices and no rights left.

At Stafford it was past midnight by the time the train arrived, but the news that the prisoner was on board had been telegraphed ahead and a large crowd was milling around. The prison had sent two warders but no vehicle, and there was no one in authority there to take charge of Palmer. There was, however, a small police detachment to keep order, one of them Tom Wool-laston, who had arrested Palmer at his home in Rugeley the previous December. In his memoirs he wrote: "On prisoner's alighting from the train, he recognised me and taking my arm asked to be allowed to walk with me, which he did the whole way." The crowd was getting larger all the time, and after a while the two warders decided to walk Palmer to the jail rather than waiting for transport, so they set off on the half-mile journey. Surrounded by policemen and a howling mob, they shuffled as fast as Palmer could go with chains around his legs. A cloak was thrown over him to hide the hand-cuffs. Woollaston continued:

> When passing up the streets, caused by the anxiety of the crowd, many were upset and trampled upon and the scene and im-proper epithets indulged in were indecent in the extreme. Pris-oner was heavily ironed and walked with difficulty. An escort of warders from the gaol met us by the way. No doubt those ought to have arrived earlier, their absence was much observed upon.

Back in London, Campbell was confident in a job well done. No one could say Palmer had not had a full trial – much longer than that of most crimi-nals, including those charged with murder. Serjeant Shee was left to rue the inadequacies of the defence, the opportunities missed, the questions not asked, and the weakness of some of those called on Palmer's behalf. There were leads the defence could have followed up, but did not do so: why, for instance, had they not found the postboy who had driven Palmer home from Stafford station on the Monday night, who would have been able to tell the court when he had got back to Rugeley and so might have discredited Newton's evidence? Why had Newton and Mills not been challenged harder, or the suggestion of widespread illness at Shrewbury races not been fol-lowed up? Meanwhile, John Smith, the solicitor, was already hard at work drawing up a petition for clemency, or at least a respite until any and all doubts had been resolved.

15

"In accordance with the voice of science and the feeling of the country"

T HE CONVICTION OF WILLIAM PALMER WAS NOT THE ONLY NEWS IN BRITISH papers at the end of May 1856. There was the Derby the day after the trial ended, "a terrific explosion" at the Woolwich Arsenal which killed six people, and celebratory firework displays across London to mark the end of the Crimean War – an event that lost something of its splendour by being crudely depicted in black-and-white drawings in the weekly illustrated press. In France on the day of the execution there would be the christening at Notre Dame of Emperor Napoleon III's son and heir, the Prince Imperial, whose life would come to a sudden end twenty-three years later when he was speared to death in an ambush on the veldt while serving with British troops during the Zulu War. Madame Jenny Goldschmidt Lind, the Swedish Nightingale, was in concert at the Exeter Hall (reserved seats: one guinea) singing selections from Rossini and Mayerbeer. And in their advertisements Messrs Crosse and Blackwell were respectfully inviting the attention of the public to their pickles, sauces and other table delicacies.

But Palmer certainly still took up a great deal of space. His trial spawned several near-verbatim transcripts, including *The Times*'s publication of its daily reports of the trial. There was also the *Illustrated Times*'s potted biography, inspired by Vizetelly. The *Illustrated Times* also got hold of Palmer's diary for 1855, which it gleefully reprinted ("The whole of his private diary up to the hour of his arrest") as part of the book. It is in fact a perfunctory appointments record, which shows just how much of his time was spent travelling, dining with friends such as Jere Smith (in November they dined together on the 12th, 16th, 17th and 21st), meeting his trainer Saunders, and making payments towards his debts. His attendance at church, whether he took communion and often who preached are also recorded on the Sundays when Palmer was at home. He did not go every week but was a fairly regular worshipper. On the day of Cook's death the entry reads: "21. Wednesday:– ++++ Cook died at 1 o'clock this morning. Jere and Wm Saunders dined. Sent Bright a three months' bill." The entries peter out the following weekend after he had dinner one last time at his mother's: "25. Sunday:– At church – Hamilton preached. Dined, Yard. 26. Monday:– Attended a PM examination on poor Cook, with Drs Harland, Mr Bamford, Newton and a Mr Devonshire." It is not clear who passed the diary on to journalists, but it was in the possession of the prosecution Treasury solicitor during and after the trial. A facsimile of the last pages was printed in the Notable British Trials series sixty years later. When George Palmer requested to have his "late unfortunate" brother's papers and diaries back that autumn, however, he was told he could not have them. He needed them because his mother was still being sued by Wright, the Birmingham moneylender, but scribbled on his letter is a note by Cockburn: "The Crown cannot give these to Mr George Palmer, even if otherwise so disposed." The most he would be allowed was to see them "on his understanding to return them".

On the whole, the newspapers' editorial writers congratulated the lawyers and the clearly impeccable British legal system for a satisfactory outcome to the trial. On the morning after the verdict *The Times* reflected on a case well tried: "Never in late times has a case of murder roused such universal interest, never have such pains been taken to insure perfect fairness in the inquiry, never have the proceedings extended to such a length," it stated, adding inaccurately – "The Crown of its own free will furnished the defence with all the evidence that it intended to bring forward." Then: "Never was a crime more cruel, treacherous and cold-blooded, never was it brought home by proof more cogent and irresistible. True, the evidence was circumstantial but in some respects circumstantial evidence is best . . . there can be little doubt as to the decision." In the justice of the verdict, it said, everyone who had followed the proceedings must fully concur. No other country, said the *Saturday Review,* "could show so excellent a specimen of perfect logic and freedom from all prejudice as this case has afforded". Others shared such views. "We gladly abstained from saying one word that could imply our belief in Palmer's guilt so long as the court had the case under consideration," proclaimed the *Illustrated Times* mendaciously in its next issue:

> But the trial itself now becomes as fair a subject of criticism as the proceedings of any other English tribunal. A prisoner with us has every chance. Ample time and leisure are given him; an Act of Parliament if need be is passed for his sake . . . the most is sure to be made of everything in his favour. Had Rugeley been a log village in the far West the man would have been hanged by the populace before Cook was buried. That his character was bad, that his circumstances were desperate, that he had easy access to poison, that Cook died in sudden striking and terrible agonies – these facts would have carried him to the tree in five minutes. But not here. His case was investigated as calmly as the question of the moon's rotation. Rabbits and guinea pigs were sacrificed like the "innocent ape" of Juvenal and the court heard with utmost consideration that Cook was of a weak constitution and had been seen drunk.

Proof that the trial had indeed absorbed the attention of the whole country can be seen in Queen Victoria's private journal entry for 28 May 1856, the day after the trial ended. The royal family had been staying at Osborne House on the Isle of Wight for most of the trial and had returned to Buckingham Palace two days earlier, but the round of guard inspections, meetings with returning Crimean veterans, sea trips, walks on the island and the arrival of the Prussian prince Frederick – Fritz – who was to be their eldest daughter Vicky's intended, plainly had not prevented the queen from keeping up with the news from the Old Bailey as well. The entry shows she was fully au fait with the case:

> We heard that after a trial of 12 days that horrible Palmer, a doctor and a black leg, well-known on the turf, has been found guilty of poisoning his unhappy friend Cook with strychnine. Everyone was convinced he had done that and also poisoned his wife and brother – all for money, but there were great fears that

would not be able to be proved. However, after one of the longest and most interesting, though horrid, trials on record the scoundrel has been convicted. The defence was bad and the witnesses quite perjured themselves. I dined alone and then dressed afterwards for a ball at the Turkish embassy.

The royal family had more than a dispassionate interest in the case: Prince Albert, after all, had bought one of Palmer's horses and Sir Benjamin Brodie was one of their physicians.

Out in the "far West", or at least in New York City, by the time the verdict was noticed by the *New York Times* nearly a month later, the paper could afford to deploy a little condescension, even some sly admiration for the guilty man, whose "horrid story . . . distances all the fancies of Bulwer's romance" – so much so that the paper devoted four articles to the Palmer case. Its readers were clearly aware of the dramatis personae in the case because the paper did not feel the need to explain who they were, and for good measure it also threw in the name of an infamous eighteenth-century thief to hallow the story with artistic verisimilitude. It added:

As this Borgia of the betting ring made a tool of Cheshire, a mere culling of Cook, a dupe of Dr Bamford and a partisan of even Coroner Ward with a versatility of resource and power which throw Jonathan Wild and such heroes into the shade, so even now he has contrived to produce a sympathy in certain very weak-minded men that the sentence upon him is the result of prejudice, not the fount of justice . . . Go where you will over London, strychnine is said to stare you in the face . . . the public entertain no moral doubt whatever about his guilt.

By the time the article appeared, Palmer was long dead. Back in Britain, specialist journals were generally satisfied with the trial's outcome. The *Association Medical Journal* (predecessor of the *British Medical Journal*) declared the verdict to be in accordance with the voice of science and the feeling of the country. And yet doubts remained among medical men, and not just the weak-minded ones. There was unease about what exactly had been proved by forensic science when Palmer was convicted even though no strychnine had been found in the body of his victim. There were also concerns about such eminent professionals disagreeing with each other so publicly when a man's life was at stake and about how complicated evidence could be presented dispassionately to a lay jury. "It is impossible that science can speak to the unskilled in language so intelligible and distinct as she does to her chosen disciples," said the *Lancet*:

> It could not be expected that twelve men relying on their general
> knowledge and that indefinable, lawless and treacherous faculty
> "common sense" should estimate accurately the value of the
> medical evidence laid before them . . . if they sought to unravel
> the scientific questions before them by the application of their
> own knowledge and common sense, they were almost sure to
> err, or to go right only by accident.

The *AMJ* said: "How can we expect the public to respect us if we will not respect each other – if we will not abstain even from using expressions which do not currently pass current in the disputes of gentlemen?" And, beneath the confidence, there was a deeper unease too: was a man going to be hanged largely as a result of the opinion of Alfred Swaine Taylor? "This is the dictum," said the *AMJ*, "of a gentleman whose test-tube has brought many a man to the gallows and it ought, we think, to be corroborated or confuted in a manner as openly as it has been given." The *Lancet* was not alone in noticing his reluctance to share his findings with those who might disagree with him.

Whatever the newspapers might say, concern about the trial extended more widely, into Parliament and to public meetings. These were against capital punishment in general, rather than in support of Palmer in particular, though his impending doom was the catalyst. One, held at the London Tavern on 9 June, was reported in the sort of lofty tone that is traditionally reserved for those whose ideas are too incredible to be taken seriously. The *Morning Chronicle* wrote it up:

> In a speech of considerable length, the chairman then proceeded
> to contend, in the first place, that capital punishment was
> against the law of God (hear, hear), secondly, by no possibility

can it have the effect of preventing or diminishing murder (hear, hear), thirdly, it has a direct tendency to increase murder (hear, hear) and fourthly that it is a punishment which a highly civilised nation ought at once to abolish (hear, hear). Murder proceeded from an unsound state of mind and experts believed that the time was coming when the nation would look on the hanging of a man with the same feelings and horror with which it now regarded the Smithfield fires and gibbeting alive (cheers, mingled with horror).

Statistics were produced showing the failure of public executions as a deterrent: of 167 malefactors condemned to death in Bristol, a Mr Henry Richards said, 164 had previously attended an execution and that had evidently not put them off from committing their offences. Public executions, far from being restraints on crime, were schools for crime, he declared, ending his remarks (to cheers) with the ringing declaration: "Down with the gallows!" There was some disagreement: a Mr Farmer suggested that opponents of capital punishment should be asked whether they were also vegetarians, but a motion for a petition declaring that capital punishment was not authorised by the spirit of Christ was heavily carried and, with a vote of thanks to the chairman, the meeting dispersed into the night.

But this was not just a meeting of eccentrics. In the Commons, William Ewart, the radical member for Dumfries Burghs – albeit one educated at Eton and Oxford – who had long campaigned against capital punishment and in favour of other absurd liberal causes such as free public libraries, succeeded in getting a debate on abolition. He wanted a select committee of inquiry and Palmer's impending execution gave him the opportunity to raise the issue. What is striking is that the arguments he deployed – that mistakes could be made, that hanging was not a deterrent, that juries were less likely to convict the guilty if it meant they would be executed, that a more certain punishment would be life imprisonment – were to be repeated endlessly for the next hundred years. So, too, was the thrust of the arguments made against him: that execution was a condign and God-sanctioned warning to would-be criminals that had worked as a suitable punishment for centuries. Ewart told the Commons:

An essential ingredient in the character of a punishment should be its reversibility; its revocable or remedial nature. It is not likely that, in these times, the execution of an innocent person can occur. Nevertheless, though not likely, it is not impossible. Even now, I am told, special trains are announced in the newspapers as about to run to and from Stafford to enable the public to witness the last moments of an expected victim. All these, the mere external evils of publicity, will be removed by the change proposed.

He was answered by Sir George Grey, the home secretary and the man on whose desk appeals for clemency for Palmer were landing. Grey was a Whig – a nephew of the prime minister who had steered through the 1832 Reform Act – but he was also a firm believer in capital punishment and he made it clear that he was not about to change his mind. He told the House:

I must express my opinion—an opinion which I strongly entertain . . . which rests on the inward conviction of every man's mind, that is not capable of being refuted—that the punishment of death is looked to with greater dread than any other punishment, and is more effectual than any other in repressing crime. Let theorists say what they will, the fear of an ignominious death as the punishment of murder does deter some persons from the perpetration of that awful crime. I believe that death is the punishment which men most dread, and that it is the right and the bounden duty of the State to inflict it for wilful and deliberate murder.

Even so, Ewart's motion secured the support of sixty-four MPs, though it was voted down by 158. The furthest anyone in authority was really prepared to go was to consider whether executions should take place in the privacy of jails, rather than in public outside them. There were still considerable reservations even about that: the bishop of Oxford, Samuel Wilberforce – the cleric who a few years later would clash with Huxley over the theory of evolution – was prepared to defend hanging as a divine institution and added that private executions would never be tolerated in Britain. Punishment, it was felt, needed to be seen to be done to have an effect – otherwise, what certainty was there that it had been carried out, and on the right person? The public torment and humiliation was part of the punishment. It would be another decade before the rowdy, indecorous behaviour of the crowds attending executions would cause a rethink and lead to them being held in private – and another 108 years before capital punishment would be abandoned altogether.

There were other voices, too. Despite its mockery of the abolition meeting, the *Morning Chronicle* had its doubts about the Palmer verdict, in contrast to many of the other papers. In an editorial it wrote: "The question of the punishment of death possesses at this moment a very peculiar interest. The public mind is agitated on the subject of the condemnation and approaching execution of a man who has been deliberately condemned notwithstanding the absence of legal proof." It was highly critical of the Commons debate for not taking the defects of the legal system seriously enough:

> This is a subject of the highest importance yet [it is] treated with indifference or levity quite unbecoming a great legislative assembly. We seem to be arriving at a state of things where unless a new law or a question for legislation be proposed by the Government it cannot command attention . . . The House of Commons becomes an utterly useless body – a mere machine moved by the government of the day. A more appropriate occasion for discussing the question of the punishment of death could scarcely be conceived.

The paper mocked Ewart – "however little that gentleman may be fitted to cope with the great social subjects on which he is so prone to discourse" – but said that his arguments deserved very grave and earnest attention. Its readers, too, lurking like modern Twitter followers behind pseudonyms, filled its correspondence columns with ruminations as diverse and inconsequential as blog commentators today. The headings of the letters give the flavour: "Pause! Reflect! Inquire!", "A Circumstantial Hanging", "How Stands the Case Now?" In one of them, "Dubitans" of London writes: "The Crown failed to prove what Palmer did with the poison he purchased and the link of the chain – ergo he gave it to Cook – legally is a non-sequitur." "Investigator", meanwhile, claimed on 9 June:

A jury well-chosen would, we feel convinced, have come to another conclusion. A jury of gentlemen would acquit, a jury of green-grocers convict. The case required the impartial consideration of men of elevated minds, men of learning, men of science, men qualified to judge . . . [the jury] were men unaccustomed to an exercise of wisdom beyond the everyday avocations of their lives . . . they were nonplussed. The people and the press can alone, by great effort, stay the hand of the law till further light has been thrown upon the case and in their hands the fate of the man who may perchance fall a victim to popular prejudice remains.

This took no account of the fact that, although there were grocers on the jury, there had also been professional men as well.

Palmer did not have any legal right of appeal so was dependent on the home secretary's clemency. In the fortnight following the trial Grey received public petitions and letters from Palmer's solicitor John Smith demanding a reprieve or at least a reconsideration of the evidence in the light of the failure to discover strychnine in Cook's organs. Grey would also have received the curious and passionate eighty-page booklet, ostensibly written by the Rev. Thomas Palmer asserting his brother's innocence and couched in the form of a letter to Lord Chief Justice Campbell. Its overwrought title and convoluted prose were a triumph of hyperventilating fervour over cool rationality and could scarcely have made a rethink of the verdict more likely. A copy still sits in the William Salt Library in Stafford. It is called: *Now Let Reason not Passion be thy Guide! Containing Remarks Upon the Conduct of the Prosecution and the Judges and with Strictures on the Charge Delivered to the Jury, Illustrative of its Dangerous Tendencies to the Long-Enjoyed Rights and Privileges of Englishmen.* Its very first sentence, in close-set type, gives a flavour of its contents:

After a struggle with internal emotions too dreadful to be described amid the tears and lamentations of my family, the bereavement of a household knit together in bonds of strongest love and amity and the smothered, not wholly concealed, indignation of rela-tives and friends – I address your lordship not only as the man who has sealed my brother's fate and borne him to the foot of the scaffold but as the judge who will have to render an account to your fellow men, to posterity and to God of your dealing towards a human being whose fate was, to a certain extent, placed in your hands and on whose destiny you operated in a manner hitherto unknown at least in our days.

It goes on to describe the trial and to include a selection of letters to the press, such as one by an anonymous author who assumed the name "May God Defend the Right": "Is there no hand to save before Palmer is gone? Let us be up and let the thing be proved before a man is ushered into another world." How Thomas Palmer allowed his name to be attached to such a counterproductive document is unclear. It seems almost certain, from the style, to have been the work of Edward Kenealy, the defence junior barrister, and if so, he was extremely lucky to escape censure on this occasion. It still rankled with Campbell when the judge wrote his memoirs:

> A most ruffianlike attempt was made by the friends of the prisoner to abuse me and to obtain a pardon or reprieve, on the ground that the prisoner had not had a fair trial. Having unbounded funds at their command, they corrupted some disreputable journals to admit their *diatribes* against me and they published a most libellous pamphlet . . . in which the Chief Justice was represented to be worse than his predecessor Jeffreys and it was asserted that there had been nothing in England like the last trial since the Bloody Assize . . . The Rev. T. Palmer has since disclaimed the pamphlet and it is said to have been written by a blackguard barrister. I bear him no enmity and he has done me no harm; but for the sake of example he ought to be disbarred.

While all this was going on, at a less exalted level a cottage industry was quickly gearing up in the Potteries north of Rugeley, where souvenir Staffordshire ware statuettes of William Palmer joined those of other such notable contemporary figures as the Duke of Wellington, Napoleon, Queen Victoria and Prince Albert. Such statuettes tended to be fairly generic at the best of times, unless the figure depicted was particularly celebrated, so Palmer standing on a flat base, dressed in frock coat and flowery waistcoat, did not look particularly like the real thing and the mould could equally have done duty for a famous statesman. This was not just a problem with the statuette but also with the illustrations appearing in public prints, as an article in the *Staffordshire Advertiser* on 7 June made clear:

> With reference to the portraits of Palmer . . . there are as you will suppose, none of them of very great accuracy; but the most atrocious of all is one which, some 12 or 13 years ago, when the CORN law agitation was at its height, did duty for a portrait of Mr Cobden. Some scoundrel of a print seller, it seems, has got hold of the plate, has hammered out the name of Cobden and inserted that of Palmer and in that condition the rude cheat is selling about the streets at a penny.[5]

Why anyone should want to have a statue of a celebrated poisoner on their mantelpiece is unclear. More generic still were little pottery models of Palmer's house in Rugeley, which were also produced at this time. There were also broadsheets and ballads being crudely printed which featured excruciating verses, potted accounts of the trial drawn from the rumour-laden newspaper reports, and woodcuts showing generalised scenes of prisoners repenting in their cells and murderers dangling from the gallows. Often these had a high moral purpose, such as *The Life, Trial and Execution of William Palmer*, printed in Bristol and illustrated with a passable portrait of the murderer, which concluded ringingly with the verse:

> Oh! What an awful sight to see,
> A murderer on a gallows tree.
> Young Men be warned by Palmer's fate,
> Repent before it is too late . . .
> . . . What gathering crowds around I see,
> Young people all be warned by me,
> Bad company and drinking shun,
> And gambling or you'll be undone.
> Relations, friends, all efforts tried,
> But justice would not be denied,
> Let's hope we all may meet in heaven,
> Forgive as you would be forgiven.

---

[5] The highly respectable radical MP Richard Cobden had been one of the leading advocates for the repeal of the Corn Laws in the 1840s.

Many of these broadsheets guessed at Palmer's state of mind and, of course, their themes were the repentance of the murderer and the anguish of his widowed mother. One entitled *The Life and Trial of Palmer* was sold at his execution:

> My poor old mother now at Rugeley,
> My awful end must now bewail
> To know her son must die with scorn
> A felon's death in Stafford jail . . .
> Dreadful is my situation,
> Before the awful bar I stand
> I might have filled a noble station
> Unfortunate unhappy man
> Infants yet unborn will mention
> When to manhood they appear
> The name of Doctor William Palmer
> Of Rugeley town in Staffordshire.

There was even a confession, of a florid sort that Palmer himself was yet to give. Called *Lamentation and Confession of Palmer*, it imaginatively pictured him despairingly throwing himself on the pallet in his cell, burying his face in his clothes, and telling the prison chaplain: "It is necessary for my soul to confess this murder. I ought also to confess to others . . . I mean my wife and brother." Perhaps the author subsequently had second thoughts, or had been told that the prisoner had, actually, not confessed, for the broadsheet continued: "He shortly after said he had neither denied nor admitted his guilt."

Some of these would doubtless have been sold in Stafford at a penny a time, though it is quite hard to imagine any of the songs being sung around the scaffold or in the inns and taverns of the town. Palmer's example was also held up in religious texts circulated at the time – an irony considering how religious he was, or purported to be. One two-sided, yellowing printed paper in the Salt Library bears the title: *William Palmer the Racer! Who is the Culprit?* It has a confiding, admonitory tone in answering its own question:

> Dear Friend – Perhaps . . . you say, the man under sentence. An-
> swer: You are right according to man's judgement but according
> to God's word thou also art the culprit for as a man is a mur-

derer if he murders but one person, so thou art a liar if thou
hast lied but once – a drunkard in God's sight if thou wast but
once drunk – a fornicator if thou wert once guilty in deed or in
thought . . . a blasphemer if thou hast but once damned thy soul,
thy body, thy neighbour, thy horse or thy dog.

It goes on to list persons who go against their parents, disobedient children,
fighters and scoffers, fierce despisers, pleasure-seekers, adulterers, traders
in whoredom, fornicators and unhappy women in chains as those who need
to hear the Word; it then comes to a strangely familiar picture and a customary offer of redemption:

Dear Friends, Years ago I stood by the gaming table on a racecourse
with a companion at the foot of whose bed afterwards I stood and
saw him struggling with death and breath[ing] his last. But long
since a loving God showed me my transgressions and I have found
a sweeter happiness than any paltry pleasure of the racecourse . . .
He will receive you and give ease to a guilty conscience.

How effective this was in converting the sinners of Stafford at Palmer's
execution may be open to doubt. The self-consciously biblical language that
was archaic even then probably did not help.

In weeks to come Palmer's name would also be invoked in improving
sermons such as that preached by the Rev. Alexander Thomson MA at
Rusholme Road Chapel in Manchester a week after Palmer's execution. He was
obviously so pleased with it – or his congregation was – that it was printed up
as a pamphlet. The subject was "a warning to young men against horseracing,
betting, gambling etc as leading to fraud, crime and self-destruction". Thomson laid it on hot and strong; they were all guilty, even Cook:

Ah! To resist the first inducements, the first approaches of the
tempter, that is the only wisdom, the only safety. William Palmer
is not a solitary criminal but as one of a class, in whom all the
tendencies of that class have attained the worst and most dreadful
development. He is no monster out of date . . . he is a birth of the
time, the mature embodiment and frightful incarnation of that
spirit of civilised, refined, gentlemanly gambling which now per-

vades certain classes of society . . . he was self-blinded and stupe-
fied by the passion that possessed him and once fairly launched
. . . he could hardly arrest himself any more than the boatman who
nears the Falls of Niagara. Has not God's word rightly termed the
wicked man a Fool? Compassion for John Parsons Cook's untimely
and cruel end must not blind us to the fact he was pursuing a
course similar to Palmer's. Whatever his character was originally,
it shares the taint of some of Palmer's dishonest deeds.

It is the sort of thing that, in happier times, seated in the family pew
at St Augustine's parish church in Rugeley, William Palmer might well have
taken notes about, as indeed he noted the contents of the sermons of the
vicar there, the Rev. Thomas Atkinson.

There was even a sort of weekly penny series called *Satan Reproving
Sin!* which consisted of an imagined dialogue between Palmer on the banks
of the River Styx and a devil – a conversation not entirely unlike C. S. Lewis's
Screwtape Letters a century later:

> *Palmer:* I saw when it was too late that I did wrong in attempting to
> bribe the postboy to upset the chaise and break the jar con-
> taining the stomach of Cook.
>
> *Devil:* Wrong? It was an act of *insanity*, that and not accounting
> for the purchase of strychnia brought you here before your
> time. Those two acts I considered the strongest points
> against you . . .

As so often, the devil seemed to have the best lines, but the series went on,
at eight closely printed pages a time, for at least six episodes.

If proof was needed that the coming execution might not deter murder, on the day before Palmer was due to hang, the *Morning Chronicle* reported
the case of Thomas Johnson, who had just been committed for poisoning
his housekeeper Mary Clarke at Winkburn near Southwell in Nottinghamshire. And already the trial had supposedly claimed a victim: a man
called Fisher, coachman to Colonel Smyth, the MP for York, committed suicide in Leeds after betting too heavily and rashly on Palmer's acquittal. He
left a wife and four children.

16

"Are you sure this damn thing's safe?"

I N STAFFORD PRISON, WILLIAM PALMER MAINTAINED HIS PRETERNATURAL calm. He ate well – plenty of salad – chatted amiably with the warders, received visits from relatives, wrote letters, read his prayers, and – as was customary with condemned men – was given a screened-off pew in the prison chapel where he attended the service twice on his last Sunday, to hear the chaplain, Goodacre, preach on the text "Let no man deceive himself". If Palmer still hoped for a reprieve, the chosen verse perhaps conveyed a different message. The execution was set for 8 a.m. on Saturday 14 June 1856; it would be held directly outside the main entrance to the prison on the portable scaffold which would be moved into place overnight.

The area in front of the prison was – and is – relatively wide, but the neighbouring houses and pubs were now preparing to open to paying visitors and to erect stands so that they could get a better view. A great crowd was expected for such a notorious criminal, and overnight excursion trains would bring spectators down from the Potteries, across from Shrewsbury, and up from Birmingham and the Black Country. The mayor of Stafford and the local magistracy accordingly issued a public notice, but not – if the handwritten and much crossed-out and corrected original in the county archives is anything to go by – without considerable cogitation and laborious revision:

> The mayor ~~and magistrates~~ require that any person who may
> intend to erect on their premises any platform or other standing
> place for spectators would give notice to him not later than

12am on Friday in order that he may instruct the town surveyor to inspect the same with a view to guarantee ~~the stability of the same and prevent the possibility of accident~~ its stability and the town surveyor will thereupon assign a notification which may be affixed to the erection.

Health and safety considerations were clearly paramount. The local records also contain a note by the surveyor, which may have been given to an unspecified property owner or was perhaps written out in case it was needed:

The surveyor of the borough has this day inspected the erection upon the premises in your occupation and he has reported that such erection was not of sufficient stability to be safe for the occupation of the Public. By direction of the Mayor therefore I give you notice either to render such erections or structures of sufficient stability or not to open them for public occupation ... you will be held legally responsible for any consequences which may ensue.

These were necessary precautions. From late on Friday afternoon, crowds were gathering outside the prison. There would be no reprieve for Palmer: Sir George Grey had responded to John Smith's last appeal with a declaration that the law would take its course. This was conveyed to Palmer in his cell by Lieutenant Colonel Dyott, the High Sheriff of Staffordshire, and his deputy. *The Times* reported: "He received this terrible intimation, which destroyed all ground for hope, in silence, and without any perceptible emotion." Later in the afternoon, George, Thomas and Sarah Palmer, his brothers and sister, visited him one last time. He had asked them not to bring his seven-year-old son Willie with them. Then, late in the evening, John Smith also arrived, on his way back from trying to lobby Grey in London. Maybe it was on this visit that Smith brought Palmer a copy of the Bible, given to him by Serjeant Shee. The interview with Smith took place in the presence of the prison governor, Major Fulford, who was still trying to persuade Palmer to confess. This was important, as if to provide a final confirmation of the legitimacy of the verdict, though the routine was always presented to prisoners as a chance for absolution, offering the hope of post-mortem redemp-

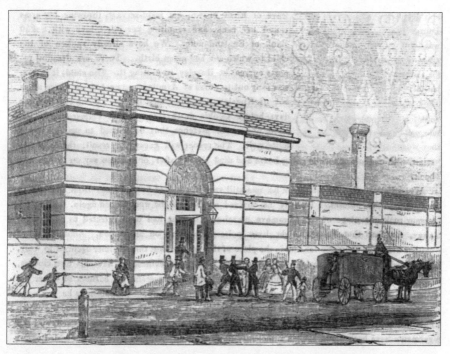

Gateway at Stafford Prison, the scene of Palmer's execution

tion. But Palmer was not going to give Fulford that satisfaction. The governor offered to withdraw while Palmer spoke to his solicitor, but he said no, on the contrary, he wanted no time to be lost in publishing his words to the world. He wanted to thank Smith for his great exertions and the officers of the prison for their kindness. Then he added that Cook did not die from strychnine. Fulford told him not to quibble "in the awful condition in which he was placed" and just to say aye or nay whether he had murdered his friend. Palmer replied as enigmatically as ever: "Lord Campbell summed up in favour of strychnine." The governor retorted that it was of no importance how the deed was done and Palmer said he had nothing else to add and was easy in his conscience. Outside the prison afterwards, Smith said that Palmer had just said: "I am innocent of poisoning Cook by strychnine and all I ask is that you will have his body examined and that you will see to my mother and boy." Palmer had handed Smith a book entitled *The Sinner's Friend*, which he had signed and dated, pointing to the couplet: "Oh! Where for refuge should I flee / If Jesus had not died for me."

This, along with every detail of the following few hours, was given in almost minute-by-minute accounts in the newspapers. Four press representatives would be admitted to the prison the following morning – the gentleman from *The Times*, representatives of the *Staffordshire Advertiser* and *Staffordshire Sentinel*, and a court reporter from the Old Bailey – but outside in the street there were at least forty other reporters from all over the country. The *Advertiser* told its readers:

> The account of the execution . . . was looked for all over the country with intense anxiety. The reporters . . . forwarded electric telegraphic dispatches to London and the other towns from which they came or proceeded by the first trains with their reports. In some few instances, we believe, the reports were sent the night before, subject to alterations. No wonder that some of the reports, prepared under such circumstances, were not very accurate. Those which represent the conduct of the spectators as having been very rude and disorderly were a gross misrepresentation; for it is admitted on all hands that nothing could be more orderly or becoming the scene than the behaviour of the immense concourse.

In this the *Advertiser* may have been allowing local pride rather to colour its view. Several of the national press reports were strikingly vivid, clear-eyed and detailed pieces of factual reporting.

As Smith and Palmer spoke for the last time, they would already have heard the crowds shouting and laughing outside the walls. Many carried baskets or knotted handkerchiefs with provisions for their vigils. It was a wet, cold night and those waiting outside the prison were soon drenched, huddling against walls, in alleyways and under trees or taking refuge in the local pubs. The *Manchester Guardian*, which devoted almost half its six editorial pages to covering the execution on the following Monday, wrote: "Considering the weather it was really a great advantage that this could be done; despite the fact that a good many men got drunk or tipsy, before they reeled off to see the sight of the morning."

Palmer must have known what a spectacle the next morning would bring. He was roused in the middle of his last night by Goodacre, the chaplain,

Topper Smith, the hangman, grimly dressed for business in his smock with his top hat close at hand

and another clergyman named Henry Sneyd, who wanted to waste no time in trying finally to secure a confession. He was soundly asleep at half past two when they woke him up and Palmer obediently joined them in prayer until 5 a.m. They returned at 6.30 a.m. for another hour. Then they broke off for a few minutes to allow Palmer to have a cup of tea and a glass of brandy. The warder who brought it asked him how he felt: "Quite comfortable," he said. Next Dyott and the under-sheriff returned – the latter formally to demand the body be handed over to the authorities after death – and Palmer at last became emotional, but still admitted nothing: "I am a murdered man, though I shall go to the gallows as a murderer. All who have taken part in my conviction, all who have aided it, are murderers." He asked instead for the warders to pray for his son. Then he relapsed into a sullen humour.

Palmer was now escorted to the press room, where the hangman "Topper" Smith pinioned his arms – Palmer asked him not to fasten the rope too tight – and then on to the chapel to receive communion. It would be a long walk to the scaffold, from the condemned cell, through the prison, down three flights of stairs and out through the main entrance. Goodacre tried one more time to get the all-important confession. It was known that prisoners sometimes admitted guilt at the very last moment, almost as the trap-door opened – Franz Muller, the first railway murderer, would do this as the white cap was placed over his head eight years later – and so there was still time. "What say you Palmer: do you now at this awful moment, admit that your sentence is just?" Palmer answered: "I do not admit it", and the chaplain replied: "Then your blood be on your own head."

Now the walk to the scaffold started, a few minutes before 8 a.m., with the prison bell tolling overhead. Palmer, it was said, walked with a light and elastic tread, some even described him as mincing: "of all who were near him he seemed the most active and full of life and certainly he alone betrayed no sign of emotion." Occasionally he murmured "murderers" to himself. As he passed the governor Fulford, he bowed his head formally "with almost a theatrical air". It was a lengthy procession: warders and turnkeys carrying black wands, Captain Hatton, the chief of police, the governor, the head turnkey, the four pressmen, the sheriff and under-sheriff, Palmer and the hangman – all following Goodacre who started intoning the funeral service. A number of stories were told of Palmer's alleged insouciance during these last few minutes: how he had been offered a glass of champagne – no doubt of the sparkling provincial variety they had all drunk so cheerily at the Raven Hotel after the races in Shrewsbury seven months before – and had blown the bubbles off the top, saying, "They always give me indigestion next morning if I drink in a hurry"; how, as they crossed the courtyard, he had side-stepped a puddle, saying he did not want to catch a cold by getting his feet wet; then, most famous of all, how, when he stepped onto the trap-door of the scaffold, he had asked: "Are you sure this damn thing's safe?" All were probably apocryphal or at least such bon mots were not reported at the time.

The tolling of the bell alerted the crowd outside the prison that the spectacle was about to begin. The crowd had grown to many thousands now: some estimates as high as 40,000, more realistically 30,000 at a time when the population of Stafford itself was only about 13,000. The rain had stopped but the morning was grey and overcast. The *Manchester Guardian*'s reporter told the paper's readers the following Monday that there had been no outrage, no gross brutality, little actual crime or accident, but also no feeling of horror at the violent death of a human being. The crowd had been good-tempered: "the hoarse hum of conversation was for hours unbroken, jokes called forth loud laughter, crushing was borne with forbearance." A character bearing a board carrying passages from the scriptures was not molested: "his singular appearance called forth but little in the shape of jeers; the crowd wanted the death act and could be complacent so long as they were not interfered with on that point."

And now it came. As the execution party mounted the scaffold, the crowd fell silent apart from the calls for hats off and umbrellas down. The prison bell stopped tolling. Palmer almost skipped up the steps. He was pale, but he managed a smile. According to the *Manchester Guardian*:

> the horrible impressiveness of his countenance was heightened by an expression as if from a smile, but which no doubt resulted from his preternatural determination not to appear appalled. And yet his air and manner were not those of sheer bravado; they seemed rather to come from an uncontrollable firmness in carrying out a purpose. Certainly he did not look a martyr, even if he attempted to act the part . . . he looked round, taking in as much of the scene as was possible without turning his head.

Goodacre was still reciting the funeral prayers in his ear. Now he stood on the trap-door, the noose brushing his collar, and Smith came forward to open the top button of his shirt and adjust the noose around his neck. Smith shook him by the hand and the condemned man could be heard to say: "God bless you" – the only public words he had said since his "Not guilty" at the Old Bailey a month earlier. The hangman stood back, then remembered he had forgotten to place the white hood over Palmer's head and returned to do so. The blowing in and out of the hood showed Palmer was breathing hard, muttering some prayers, and then the trap was sprung. The *Manchester Guardian* reported:

> The bolt was drawn and with a terrific twang and strain upon the rope, the culprit's body fell two feet and a half and remained for an instant motionless. Death must have been immediate for there appeared no room to doubt that the neck was effectually

dislocated. The body slowly turned completely round, then there came a strong convulsive start of the arms and legs; afterwards a few slight tremors ran through the trunk and legs and all was still save that the fresh breeze swayed the body to and fro.

There had no need for Smith to rush beneath the scaffold and tug at the dying man's legs.

The crowd reacted calmly, though there was some disappointment that the spectacle had been over so quickly and quietly: no struggle, no confession, no famous last words, no weeping or hysterics. And no admission or sign of repentance: it was said that that must have been to spare his family, especially his young son, the taint of disgrace, to leave open the possibility that there had been a miscarriage of justice.

The body was left hanging for an hour, as custom demanded to make sure he was really dead, and was then cut down and taken back inside the prison. Smith, the hangman, would claim the rope so that he could cut it up and sell it off in small pieces to those anxious for a memento of the execution.[6] In the prison's joinery shop where the body was taken, Palmer was found still to be clutching a handkerchief in his right hand, clenched, just as it was said Cook's hand had been.

At least two plaster casts were taken of his head. These still survive: one at the Staffordshire county museum at Shugborough Hall, the other among a collection of nineteenth-century casts of criminals' heads at Winchester prison. A third, half death mask, showing the head in profile, is in the historical display cabinet at Stafford court. They show a plump, bald man, eyes closed, mouth slightly open, and they were taken for phrenological purposes to determine what, if anything, could be discovered of his

---

[6] The rope was allegedly made 30 yards longer than was actually needed so that the profit would be greater. It would be hawked round the pubs of the Black Country by "Topper" Smith in two- and three-inch lengths for half-a-crown a piece (there were eight half-crowns to a pound). Allegedly, he was still trying to sell bits of "the rope that hanged Palmer" 10 years later, as a ballad in the local dialect noted satirically:

> Ee's a crafty owd charmer,
> Is Smith who 'anged Palmer,
> An' the rope that 'ee sowld,
> Would stretch all the road,
> From Dudley to regions much warmer.

criminal nature from the shape of his skull. One of the phrenologists, William Bally of Manchester, told the *Manchester Guardian* that he used a plaster composite of his own invention which enabled him to reproduce the texture of the skin and to create a cast of the exact size of the head: "He has taken the casts of the heads of a very large number of condemned criminals in England and Ireland, but he has not in his collection, nor has he seen, a head so contracted in the sincipital region as that of Palmer's organisation." Without going so far as to say the head showed someone of the poisoner class, Bally told the paper – with perhaps just a touch of foreknowledge of what Palmer had been like in life – that it was the head of a man who would as a rule be respectful and polite, even charitable, but who was also able to act cunningly and secretly, "perfectly indifferent to honour or truth and . . . careless what became of the most intimate acquaintance or the nearest relative". His colleague, Mr F. Bridges of Liverpool, was more emphatic about the cast he had taken: it showed "the great deficiency of the moral region and particularly the want of conscientiousness, the enormous base of the brain, the great preponderance of the selfish propensities which in such a head overruled all others . . . [a man] capable of murdering to any extent by poison . . . altogether of the worst kind . . . of the type peculiar to the class who resort to poison."

After that, the corpse was stripped naked and by 11 a.m. had been thrown, without a coffin or a shroud, into a grave next to the prison chapel, alongside other convicted prisoners. Quicklime was thrown over the body supposedly to accelerate its disintegration. There is no distinct grave and Palmer still lies with 107 other men and four women in the unmarked plot.

17

"Distinctly *not* quite composed"

P ALMER WAS DEAD, BUT THERE WERE STILL LOOSE ENDS FROM THE TRIAL TO be tied up. At the end of June Cockburn's fees book, now in the Middle Temple library, shows that he was paid £799.1s.0d for prosecuting Palmer (about half what he earned in fees that month). This payment was somewhat more prompt than in the case of the witnesses from the December and January inquests, who did not receive their expenses until the Staffordshire finance committee finally disbursed them the following month. Those costs in themselves amounted to more than the budget of the county coroner's service for the first half of 1856, but the committee consoled itself that it was right "under the peculiar circumstances of the inquests to adopt a more liberal scale of allowance than in ordinary cases". Even so, they trimmed the applications back. By and large the professional witnesses such as Taylor were paid what they asked for – Taylor got £33.4s.6d for the three investigations, paid by the Treasury. So, too, did the prosecution witnesses such as Cook's friend William Henry Jones, who had had to attend on four days and was paid £7.5s, while James Gardner, William Stephens's local solicitor, was paid the £20 he claimed. But others were only given a proportion of what they put in for. It is possible to imagine that the amount they were reimbursed was commensurate with the degree of official approval, or disapproval, each had incurred, rather than how much they were owed. Jerry Smith asked for eight guineas for his four days and received four, Cornelius Waddell wanted 15 guineas for coming all the way from Stafford for three days and was paid £6.12.9d, and Thomas Pratt, the moneylender, claimed 12 guineas for his brief appearance and received £7.5s.

Those from the servant class – Elizabeth Mills, Lavinia Barnes and Charles Newton – were paid five shillings each.

Meanwhile, in the National Archives, there is a sad little document, signed by three of the working-class trial jurors, politely requesting recompense for their lost earnings. William Ecclestone, the Stratford grocer, had it formally drawn up, in neat copperplate, on behalf of himself, Thomas Knight, the Leytonstone baker, and George Oakeshott, the West Ham confectioner. The covering letter said that they believed some of the other jurors were "so well situated as not to need or desire compensation", which was the reason there were only three names on the petition. Addressed to the Lords Commissioners of Her Majesty's Treasury, it "most humbly and earnestly" requested consideration for their case:

> This memorable trial commenced and extended over a period
> of 14 days and your memorialists were absent from their several
> occupations at very serious pecuniary loss and inconvenience,
> not to say injury to health arising from so long a confinement.

It pointed out that the trial witnesses were allowed expenses and asked that jurors be treated in the same way: "they entertain the opinion that your lordships have the power to deviate from the law when a case like that of your memorialists comes under your lordships' notice for adjudication . . . [and] earnestly rely that your lordships will be pleased to award compensation in this extraordinary exception to general cases." They pointed out that Campbell at the end of the trial had regretted his inability to award compensation and added that they would have been unwilling to make an appeal but for the length of time the trial had taken and the "serious and awful responsibility" it had imposed on them. The petitioners apologised for intruding on their lordships' attention and left the amount to their discretion: "pecuniary circumstances alone have prompted them to bring this matter under your notice . . . they humbly and earnestly confide that your lordships will be pleased graciously to comply with the prayer of this memorial." The Treasury requested the attorney general to advise. No, said Cockburn, when he got round to replying five months later, such an application could not be entertained. The note at the bottom of the petition is brusque: "so long as the law does not provide for the payment of juries, government can have no authority to select at its discretion particular cases as proper for the remuneration of the jury. It is obvious that such a practice would be objectionable in principle and liable to the grossest abuse." Perhaps it is as well that the jurors would never have known how much he had just been paid.

They were not the only ones seeking compensation. The National Archives also contain a poignant, black-edged correspondence from William Stephens to John Greenwood, the Treasury solicitor who had coordinated the prosecution, sent on 1 July, a fortnight after Palmer's hanging. It is in Stephens's handwriting from his home in Kensington:

> I pray permission to state to you that I am greatly out of pocket by the prosecution of the monster Palmer. I should not trouble you or say anything but my income is limited, my expenses just now . . . considerable and the loss with destruction of my poor stepson's betting book and other things which he must have had with him in Rugeley have involved me as his executor in great anxiety and most serious expenditure. In doing my utmost to bring Palmer to justice I am aware that I only performed a duty which was unfortunately cast upon me but the toil and anxiety which I had encountered for many weeks was immence [*sic*]. I laboured sometimes night and day. I persevered when others engaged with me were inclined to despair and if compensation for expence [*sic*] in such cases is ever allowed I trust it will not here be refused to me. I do not know where I should properly apply in the matter, if you will be so kind as to instruct me, you will confer a great obligation upon me. I am, dear Sir, your very faithful servant . . .

He obviously received a prompt, if non-committal, reply, for three days later he was writing again: "I will call on Mr Reynolds and probably send a memorial to Sir George Grey. Should you be referred to, I hope you will be so good as to give my application any support you can, in justice, afford it." It sounds as if there was bureaucratic buck-passing at the Treasury. There is no indication whether old Mr Stephens was successful, but in view of the jurors' experience it is doubtful.

Alfred Swaine Taylor was sufficiently bruised by the blows he had received to his ego and authority that he wrote a book to criticise those who had had the temerity to disagree with him and to restate his case that Cook had died from strychnine. Called *On Poisoning by Strychnia: With Comments on the Medical Evidence Given at the Trial of William Palmer for the Murder of John Parsons Cook*, it is an argumentative and self-righteous work, running to more than 150 pages and published within four months of the trial. It lays out in detail why he was perfectly correct in his diagnosis even though he had not detected any strychnine – "the allegation that no person can die from poison except the poison be found in the body is a mockery, a delusion and a snare" – and it is scathing about the chemists who maintained it could and should have been found. Taylor was particularly sensitive to the charge that he had only decided that strychnine had been involved after hearing the evidence of Palmer's purchase of the poison: not at all, he maintained, he had already reached that conclusion but had been cautious about stating it. He added:

> The great principle of jurisprudence in a criminal charge, now confirmed by the verdict in Palmer's case, is not that a poison should be invariably found in the dead body, but that there should be satisfactory evidence of the death from poison and this may be had when chemical tests, even in the hands of "adepts" fail to reveal its presence. To affirm that innocent persons may be placed in danger from the adoption of such a principle is absurd; it is equal to affirming that on a question of poisoning chemistry alone is to be relied on and that persons . . . are to be convicted or acquitted according to whether a chemist believes . . . that he has extracted the fifty thousandth of a grain of some alkaloid from the thirty-second part of a liver!

This was clearly a dig at Herapath. But Taylor reserved his greatest indignation for Serjeant Shee, whose questioning he clearly believed had gone beyond propriety:

> In dealing with the medical evidence for the prosecution . . . the learned counsel for the defence had an unfortunate failing of misstating and misrepresenting facts of the greatest importance . . . the denunciation of medical witnesses as conspirators to destroy the life of an innocent man without motive – the coarse imputations of rashness, ignorance and prejudice on men who

simply perform a duty . . . reflect disgrace on the mode in which we profess to inquire into truth. Learned counsel who are members of an honourable profession should bear in mind that the medical profession is equally honourable and that its members have a claim to be treated with proper respect.

It sounds very much as though that was the real nub of Taylor's affront: that his evidence had been questioned and not accepted unreservedly, as his eminence deserved. There is a distinct sense of lip-curling as he emphasises the "learned":

Will the learned counsel . . . be inclined to receive an opinion based . . . upon the statements of chambermaids and waitresses instead of a committee of surgeons or physicians who cannot always be present to witness an act of murder – or will he reject it as rash and indiscreet? The course pursued by the learned serjeant will, I fear, have the evil effect of stopping the expression of such a free and independent opinion as every medical man . . . not only ought to give but to be protected in giving . . . in fearlessly performing his duty to the country he cannot rely on receiving protection from violent, unjust and unmerited attacks.

Taylor's own status within the profession would, however, take a much more serious knock three years later during the case of another doctor accused of poisoning a close acquaintance. Thomas Smethurst, a 53-year-old physician, left his elderly wife in 1859 and bigamously married his mistress, a spinster named Isabella Bankes, who soon began to suffer violent retching and throat and stomach pains. When she was on the verge of death, she was presented by her husband and his lawyer with a will he had drawn up granting him all her possessions. She signed it, but even before she died, other doctors raised suspicions that she had been poisoned and on their own initiative sent specimens of her bowel fluid and faeces to Taylor, who found arsenic in them. After Bankes's death Taylor carried out a post-mortem, which discovered no arsenic in her organs, but Smethurst was arrested and committed for trial anyway. Once again, there were medical witnesses on both sides and much circumstantial evidence – Smethurst had possessed a medicine bottle containing arsenic, Bankes had been pregnant and had also

been persuaded on her deathbed to sign the will – but the case was undermined when Taylor had to admit that his finding of arsenic had been based
on faulty testing. The copper foil he had used to test the specimen – a standard procedure known as the Reinsch test – had already been contaminated
with arsenic, so his diagnosis was unreliable. The jury still convicted
Smethurst, who was not a sympathetic character, and he was sentenced to hang,
but the home secretary called in Sir Benjamin Brodie, who decided the medical evidence was inconclusive. Smethurst was pardoned and released four
days before he was due to suffer Palmer's fate. It was a great humiliation for
Taylor to admit error – he had declared in court that he had never been
found to be wrong in any diagnosis – and understandably his critics piled
in. Herapath was first, declaring in The Times that Taylor was a bungler
who had been making mistakes with his tests for twenty years. The British
Medical Journal followed, saying: "If the man who holds in his hands the
keys of life and death will not insist on the purity of his tests [then we are
returning to] the days of witchcraft when human life hung upon the lips of
any old crone." It was a terrible rebuff and one from which Taylor's reputation never quite recovered in the remaining twenty years of his life. He
died without a knighthood or other public honours.

The same could not be said either of Lord Chief Justice Campbell, who
died in harness as Lord Chancellor in 1861 shortly after attending a cabinet
meeting, or of Sir Alexander Cockburn, who eventually became Lord Chief
Justice in his own right but never got a peerage from Queen Victoria because
of his loose morals. He died, still unmarried but acknowledging his surviving
illegitimate daughter, in 1880. Serjeant Shee became the first Roman Catholic
appointed to the judiciary since the Reformation and died in 1868. The *Law
Times* said in its obituary: "so long employed in cases where able advocacy
rather than an acute knowledge of legal technicalities was required, in the
calm atmosphere of the judicial bench, [he] was not in his element and failed
to prove as effective a judge as many men of much lesser note."

As for the Palmers, Sarah, the mother of the family, died in 1861, five
years after the trial, at the age of sixty-seven; she is buried across the road
from the family home, from which she sallied forth to defend her "saintly
Billy's" honour, in the family grave behind St Augustine's parish church in
Rugeley. She was certainly not going to hide or move away. The Palmers'
vault, which also contains the bodies of old Joseph Palmer, father of the

clan, young Joseph, the oldest brother, Annie, William's wife, and their four infant children, was originally a table tomb surrounded by high wrought-iron railings, but now only the barely legible incised slab remains, flat on the ground, rather hidden in an obscure and shady spot at the side of the church behind a much more recent concrete and glass parish hall. The Rev. Thomas Palmer, who was so convinced of his brother's innocence, served as rector of Trimley St Martin at Felixstowe in Suffolk for twenty-seven years. It was a living a long way from Rugeley, bought for him by his mother at a cost of £2,493 the year before she died, and he is buried there in the churchyard under a stone cross with carved, entwined flowers. Thomas is also commemorated in the church by a stained-glass window installed in his honour after his death in 1887. George, the solicitor, died in 1866, and Sarah, the youngest sister, who married the Scottish clergyman Alexander Brodie, lived into the twentieth century. Palmer's surviving son Willie also grew up to live a respectable life, as a London solicitor, but died in his seventies in 1925 in peculiar circumstances: overcome by the fumes from an unlit gas fire in his office in the City of London. Did he commit suicide in the end, or was he just a forgetful old man who neglected to light the flame?

Many of the others involved in Palmer's trial died within a few years and are buried in the cemetery beyond the Palmers' house. Jerry Smith did not long survive his humiliation at the hands of Sir Alexander Cockburn: within eighteen months he was dead at the age of forty-seven. Charles Newton, the chemist's assistant whose evidence of giving Palmer the first grains of strychnine came so close to establishing his guilt, died aged thirty in April 1863; George Myatt, the saddler, followed two years later; and Ben Thirlby, the chemist who took over Palmer's practice, died the year after that. Thomas Masters, the landlord of the Talbot Arms, passed on, aged seventy-five, the year after the trial in 1857, and old Dr William Bamford was buried in the churchyard in 1859. James Myatt, the postboy who refused Palmer's bribe to overturn his trap, died in 1871, and Dr Salt, at whose surgery Palmer obtained the strychnine from Newton, died in 1873.

All of them now lie – as they once lived – within a few yards of each other, not half a mile from the Talbot Arms and Palmer's house. So, too, does John Parsons Cook, who is buried between the front gate of the parish church and its main entrance, a few yards round the corner from the Palmer family grave and much more prominently sited. He never was taken home to London by William Stephens to be buried with his mother – maybe the old man really was short of money after the trial, or just exhausted by it. The stone slab says his life was taken away at Rugeley in the twenty-ninth year of his age: "He was sincerely beloved and will long be lamented by his kindred and friends." But it gets the date wrong, by one day, when it says he died on the night of 22 November 1855, rather than the 21st.

The story of William Palmer, the Rugeley Poisoner, did not end either with his execution or with the deaths of most of the participants at his trial. It lingered on in folk memory, especially around the Midlands' Black Country, for many years. There was very little questioning of his guilt or wickedness, though perhaps a certain ghoulish relish, enhanced by the melodrama of Cook's death and the apparent insouciance of his murderer. The anecdotes are what survive.

One of the most enduring is of how the town authorities petitioned the prime minister Lord Palmerston to change Rugeley's name in an attempt to defuse the bad publicity the place had received. Certainly, said the prime minister, you can rename it after me: Palmer's Town. It is a good joke and has the merit of being the sort of jest the roguish old man might have relished, but of course it is not true. The witticism was first reported in the *Illustrated Times* at the end of the trial, so it is much more likely that it was coined by a bored journalist during the longueurs of Lord Chief Justice Campbell's summing-up. There is in fact no evidence that Rugeley ever wanted to change its name, even if it could have done so without becoming a laughing stock.

Palmer's trial and conviction retained their fascination throughout the Victorian period. The trial had undermined some comforting assurances offered by science: that scientists could always detect poison – that, as the *Examiner* said, "murder that does not cry out of the grave is yet able to speak ... even by the very form of the death agony" – and that dispassionate science would invariably defeat murderers. For ultimately no strychnine had been found and Palmer's refusal to admit how he had killed Cook left a troubling uncertainty hanging over the case. Experts like Taylor were perhaps not as infallible as they claimed and yet they were essential to the detection of the burgeoning crime of poisoning. The Staffordshire police had played no part in solving the case: their involvement had been restricted to guarding the prisoner, and for all the two constables and inspector at Rugeley knew, Dr Palmer could have gone on, surrounded by sudden unfortunate deaths, till kingdom come. The police in rural England did not have the resources, skills, training, experience or even inclination to deal with such a major crime. The insurance company had privately called in a famous detective from London to check out George Bates's insurance application, but he had gone away, despite the prima facie evidence of fraud and suspicious death, after telling Palmer not to try it on again and without alerting anyone else. If Cook had died in the night alone – without witnesses or a stepfather to pursue his case and with just old Dr Bamford to do what he was told and sign the death certificate – would anyone have been the wiser? Fortuitously Palmer had not got away with it, but how many had, or were doing so?

Palmer was a member of the respectable classes who had gone bad: the sort of man who would soon make his appearance in the first sensation novels – the poisonous Count Fosco in *The Woman in White* (1860), perhaps, or Mrs Henry Wood's Dr Castonel, or the brittle, middle-class money-grubbers of *Our Mutual Friend*. He was the sort of man who, tidied up and made more handsome and less plump, ruddy and *provincial*, might make the model for a Victorian genre painting: a variation on the theme of Ford Madox Brown's *Stages of Cruelty*, painted in the summer of 1856, or Abraham Solomon's *Waiting for the Verdict* (though the companion painting *The Acquittal* has a somewhat different outcome). His corruption and refusal of redemption, his willingness to prey on his family and closest friend, above all his silence and heartless recklessness, made him somehow more mysterious and amoral, seemingly accepting conviction and death as he would the loss of a horse-race.

His sanctimoniousness and religiosity made matters worse. As such he seemed to be more calculating and more wicked: the "Prince of Poisoners", suddenly the greatest murderer of the nineteenth century and a monster of depravity. His crimes were magnified: how many had he killed beyond Cook, the man for whose death alone he was tried? The figures were multiplied then and have never gone down since: even modern studies assume that he killed at least a dozen.[7] Alfred Swaine Taylor had no doubts: in his book, published just afterwards, he speaks of "three children, of a friend while on a visit, of his wife's mother and lastly of his wife" all poi-

---

[7] See, for instance, Katherine Watson's *Poisoned Lives: English poisoners and their victims* (Hambledon 2004) or Matthew Sweet, *Inventing the Victorians* (Faber and Faber 2001), which has Palmer "preying on his patients, using their faith in his professional authority to kill them with drugs from his little black bag" – stuff worthy in its inventiveness of Gus Mayhew himself.

soned – together, of course, with Cook; he might have added Walter, as most subsequent accounts have, except that, of course, Taylor could find no trace of poison in the mush of his body. For Taylor the explanation for "the extraordinary excitement produced in the public mind" by the case was to be found in "the deadly and insidious nature of the poison selected, the name of which was until then hardly known to the public, in the ingenious mode of administration, i.e. by the substitution on two successive nights of poisoned pills for pills prescribed by a medical man and in the fact that the accused was himself a member of the medical profession, a man of education and knowledge as well as a certain degree of respectability".

The alternative thesis – that Palmer was desperate and panicked and that the number of his victims may never have come near to the total supposed by rumour and innuendo – was not really considered because it did not fit the established gothic melodrama of a murderer killing by candlelight, nor did it draw the correct moral lessons from his cool and calculating wickedness. Palmer got caught and became a Terrible Warning: his curiously smiling effigy became a fixture in Madame Tussaud's Chamber of Horrors for more than a century – he did not escape that fate, though perhaps his clothes did – and he became the archetypal medical serial killer. He was only supplanted eventually, 140 years later, by Dr Harold Shipman, who quietly gave lethal injections to dozens, probably hundreds, of his aged patients in Hyde, Greater Manchester, 60 miles up the road from Rugeley, and sometimes got his colleagues to sign certificates authorising their cremation. Palmer might have liked to have had Cook cremated too, but that was not an option for disposing of corpses in Britain for another thirty years.

In time other murderers came along and superseded William Palmer in depravity, in ghastliness and rapacity, in macabre ambition and perversity. The nineteenth century remained a golden age for poisoning, particularly of inconvenient spouses and especially as a weapon of choice for medical men: after the Smethurst debacle there would be Dr Edward Pritchard of Glasgow, Dr Henry Lamson, Dr Thomas Neill Cream and Dr Robert Buchanan. It continued into the twentieth century with men like the American-born quack medicine peddler Dr Crippen, who did away with his shrewish wife and tried to flee with his mistress across the Atlantic in 1910; the calculating, miserly, rapacious insurance salesman Frederick Seddon, who poisoned his tenant in north London for her money; and – perhaps –

the hen-pecked solicitor Major Herbert Armstrong, who may have dosed his wife with weedkiller. All chose poison from recognisable, if wicked, human motives, not because they were perverts or psychopaths but because they were greedy or desperate. Their very normality was disturbing.

Just as troubling, there would be women poisoners, who might not match their husbands and lovers for strength, but could do away with them insidiously by guile: Madeleine Smith (tried for poisoning her lover the year after Palmer, though in her case the Scottish verdict of not proven was returned), Adelaide Bartlett, Florence Maybrick, Florence Bravo, Christiana Edmunds – all were middle-class – and Mary Ann Cotton, who may have poisoned twenty-one people. Unlike the others, Cotton was from the working class and was the only one of these women to be executed. Many such murders were committed for financial gain, or to escape from stifling, unhappy marriages or to relieve frustrated passion. The details, as in Palmer's case, were compelling for newspaper readers: Edmunds sending her victims chocolate creams laced with strychnine, Major Armstrong passing a rival solicitor in Hay on Wye a slice of poisoned cake with the words "Scuse fingers". In his essay *Decline of the English Murder*, George Orwell lists nine notorious murderers whose crimes "have given the greatest amount of pleasure to the British public . . . whose story is known in its general outline to almost everyone". Six of them are middle-class poisoners. Up there with Crippen and Seddon is Dr Palmer of Rugeley:

> The murderer should be a little man of the professional class –
> a dentist or a solicitor, say – living an intensely respectable life
> somewhere in the suburbs . . . he should go astray through cher-
> ishing a guilty passion for his secretary or the wife of a rival . . .
> Having decided on murder, he should plan it all with the utmost
> cunning and only slip up over some tiny, unforeseeable detail.
> The means chosen should, of course, be poison.

Palmer never got round – so far as we know – to poisoning a lover or a rival, but the arrival of William Stephens at the Talbot Arms surely constitutes the sort of tiny, unforeseeable detail specified by Orwell.

Orwell's readers may have heard of Palmer, but he is not much remembered these days. After the nineteenth century he was only occasionally written about, though his name persisted in the jokes, rumours and gossip of the

West Midlands: the drinker's greeting "What's your poison?" used to be assigned to him, and allegedly local mothers would for many years terrify their infant children with the promise that Palmer would get them if they did not do what they were told. In 1912 *The Trial of William Palmer* by George H. Knott joined the lengthening list in the Notable British Trials series, and in 1925 George Fletcher, the Palmer obsessive, finally published his magnum opus *The Life and Career of Dr William Palmer of Rugeley*.

Fletcher had spent a lifetime fascinated by the case and collecting memorabilia about it. As a small boy Fletcher had met Cook and wrote that he could remember his own father, who was a doctor, "strongly upbraiding him [Cook], a fine young man . . . telling him he was wasting his substance and his health in riotous living, racing and general dissipation, adding: 'Even now you are on your way to Worcester races with a set of blacklegs and idlers, the worst of whom is that dissolute Dr Palmer who will rob you again and again.'" Such things are likely to make a strong impression, and by the time he was a teenager Fletcher's obsession was leading him to Rugeley to watch Sarah Palmer shouting at the gawpers outside her iron gate. He revisited the town a few years later in 1865, aged eighteen, to inspect Room 10 at the Talbot Arms, and his book was based partly on interviews with people who had known Palmer or lived in Rugeley in the 1850s. Even though he did not finally get round to writing it for another sixty years, his book is probably the most authoritative on the case. "I have not only made a lifelong study of the whole of Palmer's life and various murders, as well as his trial," he admitted, "but I have had exceptional opportunities of looking into the whole matter and perhaps not made as good a use of my chances as I now wish I had." Fletcher explicitly believed Palmer was a monster and mass-murderer, with eleven victims. He espoused the theory that he had dosed Cook with antimony to incapacitate, or possibly kill him, then tried a dose of strychnine, obtained from Newton on the Monday night and, when that did not work either, finally gave him a lethal dose the following evening. Fletcher endorsed Sir James Stephen's estimation that Palmer was as "cruel, as treacherous, as greedy of money and pleasure, as brutally hard-hearted and sensual a wretch as it is possible even to imagine".

A much shorter, slighter book, *Palmer: The Rugeley Poisoner* by Dudley Barker, was published by Duckworth in its Rogues' Gallery series in 1935 and follows the Fletcher line, though in a more populist fashion. Barker had seen the Jane letters, but decided they were too coarse to print. Twenty years further on, Robert Graves, the author of *I, Claudius*, also had a go with a semi-novelised version called *They Hanged My Saintly Billy*, published at the time of the centenary of the trial in 1956, which argued counter-intuitively that "Palmer never killed nobody". Graves's interest had been aroused after his uncle Clifford Pritchard happened to take over Fletcher's medical practice, and the book is an uneasy mix of fact and fiction in which authentic quotations are mingled with invented, novelistic ones. It is also written in a slightly arch style and blames everyone except Palmer for the crimes, even suggesting, incredibly, that his wife Annie poisoned herself in order to get him out of debt by her life insurance policy: "the only theory that covers all the facts." Graves knew of the Jane letters but had not seen them and believed they had disappeared, so he could not incorporate them in the mix. The book is not one of his more memorable efforts. Most recently, Dave Lewis, a local primary school teacher, published a thorough and accessible monograph of 1,000 copies, to coincide with a small exhibition about Palmer at the museum in the Elizabethan Ancient High House in Stafford in 2003. Lewis also has devised a William Palmer website. Palmer pops up occasionally and briefly in books about Victorian murder and even receives a name-check in the Sherlock Holmes short story 'The Adventure of the Speckled Band', written in 1892, when Holmes remarks to Watson, apropos of the villain Dr Grimesby Roylott: "Subtle enough and horrible enough. When a doctor does go wrong he is the first of criminals. He has nerve and he has knowledge. Palmer and Pritchard were among the heads of their profession . . . " – which is flattering to Palmer since he lost his nerve and was never at the head of his profession, even as a poisoner.

The brutal and fiendish Roylott in the story is a model for how Palmer has generally been portrayed on the rare occasions that his story has featured in true-crime documentaries on television, such as in part of a *Forensic Casebook* episode in 2001. The actor Keith Allen was called in to give a typically rip-roaring melodramatic performance as a villainous Palmer in a rather successful three-part television drama made by Yorkshire Television in 1998: sinister and snarling and not looking much like the real man, but compelling as the wicked and devious murderer.

Palmer was not done any favours by the line drawings of him which were made at the time of the trial. The best of them, entitled "The Only Authentic

Likeness of William Palmer", formed the frontispiece of the *Illustrated Times* biography and shows Palmer, dapperly dressed in top hat (complete with broad mourning band in commemoration of his dead wife) and morning coat, betting book in hand, at a race-course with a stable-boy leading a racehorse in the background. Palmer does indeed look sinister and calculating, with small, piggy eyes and a downturned mouth. Fletcher's book has a similar portrait, showing a more portly and more benign Palmer, also in top hat and suit and making notes in his betting book as a horse is led past in the distance, though in this one Palmer has turned slightly and is in profile. There is a possibility that he was also photographed. It would have been quite possible as daguerreotype portraits were becoming common even in the provinces in the 1850s, and – as we have seen – a photographer set up a studio in Palmer's back garden in 1856, soon after his arrest. A head-and-shoulders picture labelled as a photograph appears in Fletcher's book and looks as though it might well be authentic (it is reproduced on page 7) – and if anyone had acquired such an artefact, Fletcher would have done – but it is heavily retouched in the reproduction and its provenance, date and current whereabouts are unknown. Fletcher also published in his book a photograph of Palmer's house, complete with a maidservant standing in a doorway, which he dated to 1855 – which, if true, might well show Eliza Tharme – but the dating on the face of it seems unlikely: why would the property have been photographed, seemingly in summer, *before* his arrest? Afterwards the house was shut up. The house in the photograph is covered in ivy or some other creeper, which none of the contemporary line drawings show. The maid also appears to be wearing a sort of uniform, which would have been unusual for such a household in the 1850s, so the photograph may have been taken much later in the Victorian period. The house would not have changed its appearance much, however, set slightly back from the road behind wrought-iron railings, with three large, paned windows on the first floor, through one of which Palmer answered the fateful call from Elizabeth Mills for him to go and help Cook in his dying agony.

Poisoning only died out as a relatively common means of murder with the increasing certainty of forensic detection – Taylor was right there, though it took a long time to happen – and with the introduction of more stringent rules regulating over-the-counter sales of poison. Divorce-law reform, making it easier to escape a disastrous marriage or malign partner, also eventually helped.

18

"Poisoning is just not very popular these days"

NOWADAYS, ALTHOUGH SELF-POISONING THROUGH MEDICINAL OVERDOSES or drugs occurs, homicide by poisoning is very rare – though Shipman single-handedly inflated the statistics. "I must have done 1,500 post-mortems and I don't think I have ever seen a homicidal poisoning," Suzy Lishman, the vice-president of the Royal College of Pathologists, told me when I was researching this book. "Poisoning is just not very popular these days. You can detect most things now. Modern text-books scarcely mention poisons."

The types of poison that kill people nowadays are different from those of the nineteenth century: they may involve prescription or recreational drugs, or household and industrial chemicals. People still die from accidental poisoning: just as arsenic was sometimes mistaken for sugar or flour in those days, now people sometimes drink weed-killer or bleach that has been stored in fizzy-drinks bottles. So poisoning using strychnine or antimony, says Dr Lishman, is the equivalent of overdosing on modern prescription drugs such as paracetamol – drugs that have therapeutic effects in small doses but can prove fatal if too much is taken. Unfortunately for Cook, strychnine is very potent, and substances such as strychnine and arsenic are now carefully controlled. They have fallen out of fashion both as therapeutic drugs and as methods of poisoning. The leading forensic pathology text-book, *Simpson's Forensic Medicine*, included a section on strychnine poisoning as recently as 1997, but it has now been omitted.

Poisoning was so popular in the nineteenth century perhaps because poisons were unwanted by-products of increasing industrial activity and so were easily available and inexpensive. Restrictive laws were slow to be introduced and rarely strictly enforced. Many poisons had legitimate uses, such as poisoning rats, or they were used in cosmetics so could be easily bought. Chemical tests at the time were not as sensitive or as accurate as modern tests and were not routinely performed, so detection was less likely. The symptoms of poison were also in many cases similar to those of common infectious diseases such as cholera and so could be easily passed off as having natural causes.

Dr Lishman had not heard of Palmer when she agreed to deploy her professional skills to give a modern forensic analysis of the case, based on the court transcript. If ever there was a cold case, it was this one. Her view was striking: that Taylor ought to have been able to find traces of strychnine poisoning and that it would have been measurable even if the body had been exhumed again:

> I am surprised that no strychnine was found as the evidence points very strongly to it being the cause of Cook's death. Even following the loss of the stomach contents, if strychnine had been ingested, I would have expected it to be detected in the blood, liver and kidneys. The failure to detect strychnine does not rule it out not only because of the haphazard way the post-mortem was carried out but because the chemical tests at the time were not particularly reliable. Physicians then performed their own chemical tests, which relied on the quality of the available reagents and the skill of the doctor. Nowadays physicians do not test samples themselves but send them to expert pathologists for analysis.

She wondered why the other specialists had not examined the body themselves – it does not seem to have been considered and the defence experts were recruited late – and has a different thought about that:

> The fact that no one suggested testing again suggests that they thought it might be positive – it wasn't in the defence's interest to identify strychnine, just to try to discredit Taylor. As several people pointed out during the trial, strychnine can be detected in organs, even after putrefaction – why then were not further

tests done by one of the other experts? Unless Cook's remains had been completely destroyed, I would expect strychnine to have been detected if it was there. The comments about it being absorbed so not present in the stomach are a red herring – it would have circulated around the body in the blood.

Dr Lishman did not find the alternative explanations of Cook's death convincing. The symptoms were nothing like angina and epilepsy. Nor was Dr Bamford's diagnosis of apoplexy – a stroke – at all likely: Cook did not have any of the symptoms – slurred speech, one-sided limb weakness, drooping face – and his illness was not devastatingly sudden. The experts at the trial spent a great deal of time trying to differentiate between supposedly different forms of idiopathic and traumatic tetanus, but this was unnecessary. There is, in fact, no such thing as idiopathic tetanus, where the cause is unknown. The bacillus *Clostridium tetani*, which causes tetanus typically by entering through a wound, was not discovered for another thirty years. Nor is there strychnine tetanus. Although the symptoms are similar, strychnine does not cause tetanic convulsions and the progress of poisoning is very different, as some of the experts pointed out at the trial: strychnine is very much more rapid and relentless in its effect. Cook's post-mortem appearance is also distinctive in this respect: with strychnine poisoning, rigor mortis sets in immediately after death rather than several hours afterwards, which might account for why Mary Keeling, laying out the body soon after Cook died, found it to be so rigid already. Similarly, the long argument about the effect of antimony was also probably irrelevant, as Cook's symptoms do not coincide. Nor does the lengthy debate at the trial about Cook's heart being empty of blood have any relevance to the cause of his death: "it is now regarded as meaningless and I have never recorded it," she said. Dr Lishman was surprised that, although Taylor carried out chemical tests on Cook's organs, he does not seem to have examined samples under a microscope, which he could have done:

> If I was investigating Cook's death, I would take samples of the heart at the very least, probably also liver, lung and kidney. Given the concern about the granules on the spinal cord, I'd probably have sampled that as well. The study of tissue under the micro-

scope developed rapidly in the nineteenth century with advances in staining techniques and lens – and therefore microscope – manufacture. The standard size for a microscope slide was decided in 1839 [but] I presume that it wasn't a technique in routine use in forensic cases in the mid-century.

Dr Lishman continued:

They slaughtered a lot of animals, didn't they? It seems like thousands. The sort of experiments they were doing were so random – they weren't comparing like with like: rabbits and dogs . . . those sorts of tests would not be acceptable or appropriate today. Nowadays the use of animals is strictly controlled and they are only used when absolutely necessary. The experiments described at the trial appear to have had no controls or standardisation. I am amazed, frankly, that the jury could follow the evidence. It would have been very confusing – with just the medical evidence on its own you would have been totally baffled.

Then she added: "Do you know, I think the best testimony of the whole lot was the housemaid's. She just described what she saw, she was not trying to shoehorn the symptoms into a preconceived pattern. I would have much more trust in a lay person's evidence in those circumstances." So much for the snobbish sneering of Serjeant Shee and Professor Taylor about taking the word of a servant over an expert!

Professor Adam Hargreaves, a toxicologic pathologist with AstraZeneca Pharmaceuticals and professor of medicine at the University of Surrey, also studied the trial transcript. He has never seen a case of strychnine poisoning – "modern poisons tend to be antifreeze and paracetamol" – and he also ruled out Cook's death being caused by tetanus: "definitely not, it comes on gradually, not with a distinct, rapid onset. It must have been a poison of some sort."

Hargreaves was impressed by Taylor and more cautious about saying he should have detected strychnine:

It tends to be quite corrosive and the fact that he did not detect it does not necessarily rule it out. I think in the nineteenth century they were more adept at testing for metallic poisons like arsenic. But overall I like the way Taylor comes across: he was quite realistic and it was not an exact science in those days. These days you would take samples from the organs and use mass spectrometry to break them down into their individual components, into molecules to check the peaks in the spectrum. That would detect what it was.

And Professor Hargreaves has an even more intriguing possibility for the poison that killed Cook. He thinks it could have been prussic acid – hydrogen cyanide – and not strychnine at all. Remember Palmer's constant denials and his statements to the prison governor Fulford: "The Lord Chief Justice summed up for strychnine" and "Cook did not die from strychnine". And remember, too, the evidence of Charles Roberts, the apprentice to the druggist Mr Hawkins, delivered on the third day of the trial that Palmer bought not just six grains of strychnine and two drachms of Batley's Sedative but also two drachms of prussic acid. Two drachms – two teaspoons full – would have been enough to kill a man, says Professor Hargreaves. The symptoms would have been similar too: they can come on very quickly, if cyanide is inhaled or exposed to the skin, or be delayed for up to an hour: the time of onset depends on the concentration and duration of exposure. The short-term effects of ingesting cyanide include light-headedness, giddiness, rapid breathing, nausea and vomiting, as well as a feeling of neck constriction and suffocation, confusion, restlessness and anxiety. Rapid breathing is followed by respiratory depression or the stopping of breath altogether. In severe cases the symptoms progress to stupor, coma and muscle spasms in which the head, neck and spine are arched backwards, followed by convulsions, fixed and dilated pupils, and death. The skin becomes cold, clammy and diaphoretic – sweaty – and there may be a blue discolouration of the skin. Some of these symptoms appear very like those suffered by Cook. There would probably have been – though no one mentioned it at the time – an almond smell around the body.

Maybe Taylor could have discovered prussic acid residue if he had looked for it, or maybe it was lost during the botched post-mortem.

"Some of the tests were very hit and miss and I agree – residues may have been missed," says Professor Hargreaves. "I certainly think that it warrants a mention."

Roberts's evidence was glossed over quickly during the trial and he was not closely questioned, nor was the sale of prussic acid much mentioned. Was this because it was another poison that Taylor had failed to find? Or was it thought that suggesting two alternative poisons would unnecessarily complicate matters and undermine the prosecution's contention that Cook had been poisoned with strychnine? Was Palmer simply lying when he repeatedly denied that strychnine had been used? Or was he telling the truth? If he used multiple different poisons to kill his victims – antimony, perhaps, for Annie and possibly Walter and antimony, strychnine or cyanide for Cook – then he really might have been the Prince of Poisoners after all.

"The case against Palmer, albeit based on circumstantial evidence, was very strong," Brian O'Neill QC told me. He, too, was basing his thoughts on the transcript:

> If he was being tried today he would find himself facing an indictment accusing him of the other murders of which he was suspected as well as perhaps the fraud and forgery allegations. That couldn't happen in 1856 because the rules of the time did not permit it, and whilst there was some reference to those matters in order to put the instant allegation in context it was never suggested in court that he was guilty of anything other than the single murder for which he was being tried.

O'Neill is a criminal lawyer, but he also sits as a Recorder – part-time judge – at the Old Bailey, and on the day we met he had been sitting in Court One, the very place (though no longer the same room) where Palmer was tried 157 years earlier. We met in the judges' room along the corridor behind the courts, and after the day's sitting, he took me up to the bench to look down and across the famous court-room. I had covered cases there from the press bench, but from the judges' much higher vantage-point, looking down across the green-leather benches and to the distant dock, it all seems much bigger and more expansive. O'Neill continued:

Today Palmer would not have had the luxury of being represented at trial by four counsel, including the equivalent of two Queen's Counsel. And in addition to the extensive legal representation he had he was able to call a large number of expert witnesses. Neither of those facilities would be afforded him today. The Attorney General's opening speech was masterful, full of detail yet very easy to follow. Shee, quite frankly, wasn't in the same league. His opening speech went on for ever. He said he would go foot to foot with the prosecution, but he didn't. He set himself tasks which he did not need to and could not discharge and he was much less persuasive. He kept saying he believed in his client's innocence and he was rightly hauled over the coals for it.

It is very hard to argue that Palmer did not get a fair trial. He was not unfairly treated by the standards of the day – or today for that matter. If he was being tried now, the pre-trial publicity would be less acute and less prejudicial, but with a sensational case there would still be a considerable amount in the media. The court made every effort to counter that by moving the case away from the local area to be tried at the Old Bailey; a device which is still used today where there is a danger of a defendant not receiving a fair trial because of local prejudice.

There was more judicial comment from the Lord Chief Justice than would be appropriate today, his views were clear for all to see; occasionally one still sees that, but it is less and less frequent, certainly much less than when I started in practice 25 years ago. I don't think he overstepped the bounds though: even today it would be very difficult to argue on appeal that the level of judicial comment rendered the conviction unsafe.

Then he added wryly: "The jury was really put to work. Ten till six, six days a week and sequestered all that time, no wonder they returned their verdict so quickly."

Suzy Lishman said a sobering thing:

You know, if there was a death like this today, we would not necessarily check for strychnine or other poison unless we had reason to believe the deceased had taken something. Most people die from natural causes so there is no reason for toxicological tests routinely. If he died in the night with no one watching and then no relatives turned up, you wouldn't check for it. In a case like Cook's any of the medically qualified men who attended him could sign the death certificate, as happened then. Now, as then, that would have been the end of it, if a relative did not come forward with concerns. In Cook's case it seems likely that a general pathologist would be asked to perform the PM [post-mortem] unless Stephens had very good evidence that there was an unnatural cause of death. I think it is unlikely that the coroner would have ordered a forensic PM on Cook unless the police supported Stephens's concerns. Forensic PMs are much more expensive than regular ones and take much longer – so they're kept to a minimum.

Post-mortems these days are not, fortunately, done by drunken medical students slitting open the body on an inn table. They would usually be carried out in a hospital mortuary with the pathologist starting by describing the state of the body: height, weight, hair length and colour, presence of scars, tattoos and other distinguishing marks. The back would be examined and then an incision made down the centre of the chest and abdomen. In the National Health Service an anatomical pathology technologist usually removes the organs, though in forensic post-mortems it is more usual for the pathologists themselves to do it. The intestines are tied at each end and removed, and then the rest of the internal organs are taken out altogether in a single block – trachea, oesophagus, heart, lungs, spleen, liver, stomach, pancreas, kidneys and bladder – and removed to a separate table to be examined and dissected. Each organ is weighed separately and the contents of the stomach are emptied into a bowl and the volume measured – if there is no suspicion of poisoning, the contents would not be retained. As each organ is examined, any blood present is washed out and away down the drain. The spinal cord is not routinely examined unless there is an obvious trauma like a broken neck. If no cause of death is found, tissue is taken for microscopic examination as subtle changes may not be obvious to the eye. Samples of body fluids, urine, blood and stomach contents and small cubes of liver are taken and kept for analysis. Other samples may also be taken, though they are not necessarily tested. The coroner holds an inquest only in a minority of deaths referred to him. Most are signed off following a post-mortem; a few are heard in the coroner's court, often several months after the death.

Yes, said Dr Lishman, if Cook died in the night today with no one watching and if his death was certified the next morning by a medical man and no relative turned up, it is doubtful that there would be a post-mortem and unlikely that we would check for poison. That's how Shipman got away with it for so long, wasn't it?

If William Palmer were to go back to Rugeley today, he would still be able to find his way about. His mother's house and St Augustine's parish church opposite are much as they were, and a short walk would bring him to Market Street. He would probably recognise his old house, though it has been much altered. The roofline remains the same but there are two modern shops downstairs: a tanning centre and a pet shop. Round the back of his house, he would probably recognise the roofline, a jumble of ancient walls and chimney stacks, but the garden has long since been concreted over and disappeared under the detritus of commercial skips and storage cages. Next door to his old house the pub where Palmer's cleaning lady Matilda Bradshaw was said to have run to announce that he had done away with another child after his fourth baby died is now a Chinese restaurant and takeaway. Further up the street there are the normal sorts of charity shops, betting shops and gaming arcades that now occupy dispiriting premises in so many small English country towns. At least he would still recognise the names of the streets, which remain the same: there is still a Horse Fair and Market Street is still Market Street. William Palmer would not need to go all the way to London to settle his bets at Tattersall's these days: he could pop into one of the local bookmakers or wander over to the gaming arcade to try the one-armed bandits. "Grab £500 for Free!" proclaimed a poster in the front window of a betting shop on the day I wandered past: it showed a grinning, jubilant man, fists aloft, so Palmer might have been tempted. Or he could pawn any gold or silver jewellery he, or his wife, had at the shop on the corner, just a few yards from his house – it advertises that top prices are paid.

Palmer would recognise the Talbot Arms directly across the road from his old house too. It has gone through several names since his day, including the Shrewsbury Arms, but now that has been shortened to the Shrew. The old coaching inn's façade is still more or less as it was, but the pub now nestles between a couple of supermarkets. The entrance has been changed slightly, but there is still a short flight of steps to enter the pub. Unfortunately, when I was there last, the place had plainly seen better days. The décor was faded and dusty, the walls a gloomy red, the chairs battered, and the atmosphere stale and seedy. A review on an eating-out website said ruthlessly but, unfortunately, possibly accurately: "This is not just the worst pub in Rugeley. No, this is the worst pub in Staffordshire. It's awful." It was perhaps a reflection of its sense of abandonment that, nearly two years on, no one had contested the comment. The latest reference to the pub was in the local *Sunday Mercury* in February 2012, illustrated with a photograph of the leaseholder Gavin Houston and three brawny bouncers. The newspaper claimed then that it was the only pub in Britain that had more bouncers than boozers – a touch of which Gus Mayhew 156 years earlier would have been proud. Mr Houston accused the police of harassing the place. Old Tom Masters must be turning in his grave.

On the midweek afternoon when Dave Lewis, the Palmer specialist, and I visited the place, it was quiet enough. A few morose, elderly drinkers were scattered about and the barmaid – Elizabeth Mills's distant successor – was wearing a baseball cap as she pulled the pints. John Stead, the landlord, shaven-headed and wearing an anorak, was genial enough and said we could go up to Room 10, so we wended our way through a maze of grubby, half-partitioned corridors and up a scruffy, bare staircase to reach the first floor. The builders had been in, but had dropped their tools and bits of plank and timber and disappeared again. Room 10 itself was bare and unused, much smaller now than it must have been when Cook stayed there, with partition walls and a naked light bulb swinging from the ceiling. Possibly the only recognisable feature was the sash-window looking out across to Palmer's house. If I had thought there might be some sort of atmosphere, or even a vestige of the room it must once have been, I was mistaken.

We went back to the bar without a shudder. Mr Stead was still there. "There's definitely a funny feeling up there, isn't there?" he said. "Me babby used to play in there, but he always said it was cold, though I've never noticed it myself. You get strange things happening. You get glasses smash sometimes and I've heard footsteps in the corridor when there's no one there. People do ask occasionally. The barmaids don't like going up there much." "Nah," said the girl in the baseball cap, "I don't mind it."

By now we had been joined by one of the elderly drinkers who had heard us talking. He was chewing gum and held a pint of lager in his hand. "That Palmer," he said, slurring slightly. "I believe he was innocent of those deaths. I mean, they just died in those days, didn't they? He never killed them. He was 100 per cent innocent. That bloke, Cook, he didn't die from strychnine. He may have given him something just to make him bad, know what I mean?" It was hard to stop him now. "I mean, look at Jack the Ripper . . . I believe he was the Queen's doctor, Sir William Gull," he added, choosing possibly the least likely candidate for the East End psychopath. We started edging away. "I mean, the police knew who it was all the time, didn't they? No, Palmer never killed anyone."

For a more sober view, I called on Prebendary Michael Newman, who has been the vicar of Rugeley since 1989. We met in the vestry of St Augustine's, where the Palmer family had a pew. It was plain that he had not given his church's most infamous parishioner much thought over the years – and why, indeed, should he? "Most people who want to know about him are coming from outside, like you," he said severely:

> Locally, I must admit, I've not heard him spoken of very much.
> To my knowledge he's not mentioned in the school – local history: coal mines, the industrial revolution, Cannock Chase, yes, but not Palmer. When we have school groups in the church, there's always an opportunity for them to ask me questions and I've never had one about him. I suppose there's a recognition that he was a nasty piece of work, if he's spoken about at all . . . almost in hushed tones. I suppose you'd say there's an ambivalence . . .

Perhaps that is for the best. It is clear that Palmer was a villain and almost certainly a murderer, but maybe the image he has carried all these years of being a ruthless, predatory serial killer is overblown. He may have killed his earlier racing companion Leonard Bladen in 1850, and if he did, to get himself out of a financial hole, he got away with it. I think it is more likely that he poisoned his wife Annie, because of the antimony found by Taylor in her body – though that may have been due to the tartar emetic with which she had been dosed during her sickness – and he certainly benefited from the insurance he had taken out on her life only shortly before. He would have been far from alone in doing that, as the insurance companies quietly admitted to Henry Mayhew a few months later.

He may have hastened the passing of his brother Walter by plying him with drink, though Walter was making a pretty good attempt to drink himself to death anyway. Walter's death scarcely eased his troubles since the insurance company refused to pay up, so all it did was increase the lurking suspicions about what William Palmer was doing. It seems certain that by the autumn of 1855 the threats and pressure being exerted by the money-lenders Pratt, Padwick and Wright were pushing Palmer towards ever greater extremes of desperation and ruin. He owed them an enormous sum of money, which he could not hope to repay, and he faced professional and personal disgrace imminently by that November and the prospect of imprisonment or even transportation. Not only he but his family would be ruined.

There was just one slim, desperate chance of staving off disaster: if his horse The Chicken won at Shrewsbury. It might not have been enough, but it would have bought him some time. Instead, his best friend Cook's horse Polestar won its race; and then The Chicken lost, pitching Palmer even deeper into the mire. He may have started the week intending no ill to Cook at all, but suddenly a temptation and an opportunity opened up. Perhaps initially he just wanted to make Cook too ill to collect his winnings, so that he could embezzle them instead, and then, maybe, he realised he would have to do away with him, or be discovered. In that case, perhaps he did dose Cook with a small quantity of strychnine on the Monday night and, when that did not work, procured more the next day to finish him off. Or perhaps he had in mind using the prussic acid he had bought at Hawkins's. If that was so, the arrival of Dr Jones and his staying in Cook's bedroom overnight would have made things much more difficult. Possibly he had hoped to finish Cook off before Jones arrived, which would have made explanations about his fatal illness simpler if his fellow doctor had not seen it for himself. Perhaps the strychnine or prussic acid administered on the Monday night was adulterated, as Fletcher thought, or perhaps Palmer miscalculated the dose, which might account for his discussion with Newton later in the week about how much would be needed to kill a dog. Or was that just a ruse to indicate to the chemist's assistant that he was ignorant of the poison's lethality? Jones's presence at the deathbed changed things, and it seems that Palmer adopted strategies to convince him that Cook's death was natural – caused by epileptic convulsions or tetanus. It would have taken some explaining, but both Jones and Bamford were prepared to accept that the death had natural causes: murder is not necessarily the first thing you suspect of a friend.

But the arrival of the suspicious stepfather William Stephens – already half-convinced from reading about other cases in the newspapers that his dear boy must have been poisoned and determined to find out what had happened to him and where his betting book had got to – clearly sent Palmer into a full panic. There can be no other explanation for his maladroit interference at the post-mortem and desperate attempts to bribe the coroner. He was being driven ever further into a corner, reliant at the last on the local network of cronies and contacts to get him off the hook, to return a verdict in defiance of the London professor. But by then it was too late: the Rugeley poisoning was no longer a local matter but of national interest, and he was trapped. Just as twenty years earlier he could not have buzzed around the race-courses of the country, betting out of his depth, or nipped down to London for the day to see Pratt and pick up Cook's winnings at Tattersall's, because there would not have been a train to take him, neither in earlier days would there have been so much national press interest, bringing his quiet little stratagems to the attention of the entire country and sucking him remorselessly down into a vortex of his own making and folly. If this reading is correct, then William Palmer was not the greatest villain of the nineteenth century, but a desperate man, floundering out of his depth and ruthlessly exposed and destroyed. As such, his story, touching on so many of the seamier sides of mid-Victorian life, is not so much about an arch criminal mastermind as an ordinary man brought low by his own venality, by chance and fate. How many men, like him but cleverer and luckier, shifted uneasily in their chairs as they read the daily details of his downfall?

The last person who could reliably have been said to know William Palmer was a woman called Emma Price, who gave an interview to a local paper when she reached the age of a hundred in January 1944. She had lived locally all her life and been a farmer's wife up on the Chase. When the reporter visited, he found her busily engaged in her principal pastime, knitting:

Mrs Price's only serious defect is the fact that she is slightly deaf but she can read and twice every day she peruses her prayer book and the New Testament. There are not many texts in the latter which she cannot remember. She told our representative that she had seen Dr Palmer in the flesh and in death, as many years after he was hanged at Stafford she went to Madame Tussauds in London. In her childhood, she said, she remembered Palmer as a handsome man wearing a silk shirt and to her he appeared kind and gentle.

Her mother had taken her to see him because she had an injured finger and he had made it better. It looks as though the reporter had taken the story from an interview the old lady had given to the *Rugeley Times* the previous year, on her ninety-ninth birthday. The same quotes seem to have been repeated anyway – perhaps she was so used to telling the story that she had memorised it verbatim, or perhaps she was too senile to remember any more. "Poor Dr Palmer," she sighed. "He was such a tall, handsome man you know, with such rosy cheeks. Some say he poisoned his wife and other people, but I don't know."

Notes

1 Stafford, 14 June 1856

Details of Palmer's last night and execution are taken from newspaper accounts over the following days, especially the *Staffordshire Advertiser*, which published an edition that weekend, the *Observer*'s edition of Sunday 15 June, and *The Times* and the *Manchester Guardian* of Monday 16 June. The *New York Times*'s reference to Palmer as "the Borgia of the betting ring" was in an article about the trial published on 27 June 1856. Details of George "Topper" Smith's career are in Dave Lewis, *The Rugeley Poisoner*, pp. 155–7 and in *Black Country Characters* by Aristotle Trump.

2 "Oh doctor, I shall die!"

Cook's death was detailed at Palmer's trial, from which the witness statements are taken, as reported in the *Manchester Guardian*, 15—18 May 1856, *The Times Illustrated and Unabridged Report of the Trial of William Palmer*, published in book form by Ward Lock in 1856, and *Trial of William Palmer*, edited by E. R. Watson in the Notable British Trials series, 3rd edition 1952. Charles Dickens's description of Inspector Field is from his article "Detective Police" in *Household Words*, 27 July 1850, which names the lightly disguised officer as "Inspector Wield"; by the following year the pseudonym had been dropped and he was indeed named Field. The archway for coaches at the side of the Talbot Arms has now been replaced by a supermarket.

3 "They won't hang us yet"

William Stephens's background is hard to discover. There are some basic details in the 1851 and 1861 censuses, available online, and more from the written statements in the Palmer boxes at the National Archives at Kew, TS25/922 and 927 and TS11/430–4, including his statement describing his immediate belief that his son must have been poisoned. Henry Savage's letter about Cook's previous health is also in the Palmer boxes. The account of Palmer's arrest is in Thomas Woollaston's memoir.

4 "The great days of England"

The account of reactions to the Great Exhibition of 1851, including Charlotte Brontë's "only magic" quotation, is in *The World for a Shilling* by Michael Leapman, p. 165. Macaulay's ringing phrase about "The history of our country . . . intellectual improvement" is stated in his declaration of purpose at the start of *The History of England. The Times*: "Thirty years ago . . . spent the day there" is from an article that appeared on 12 January 1850, quoted in *Fire and Steam* by Christian Wolmar. Charles Dickens: "physical force breaking out all around me", see *Charles Dickens: A life* by Claire Tomalin. R. S. Surtees's description of Soapey Sponge – "a rather vulgar-looking man" – is in chapter 1 of *Mr Sponge's Sporting Tour*; "gentlemen . . . having nothing a year, paid quarterly" is in chapter 24. Dickens's article "The Demeanour of Murderers" was published in *Household Words* on 14 June 1856, the day of Palmer's execution, and his description "everywhere I see the late Mr Palmer" was in a letter of the same period to his friend John Forster. Charles Greville's description of the trial as provoking "interest almost unprecedented" appears in his diary entry for 28 May 1856, the day after Palmer's conviction; see *The Diaries of Charles Greville*, edited by Edward Pearce. James Hannay's quote in the *New York Tribune* about "hoofs in patent leather" is cited in Thomas Boyle's *Black Swine in the Sewers of Hampstead*. Lord Campbell's reference to the trial is in his diary on 28 June 1856, published as part of his *Memoirs*. Sir James Fitzjames Stephen devoted a chapter to the Palmer case in his book *A General View of the Criminal Law of England*, published in 1890, with his description of Palmer on page 272.

5 "A thoroughly bad boy"

The account of Palmer's family background and antecedents is taken partly from George Fletcher's *The Life and Career of William Palmer* but also from the family descendant Ian Brodie's researches into his ancestry. Fletcher claimed to have witnessed Sarah Palmer's "saintly Billy" remark. Where Fletcher's factual statements can be cross-checked with other sources such as parish and court records, they tend to be accurate. Some of the family details and references to other local figures such as Dr Tylecote can be verified from the 1841 and 1851 censuses. The account of conditions in the Palmers' coal-mines is drawn from the 1842 Parliamentary Commission report on *Young Persons in the Coal Mines of North Staffordshire and Cheshire and the condition and treatment of such children and young persons*: evidence given on 26 March 1842. The references to medical training are largely taken from Douglas Guthrie's *A History of Medicine*, as is his felicitous reference to Victorian surgeons' practice of "physical carpentry". Palmer's student medical notebook is in the files at the National Archives. Vizetelly's account of choosing pictures for his Palmer biography are in his memoirs, *Glances Back through Seventy Years*, vol. 1, p. 419.

6 If public rumour be worthy of credit

Accounts of the death of Abley and the others are in most histories of the Palmer story; the most authentic and likely are in Fletcher and Lewis, but the *Illustrated Times* was the first to air them in its special Rugeley edition of 2 February 1856. The graves of Abley and Bladen are still visible in Colwich and Rugeley churchyards. Kell syndrome is now a medically recognised condition. Eliza Tharme's statement and the legal opinions scrawled on it are in the Palmer boxes at the National Archives. For Liverpool death rates in 1840, see *The Sanitary Condition of the Labouring Population of Great Britain* by Edwin Chadwick, p. 225. Details of Palmer's insurance dealings were outlined in the *Post and Insurance Monitor*, 5 January 1856. Information about the Victorian insurance industry and its expansion is in *The British Insurance Business* by H. A. L. Cockerell and Edwin Green. Pratt's self-exculpatory letter was carried in the *Morning Post* on 8 January 1856. Walkenden's statement was made at Walter Palmer's inquest in January 1856.

7 "On – on! Like the rushing whirlwind"

For information on Victorian horse-racing, I consulted Professor Wray Vamplew, especially his book *The Turf: A social and economic history of horseracing*, and articles by M. Huggins in *The International Journal of the History of Sport*. Details of William Powell Frith's painting *The Derby Day* are drawn from the catalogue of the painter's exhibition at the London Guildhall in 2006. The *Morning Chronicle*'s account of the Derby Day accident was published in the paper on 28 May 1856. Details of Palmer's horses and their sale are given in *Trial of William Palmer*, edited by E. R. Watson in the Notable British Trials series, 3rd edition 1952. Padwick's career is outlined in the Findon, Sussex website (www.findonvillage.com). The Pratt–Palmer correspondence is in the pre-trial bundles in the Palmer files at the National Archives.

8 "The man is as silent as death"

The thirty-four Jane letters are kept at the William Salt Library in Stafford (Ref: D1548). Kettle's article is in *Transactions of the Stafford Historical and Civic Society* (1971), also in the Salt Library.

9 "Dreadful reports current at Rugeley"

Accounts of Palmer's brief hunger strike were reported in many papers, including the *Morning Chronicle* on 12 January 1856. Annie and Walter's inquests were reported in the *Staffordshire Advertiser* and picked up by the *Manchester Guardian*, 14 January 1856 and 24 January 1856. Devonshire's post-mortem report on Cook is in the National Archives at Kew and Harland's statement is drawn from his evidence at Palmer's trial on 16 May 1856. The *Rugeley Times* article about Palmer's grandfather clock was printed on 7 August 1971. The Queen's Bench hearing on possible prejudice at Palmer's trial was reported in *Ellis and Blackburn's Law Reports* (1856), p. 1024, now in the Middle Temple law library. The Trial of Offences Bill, CAP XVI, debates and readings were reported in *Hansard* (1856): first reading, Lords, 5 February 1856; second reading, Lords, 11 February; second reading, Commons, 3 March; Royal Assent to Act, 11 April 1856. A copy of the Act is in the William Salt Library. A copy of the grand jury's indictment of Palmer is in the National Archives.

10 "History when properly written"

The *Staffordshire Advertiser*'s first mention of Cook's death was in its edition of 1 December 1855, on microfilm at the British Library's Newspaper Library at Colindale. *The Times* and *Manchester Guardian*'s editions for the period are both accessible through the papers' websites (*The Times*'s is more easily accessed, but is behind a paywall). Delane's hand-written memoranda to his staff are in the files of *The Times*'s archive at Enfield (appointment needed). Whitty's authorship of the *Leader*'s reporting on Rugeley was identified by Thomas Boyle in *Black Swine in the Sewers of Hampstead*. Gus Mayhew's role at the *Illustrated Times* was first identified in Shee's cross-examination of Taylor in the verbatim trial transcript, and subsequently confirmed in Vizetelly's *Glances Back* memoir, which is a mine of information both on the trial and on mid-Victorian journalistic mores. The Mayhews' literary efforts are discussed in Judith Flanders's *The Victorian House*. Henry Mayhew's exposé of the insurance industry was carried in the *Illustrated Times*'s Rugeley edition of 2 February 1856. Taylor's published letter in the *Lancet* appeared on 2 February 1856, and his stronger, private letters about the case to the Treasury solicitors Greenwood and Reynolds – including the "impudent fellow" reference on 26 March 1856 – are in the Palmer files at Kew.

11 "As calmly as the question of the moon's rotation"

Taylor's background and pioneering achievements are listed in his entry in the *Dictionary of National Biography* and biographical articles in *Clinical Chemistry* and the *Cambridge Journal of Medical History*; his career is also discussed in Whorton, *The Arsenic Century*, and in Burney, *Poison, Detection and the Victorian Imagination*, which fully discusses the medical evidence and its shortcomings in the Palmer case. The lawyers' careers are detailed in their *DNB* entries and their obituaries in *The Times* and various law journals. In addition, Campbell wrote a memoir, published after his death with a selection from his diary and letters. George Shee wrote a poignant memorial article about his father in *Law Magazine and Review*, vol. 1, April 1872. Cockburn's fees books are kept in the Middle Temple library, as is the manuscript of his youthful novel, the plot of which has been helpfully outlined in a note written by Sian Busby in February 2005, which saves anyone else from having to wade through it ever again. Kenealy's vivid description of Palmer is related in his memoirs, published by his daughter long after his death, pp. 161–2. The disaster of his defence of the Tichborne Claimant is related in *The Man who Lost Himself* by Robyn Annear. The pamphlet supposedly written by the Rev. Thomas Palmer to try and save his brother's life is in the William Salt Library. The contemporary legal background to murder trials is taken from John Hostettler's *History of Criminal Justice* and Clive Emsley's *Crime and Society in England*. The *Times*'s quote – "Strangers who came to London . . . " – appears in its obituary of Cockburn published on 22 November 1880.

12 "Extraordinary disclosures of a most frightful character"
13 "The most memorable proceedings for the last 50 years"
14 "It was the riding that did it"
The accounts of Palmer's trial are very full: in the daily reports of papers such as *The Times*, the *Manchester Guardian* and the *Morning Chronicle*; in *The Times*'s subsequent separately published verbatim account; and in the more truncated Palmer volume in the Notable British Trials series, which, however, misses some salient points. Vizetelly's *Glances Back*, vol. 1, devotes most of chapter 20 to his vivid reminiscences of the case. For length of Victorian trials, Emsley, *Crime and Society in England*, p. 213, quotes Edward Carpenter (*Prisons, Police and Punishment*, published 1905) as saying most magistrates' cases took three minutes or less. A photograph of Palmer's note in court to Smith saying he'd like to poison Campbell is reproduced in Notable British Trials; other notes were recalled by Kenealy in his memoirs. The *Morning Chronicle* carried the report of Palmer's meeting with his brother George on 27 May 1856, and the quote "that don't satisfy me" in its report of the end of the trial the following day. The *Illustrated Times* carried gossipy paragraphs about the proceedings as well as its full round-up in its edition of 28 May 1856. Woollaston's memoir of Palmer's return to Stafford was published by the Berkswich Historical Society in 2007.

15 "In accordance with the voice of science and the feeling
 of the country"
An account of the scientific debate following the trial is in Burney's *Poison, Detection and the Victorian Imagination* and in Flanders's *The Invention of Murder*. Queen Victoria's reference to Palmer was written in her journal on 28 May 1856, available online. William Ewart's career is outlined in the *DNB*, and the capital punishment debate in the Commons on 10 June 1856 is in the Hansard archive, available online. The *Morning Chronicle*'s editorial was published on 11 June 1856, and Investigator's letter about recruiting a jury of gentlemen on 9 June. The pamphlets about the

case, circulated at Palmer's execution and afterwards, such as *Satan Reproving Sin!*, are in the William Salt Library. Several broadsheets about Palmer and his execution are in the Borowitz Collection at Kent State University, Ohio.

16   "Are you sure this damn thing's safe?"
The mayor of Stafford's concerns about safety at the execution and the licensing arrangements for the public stands are in the Stafford County Record Office, as are the Staffordshire finance committee minutes of its meeting in June 1856 which decided on the coroners' courts expenses and the reimbursement of witnesses.

17   "Distinctly *not* quite composed"
18   "Poisoning is just not very popular these days"
George Palmer's request to consult his brother's files, William Stephens's request for compensation and the jurors' plea for recompense submitted on 4 July 1856 (and Cockburn's brief reply, dated 8 November 1856) are all in the files of the National Archives. The Smethurst case is discussed in Whorton, *The Arsenic Century*, pp. 103–12. The deaths of the Palmer case participants are listed in Fletcher, pp. 22–3. The subsequent life of Palmer's sister Sarah Brodie is taken from Ian Brodie's research. *The Life and Crimes of William Palmer*, a three-part drama by Yorkshire Television "based on a true story", was broadcast in 1998 and subsequently released on video. The *Forensic Casebook* episode which mentions the Palmer case was made in 2001 (see www.silverglade.co.uk).

The quotations by Suzy Lishman, Adam Hargreaves and Brian O'Neill QC were made in interviews with the author in March and April 2013. The *Sunday Mercury*'s claim that there were "more bouncers than boozers" at the Shrew was made in a story published on 12 February 2012, and the accusation that it was "the worst pub in Staffordshire" was made online in a review on the yelp.co.uk site on 3 October 2012: more than a year later it was still prominently displayed. Emma Price's interviews were carried in the *Rugeley Times* on 23 January 1943 and subsequently the following year, on her hundredth birthday, in the *Birmingham Mercury* on 14 January 1944.

Bibliography

National Archives, Kew

TS25/922 & 927

TS11/430–434

William Salt Library, Stafford

D (W) 1548/1

D (W) 1548/2/3/4/5/6/7/1–34

Palmer Act: Cap XVI: An Act to empower the Court of Queen's Bench to order certain offenders to be tried at the Central Criminal Court

Rev. Thomas Palmer's letter to the Lord Chief Justice: "Now Let reason, not Passion be your guide."

William Palmer pamphlets, c3.21:

William Palmer the Racer!

'William Palmer: A Warning to Young Men Against Horse Racing, Betting etc': Sermon by Rev. Alexander Thomson

Satan Reproving Sin! A Dialogue between the Devil and Dr Palmer

"Jane" Letters: Ref: D 1548

Staffordshire Record Office

Indictments at Stafford: January–July 1856

Staffordshire finance committee minutes, June sessions 1856

Documents related to Palmer's execution

Middle Temple Library

Sir Alexander Cockburn papers and fees book

Ellis and Blackburn Law Reports 1856, p. 1024: Queen's Bench Court, Regina *v* Palmer

The Times Newspaper Archive, Enfield

Correspondence and memoranda files of John Thadeus Delane, 1855–6

Parliamentary and Official Papers

Hansard 1856: 11 February, 3 March, 10 June 1856

Children's Employment Commission 1842: On employment of children in the coal mines of north Staffordshire

Census 1851, 1861

Newspapers

Birmingham Mercury

Examiner

Illustrated Times

Law Journal

Law Times

Manchester Guardian

Morning Chronicle

New York Times

Observer

Post Magazine and Insurance Monitor

Rugeley Chronicle

Rugeley Times

Solicitors' Journal and Reporter

Staffordshire Advertiser

Sunday Mercury

The Times

Journal articles

Berkswich History Society, Stafford, 2007: Thomas Woollaston, *Police Experiences*

Cambridge Journal of Medical History, vol. 35/4 (1991): N. G. Coley, "Alfred Swaine Taylor MD: Forensic toxicologist"

Clinical Chemistry, vol. 31/7 (1985): L. Rosenfeld, "Alfred Swaine Taylor: Pioneer toxicologist – and a slight case of murder"

International Journal of the History of Sport, vol. 11 (1994): M. Huggins, "Class Culture and Respectability: Racing and the middle classes in 19th-century England"

International Journal of the History of Sport, vol. 13 (1996): M. Huggins, "Lord Bentinck, the Jockey Club and Racing Morality in mid-19th-century England"

Royal College of Physicians: 'Lives of the Fellows'

Stafford Historical and Civic Society Transactions, 1971–3: Ann J. Kettle, "William Palmer and Stafford: The Jane letters", pp. 22–6

Sport in History, vol. 23 (2003): J. Tolson and W. Vamplew, "Railways and British Flat Racing 1830–1914"

Sport in History, vol. 33 (2013): M. Huggins, "Art, Horse Racing and the Sporting Gaze"

Websites

Oxford Dictionary of National Biography: entries for William Palmer, Sir Alexander Cockburn, Lord Chief Justice Campbell, Sir William Shee, William Herapath

www.williampalmer.co.uk

www.staffspasttrack.org

www.findonvillage.com

www.queenvictoriasjournals.org

Wikipedia: various entries

Books

Peter Ackroyd, *Wilkie Collins*, Chatto and Windus 2012

Richard D. Altick, *Victorian Studies in Scarlet*, Norton 1970

Robyn Annear, *The Man who Lost Himself*, Robinson 2002

J. B. Atlay, *The Victorian Chancellors*, vol. 2, Smith Elder and Co. 1908

David Ayerst, *Guardian: Biography of a newspaper*, Collins 1971

Dudley Barker, *Palmer: The Rugeley Poisoner*, Duckworth 1935

Mark Bills and Vivien Knight, *William Powell Frith: Painting the Victorian Age*, Yale University Press 2006

Thomas Boyle, *Black Swine in the Sewers of Hampstead*, Viking 1989

Simon Bradley and Nikolaus Pevsner, *The City of London*, Penguin 1997

Ian Burney, *Poison, Detection and the Victorian Imagination*, Manchester University Press 2006

Edwin Chadwick, *Report on the Sanitary Condition of the Labouring Population of Great Britain*, Edinburgh University Press 1964

H. A. L. Cockerell and Edwin Green, *The British Insurance Business*, Sheffield Academic Press 1976

Kate Colquhoun, *Mr Briggs' Hat: Britain's first railway murder*, Little Brown 2011

Sir Edward Cook, *Delane of the Times*, Constable 1916

Rosalind Crone, *Violent Victorians*, Manchester University Press 2012

Michael Diamond, *Victorian Sensation*, Anthem 2003

Charles Dickens, *Dickens's London*, Folio Society edition, 1966

Charles Dickens, *Little Dorrit*, Penguin edition, 1986

Charles Dickens, *Selected Journalism, 1850–1870*, Penguin edition, 1997

Charles Dickens, *Sketches by Boz*, Penguin edition, 1995

Clive Emsley, *Crime and Society in England, 1750–1900*, Longman 2010

Michael Farrell, *Poisons and Poisoners*, Bantam 1994

Judith Flanders, *The Victorian House*, Harper Perennial 2003

Judith Flanders, *The Invention of Murder*, Harper Press 2011

George Fletcher, *The Life and Career of Dr William Palmer of Rugeley*, T. Fisher Unwin 1925

Nicholas Foulkes, *Gentlemen and Blackguards*, Weidenfeld and Nicolson 2010

V. A. C. Gatrell, *The Hanging Tree: Execution and the English people, 1770–1868*, Oxford University Press 1994

Robert Graves, *They Hanged My Saintly Billy*, Doubleday and Co. 1957

Adrian Gray, *Crime and Criminals of Victorian England*, History Press 2011

Charles Greville, *The Diaries of Charles Greville*, ed. Edward Pearce, Pimlico 2006

Douglas Guthrie, *A History of Medicine*, Thomas Nelson 1960

Hon. Mrs Hardcastle, *Life of John, Lord Campbell: Autobiography, diary and letters*, John Murray 1881

Alan Hayhurst, *Staffordshire Murders*, History Press 2009

The History of The Times: The tradition established, 1841–84, Office of the Times 1939

John Hostettler, *A History of Criminal Justice in England and Wales*, Waterside 2009

Anne Humphreys, *Travels into the Poor Man's Country*, University of Georgia Press 1977

Anthony Hunt, *More Murder and Mayhem around the Chase*, Mount Chase Press 2013

Anthony Hunt and John Griffiths, *Hednesford's Horse Racing History*, Mount Chase Press 2010

Illustrated Life, Career and Trial of William Palmer of Rugeley, Ward Lock 1856

Arabella Kenealy, *The Memoirs of Edward Vaughan Kenealy LL.D by his Daughter*, John Long 1908

George H. Knott and E. R. Watson, *Trial of William Palmer*, Notable British Trials series, William Hodge and Co. 1923

Stephen Koss, *The Rise and Fall of the Political Press in Britain*, Fontana 1984

George Lawson, *Surgeon in the Crimea*, Military Book Society 1968

Dave Lewis, *The Rugeley Poisoner*, Artloaf 2003

Henry Mayhew, *London Labour and the London Poor*, Penguin 1985

George Orwell, *Shooting an Elephant and Other Essays*, Penguin 2003

Roy Porter, *Quacks: Fakers and charlatans in English medicine*, Tempus 2001

The Pre-Raphaelites, Penguin Books catalogue of Tate Gallery exhibition, 1984

Thea Randall and Joan Anslow, *Around Rugeley from Old Photographs*, Amberley 2010

Giles St Aubyn, *Infamous Victorians*, Constable 1971

Paul Schlicke, *The Oxford Companion to Charles Dickens*, Oxford University Press 2011

Gavin Stamp, *The Changing Metropolis*, Viking 1984

Sir James Fitzjames Stephen, *A General View of the Criminal Law of England*, Macmillan 1890

Robert S. Surtees, *Mr Sponge's Sporting Tour*, Nonesuch 2006

Alfred Swaine Taylor, *On Poisoning by Strychnia: With comments on the medical evidence given at the trial of William Palmer for the murder of John Parsons Cook*, Longman, Brown, Green, Longmans and Roberts 1856, Nabu Public Domain Reprint 2013

Matthew Sweet, *Inventing the Victorians*, Faber and Faber 2001

Wray Vamplew, *The Turf: A social and economic history of horse racing*, Allen Lane 1976

Henry Vizetelly, *Glances Back through Seventy Years*, vol. 1, Kegan Paul, Trench,

Trubner and Co. 1893, Forgotten Books 2013

Katharine Watson, *Poisoned Lives: English poisoners and their victims*, Hambledon 2004

James C. Whorton, *The Arsenic Century*, Oxford University Press 2010

Colin Wilson and Pat Pitman, *Encyclopaedia of Murder*, Pan Books 1964

Thomas Woollaston, *Memoir: Assistance rendered during investigation of murder by William Palmer. Notes and recollections thereon etc*, published by Berkswich History Society Stafford 2007, courtesy of Martin Woollaston.

Television

The Life and Crimes of William Palmer, Yorkshire Television, 1998

Forensic Casebook, 2001: www.silverglade.co.uk

Acknowledgements

A GREAT MANY PEOPLE GENEROUSLY AND FREELY HELPED ME WITH MY research, but of these the first I must thank is Dave Lewis, whose book *The Rugeley Poisoner* (2003), printed in a limited edition of 1,000 copies, is the only significant modern study devoted to William Palmer. Dave was a source of anecdotes, fact verification and gossip, and generously drove me round all the sites around Rugeley and Stafford that can be associated with Palmer. Ian Brodie, a direct descendant of Palmer's sister Sarah, and his wife Val, who live in Warwickshire, were very helpful about the Brodie side of the family and Palmer's parents and were extremely hospitable hosts: were they upset to discover they had a murderer in the family, I asked: "Not bloody likely," Ian replied cheerily, showing the true family spirit. The Rev. Val White and the Rev. Chris Leffler, current and immediate past incumbents of Thomas Palmer's parish at Trimley St Martin, Suffolk, helped me with information about their Victorian predecessor: Thomas never married and grew eccentric in his dress, according to the parish records. In Rugeley Prebendary Michael Newman, the current vicar of St Augustine's parish church, gave me an interview, as did John Stead, the current landlord of the Shrew, formerly the Talbot Arms. Margaret Neal and Marion Kettle of the Landor Society of Rugeley were also founts of local knowledge and local author Anthony Hunt sent me copies of his research.

In London, my former Guardian colleague, the paper's crime editor Sandra Laville, put me in touch with her brother-in-law, the criminal barrister and Old Bailey Recorder Brian O'Neill QC, who kindly spared the time to read the trial transcript and comment on the way Palmer was tried – and how he might be tried today. He did not have much doubt that Palmer would be put away for a long stretch today – though not, thankfully, the sort of stretch that Palmer endured when he was executed in public. I am hugely grateful to the Royal College of Pathologists for putting me on to Suzy Lishman, the vice-president, and Adam Hargreaves, the toxicology specialist, and thank both for their comments on the case. Their enthusiastic and most helpful participation included reading the transcript and wading through Swaine Taylor's self-justificatory book: how astonishing it is that Suzy believes Palmer might well have got away with murder today, just as he so nearly did 158 years ago.

Professor Wray Vamplew of Stirling University, the leading historian of sport, not only generously loaned me his copy of his own book on Victorian racing when it proved impossible for me to acquire a copy for myself, but also read and commented on the racing chapter in this book.

A number of librarians were extremely helpful, particularly the staff at the British Newspaper Library in Colindale, Nick Mays and Anne Jensen of *The Times*'s archive in Enfield, Richard Nelsson, Jason Rodrigues and Marian Yamin at the *Guardian* archive, Hannah West at the Chartered Insurance Institute Library in the City of London, Frances Bellis, assistant librarian at Lincoln's Inn and Lesley Whitelaw of the Middle Temple library.

My gratitude is also due to Jon Jackson, former publishing director at Duckworth, who was enthusiastic in commissioning the project, as were Dan Crissman of Overlook in New York and Andrew Lockett, Jon's successor at Duckworth in London. Special thanks are due to my agent Charlie Viney, of the Viney Agency, who has been immensely supportive and proactive with this and my other projects and saw the merits of retelling the Palmer story from the start: he is a terrific and enthusiastic support. Ben Dupré was, as ever, a terrific copy-editor. Lastly, thanks are due to my family: wife Alice, daughter Helena and her husband Gareth, and sons Tim and Philip.

Index

Stephen Bates read Modern History at New College, Oxford before working as a journalist for the BBC, *Daily Telegraph*, *Daily Mail* and *Guardian*, where for twenty-three years he was successively a political correspondent, European Affairs editor and religious and royal correspondent. This is his sixth book. He is married with three children and lives in Kent.